Contents

Foreword

Journalists have always been an important and integral part of the travel industry. They were the mouthpiece of those who created the package tour between the 1950s and mid-1960s, right through to the crazy days of no-holds-barred entrepreneurship that followed and also during the coming of regulation in the mid-1970s, designed to protect the public from the industry's worst excesses.

Travel was, and still is, an industry where growth is everything, where common sense and logic seemingly play no part. The public eagerly participates by believing the message that the dream of worldwide travel at a cost of next to nothing is its God-given right.

Nothing, except perhaps trading in stocks and commodities, can match the adrenaline rush created by the risk involved in attempting to fill an aircraft week after week, to transport the travelling public to some faraway place. Single-handedly, the early travel entrepreneurs created unexpected wealth for overseas destinations from a totally unknown source. Spain, Portugal, Italy, Greece and a host of other countries found that tourism became their primary source of wealth – initially due to the popularity of the package holiday and, now, through the no-frills airlines that have continued in the same tradition.

Competition has always been cut-throat, and margins have always been slim-to-non-existent, but the eternal optimism is always there. Somehow, it seems, next year will be better than the last, past mistakes can be forgotten and disaster will always be averted.

I came into the travel industry – by sheer fluke – around 1970, as everyone in my generation seemed to do. Being a tour operator was not regarded as a proper job, but something one drifted into. No qualifications were required and, in the early days, no money either;

the cash would come rolling in, to be used for whatever purpose required, in the sure knowledge that perpetual growth would simply bring in more cash tomorrow.

I cannot remember a time when the author, Dave Richardson, was not around; never excitable, always measured, persistent, always probing with his questions. You sensed that he would know if you weren't telling the truth. It's rare for any tour operator or travel agent ever to say that bookings are not dramatically up compared with the previous year, because eternal optimism is what makes this industry tick. But you couldn't pull the wool over Dave's eyes. He would listen to the hype and bluster, and then would pose a question that made you realise he'd seen through the whole performance.

Everyone in the travel industry loves talking to a journalist because it's journalists who bring in business by extolling, by describing, by persuading the public to travel. But not all journalists understand the travel trade, and how it works and thinks.

In *Let's Go*, Dave Richardson captures, in a light-hearted and pragmatic manner, the years between the creation of the package holiday in the 1950s and the arrival of the no-frills carriers and the internet entrepreneurs that have transformed the industry yet again in the past ten years. Here is someone who really understands the industry, has watched it develop and change, and can put it all into perspective.

What brings the book alive is the fact that Dave has lived through many of the years he describes – after all, this is a young industry – and can write from personal experience of the many colourful characters that have shaped the travel sector. He can quote from the countless interviews he has conducted and can therefore reveal, first hand, what was in their minds. This book enables us to see travel through the eyes of those who were actively involved in creation of the dream. They are quoted liberally throughout the book, and several of them look back on their mistakes – mistakes that affected tens of thousands of people.

There are of course more academic works describing the growth and development of the tourism industry, but the interested reader and student alike will find *Let's Go* both informative and entertaining in equal measure. It is well researched, it is accurate and it captures the excitement of those who built the travel industry over the past sixty-five years.

What this book details particularly clearly is that it is individuals – the personalities who formed the UK travel industry, and their strokes of genius and entrepreneurship – who created the trends and ways of working. These rippled out from our country and have now insinuated themselves into the worldwide travel and tourism industry. The UK's pioneers developed what is now seen to be the most sophisticated and diverse travel market in the world.

In the twenty-first century, it's our challenge to protect and nurture the thousands of destinations worldwide into which tourism's tentacles reach. We need to ensure that host countries are both protected from tourism's worst excesses and that tourism's undoubted benefits are spread fairly, trickling down to as many people as possible. It's also a key challenge to encourage consumers to see that endless cheap flights for weekend trips to places they've never heard of are not good, long-term, for the environment. But that is definitely the role of another book...

Noel Josephides
Chairman, Sunvil (www.sunvil.co.uk)
Chairman, ABTA (www.abta.com)
January 2016

Acknowledgements

First of all I must thank more than sixty people who agreed to be interviewed for this book, a mixture of travel industry pioneers and leaders, and those at the sharp end of serving the public. Nearly everyone approached was keen to tell their story even when discussing the bad times, although overall it's a story that has brought great happiness, even wealth, to countless people. Thanks in particular to ABTA chairman Noel Josephides, and to Dan Pearce and Pippa Jacks from *Travel Trade Gazette* (TTG), where I started work in 1974. TTG has been published every week since 1953 and now has a thriving website (www.ttgdigital.com), and TTG's archives of back issues, which it is hoping to digitise, are a treasure trove of history. Its journalists have written fearlessly about the travel industry for over sixty years and I am proud to be still writing for TTG in 2016.

There have been few books about tour operators (but plenty about airlines, cruise lines and so on), but the most helpful to me was *Flight to the Sun* by Roger Bray and Vladimir Raitz (Continuum, 2001). Others I found particularly useful were *ABTA: The First Fifty Years* (ABTA, 2000); *Aiming High: The Life of Ski Pioneer Erna Low*, by Mark Frary (Matador, 2012); *Chandler's Travels*, by John Carter (Quiller Press, 1985); *Return Ticket Home*, by Philip Morrell (Magna Carter, 2014); *Thomas Cook: 150 Years of Popular Tourism*, by Piers Brendon (Martin Secker & Warburg, 1991); and *Unfinished Journey*, by Aubrey Morris (The Polemicist/Artery Publications, 2006).

Thanks also to all those who provided pictures, either from company records or their attics, and in particular to Paul Smith, company archivist of Thomas Cook Group, whose splendid digital library includes the images on the front and back covers. It hasn't been possible to include every person and company who has played a role in creating the package holiday and escorted tour business, and of course *Let's Go* is only up-to-date to the point when it was finished. But I invite everyone interested in the history of the travel industry to look at my website, www.historyofpackagetours.co.uk, for updates, links, company profiles and what I hope will be a lively and entertaining forum.

Finally, may I thank my wife Victoria for all her forbearance, and let's look forward to many more trips together!

Dave Richardson

January 2016

www.historyofpackagetours.co.uk

Take-Off

Are your seat belts fastened? I'm your pilot and I'm taking you on holiday, and it's going to be an exhilarating, if sometimes bumpy ride. We'll be meeting all kinds of people, from fly-by-nights and multi-millionaires to reps, tour managers and the people who try to help when a holiday goes wrong. But that won't happen to us, of course!

This is your story too, whether you're going to lie in the sun on a package holiday or do something more cultural on an escorted tour. During this trip you're going to change completely from someone rather shy and pale-skinned, who's never been abroad before, to the outgoing, suntanned man or woman of the world that you always wanted to be. Instead of eating fish and chips or pie and mash, you'll be dining on seafood paella or moussaka, and you'll be washing it down with lots of different wines rather than beer or lemonade. And when you get home, your tastes and outlook on life will be changed forever.

The holidays we take reflect the people we are – or aspire to be. The image of package holidays dating from the 1960s means many people turn up their noses at the thought of it, and don't always realise they're on a package when they're relaxing in some distant part of the world, or sightseeing in a vibrant city. There's a serious side to this too as the package is now threatened as never before, and we don't enjoy the same level of security on a do-it-yourself holiday.

But let's leave that till later. It's the early 1950s and we're off to sunny Spain. It's going to take four hours to get there because this plane can't fly over the Alps and has to take the long way round, and we'll have to stop to refuel. When we get there no one will speak English, and, as we don't speak any foreign languages, we'll have to point at things. We might be going camping or to a small hotel but don't worry – bigger hotels with private bathrooms are coming, and that's something we don't all have at home.

All set? Then hang on tight and let's go!

PART I

Package Holidays

1

1950–1965: The Pioneers

How did package holidays get started? There are various claims to have been the first, but the most persuasive is by a Russian émigré called Vladimir Raitz who started Horizon Holidays in 1950. The attraction was not only sun, but meat. In the long years of austerity after the Second World War food rationing meant meat was off the menu on most days, unless you were on a Horizon holiday to a campsite in Corsica.

Another of the pioneers, Travel Club of Upminster, chose Switzerland as its first post-war holiday destination in 1947 because it was a land of plenty. Its founder, Harry Chandler, wrote:

> I painted a glowing picture of what Switzerland was like – plenty of food, shops full of goods, virtually pre-war conditions and a complete contrast to England at that time with its shortages, electricity cuts and hard times.

But while Travel Club's customers faced a gruelling journey by cross-Channel ferry, and then by train through war-torn France, Horizon pioneered a concept that soon became the norm for package holiday operators. It chartered a series of weekly flights, with fixed holiday durations of seven or fourteen nights by the beach. Whether Raitz really was the first will probably never be known for sure, as Thomas Cook – which shied away from mass tourism until much later – had advertised an eight-week series of summer charter flights to Cannes in the South of France more than a decade earlier. Holiday prices including all meals were from £15 5s staying at the Hotel Londres. Even Thomas Cook can't be sure those flights actually operated, however. The year was 1939 and Europe was on the brink of war.

The package holiday pioneers were a mixture of astute businessmen who spotted that air travel was about to literally take off, and amateurs who liked taking holidays themselves and rather fancied having a go at organising them. But, whoever they were, the challenges were immense. There might have been plenty of aircraft around to charter, many of them converted from military use after the war. But a strict licensing regime was in place to protect airlines such as British European Airways (BEA), a predecessor of British Airways, which operated regular scheduled flights. Air travel was a luxury and way beyond the pocket of the average person.

But there was pent-up demand for travel abroad, as Britain's economic prospects started to improve, and people wanted to revisit the places they had served in during the war, or on National Service. Until now, the vast majority of people who went on holiday abroad went for the experience, to better their minds. A few wealthy people might have gone to the grand hotels of Europe to enjoy the sea or a few rounds of golf, but the idea of going abroad primarily to soak up the sun – with an adventure in food, drink and possibly romance thrown in – was beyond most people's pockets, and imaginations. People went to the British seaside for that, and Butlins – whose first holiday camp opened at Skegness in 1936 – offered a kind of holiday package. But people often didn't see the sun, and the food and drink were the same dull fare as at home. As for romance, the saucy seaside postcard nudged, winked but often didn't deliver.

Vladimir Raitz was working for the Reuters news agency in London, when his own holiday to Corsica in 1949 involved an almost 48-hour journey in each direction, by train through France then a six-hour ferry trip from Marseille to Calvi. He had the idea of setting up a holiday company, but wanted a better experience for his customers – and that meant flying. This was before the jet age, and the larger aircraft that would transform the economics of holidays by air. The workhorse of the skies was the Douglas DC-3, later known as the Dakota, which first entered service in 1936. It stood on the tarmac at an angle of about 30 degrees, meaning anyone sitting towards the front faced a steep climb up the aisle from the door at the rear – enough to make some passengers feel sick even before getting airborne! Raitz saw an opportunity, but he hadn't reckoned with officialdom.

The licensing rules stated that package holidays could not be sold for less than the normal return air fare, which was £70 to Nice in the South of France, the nearest airport to Corsica served by BEA. Horizon wanted to charge less than half that, £32 10s for a week all-in, including camping, all meals and unlimited wine – a stark example of how expensive air travel was in 1950. The licensing authorities said no, but in the end it agreed as long as Horizon sold only to members of a club, in this case students and teachers.

Horizon's first flight took off in May 1950, with a target of 350 passengers to break even during sixteen weekly flights. With a top speed of 170 mph, the trusty DC-3 reached Lyon in three hours, where it had to refuel. Six hours after leaving Gatwick – 'there was hardly another plane on the tarmac', Raitz related – the group arrived in Calvi to be greeted by the municipal band. He may not have realised it at the time, but the package holiday age had begun.

Why would people who could afford to travel by air in these early days want to stay in a campsite rather than a hotel – with only a 'primitive open air dining room' and sanitary block? Cost was one consideration, but another was that there were few affordable hotels of good standard in coastal resorts. Raitz had also checked out Mallorca, which would soon become a mainstay of the package holiday business, but found only a few old hotels and deserted beaches. Corsica it was, then, and Horizon's first holidaymakers had a great time although the company lost money in the first season.

By 1952 the red tape had been eased, the students and teachers restriction no longer applied, and the stage was set for growth not only by Horizon, but some of the larger travel companies of the time. But the restriction on package holiday prices not undercutting the regular air fare remained for about twenty years, as state-owned airlines were protected by their governments. In 1952 Horizon started flying to Mallorca, despite objections from BEA, and by the end of 1953 it had made enough money to contemplate serious expansion, with flights added to the Costa Brava in northern Spain and Sardinia, and many other destinations under consideration. 'When I went to Menorca there was just one hotel,' recalled Raitz. 'When I first went to Benidorm there was just one hotel owned by the Mayor – everything was virgin territory.'

Thomas Cook was well established but its main focus was escorted tours, air, rail and sea tickets, and foreign currency. Other major travel companies of that time included Sir Henry Lunn and the Polytechnic Touring Association, which could both could trace their roots to the nineteenth century as organisers of travel for health, sport and education. When they merged in the 1960s to create Lunn Poly, it established a name that lasted half a century as the largest chain of retail travel agents in the 1980s and 1990s.

In 1953 a major new competitor to Horizon emerged, to focus on beach holidays as well as escorted tours. Universal Sky Tours, later simply Skytours, fought many battles with the licensing authorities, and had to fly to Mallorca via Maastricht in Holland, with some other flights operating from Blackbushe airport in Hampshire so not to compete in BEA's catchment area around London. The founder of Universal Sky Tours was a mercurial character called Ted Langton, who had made his name running coach tours before the war and now wanted to take advantage of the many aircraft available for charter.

Those early charter flights were often hair-raising, with safety concerns meaning that some airlines were stripped of their operating licences. Delays caused by faulty equipment were commonplace, and accidents occurred although few were fatal. Noisy, unpressurised aircraft such as the DC-3 offered a very uncomfortable ride in bad weather and could not fly at high altitude, meaning they had to go 'the long way round' to avoid the Alps. When the pressurised, thirty-two-seat Vickers Viscount aircraft was introduced in 1953, powered by turboprop rather than piston engines, Harry Chandler's Travel Club of Upminster switched from rail tours to flying. 'I was able to write in my brochure lyrical accounts of travelling on a Viscount, describing how you could actually balance a halfpenny on the table in front of you as the aircraft sped through the skies at 300 mph,' he wrote. 'Such simple explanations as this, I felt sure, convinced many people that flying was comfortable and safe. The age of mass holiday travel by air was dawning.'

Travel Club was still focusing on mountain resorts rather than sunshine holidays, booking passengers on scheduled airlines such as BEA, Air France and Swissair rather than taking on the much greater risk of chartering its own flights. Its first charter, with Swissair, came in 1956 – allowing a dramatic cut in prices, but risking financial collapse if the holidays failed to sell.

'We had forty-four seats on the aircraft, a forty-four-seater coach to carry out the transfer from Basle to Seefeld, and eighty-eight beds in the Hotel Karwendelhof,' recalled Chandler. 'With a combination like that, anything over a 90 per cent load factor meant that we could not fail. We did not fail, and I decided then and there that charter flights were, to quote Lord Thomson, a "licence to print money".'

Expansion to Italy and Spain followed, and in 1960 Chandler took another big step forward and claimed a travel industry 'first' by chartering a jet aircraft – an Air France Caravelle. The French-built aircraft was faster than turboprops and could carry eighty passengers, and Travel Club squeezed two daily return flights out of it – from Heathrow to Basle and later from Heathrow to Perpignan. Flights were on Saturdays, when the aircraft would otherwise have been idle, so prices were keen. This established another pattern, which tour operators used for decades, while today low-cost airlines can often squeeze in three return trips.

Few tour operators relied only on sunshine holidays, one reason being a shortage of hotels and another being that many people also wanted to fly to enjoy mountain resorts and cultural tours. When another new company, appropriately called Wings, was set up by the Ramblers Association in 1956, it hedged its bets. It sold holidays to resorts in the Alps, plus coach tours of Spain and Italy, in addition to the sunshine resorts of Palma, Mallorca and Laiguelia in Italy.

Eyewitness: Stewart Wild
He first came to Clarksons Tours during school holidays in 1959 as a sixteen-year-old office boy, joining full-time in 1968. He was a director by the time of Clarksons' catastrophic collapse in 1974, and later joined a management team for American Express tour operations.

Clarksons started as a respected shipbroker and air freight company, but then it was asked to arrange an air charter to the World's Fair in Brussels in 1958 where people had a great day out for £5, flying in a DC-3 from Southend to Ostend. Tom Gullick had joined the company from the Navy when he was twenty-seven, and by 1960 he was operating day and weekend trips by air for groups to the Dutch bulbfields, Paris and the Rhine Valley. 1964 was our first summer operating to Spain and I worked as a rep. Clients paid 27 guineas for a week's full board at the Centrico Hotel in Calella, Costa Dorada, but flew only as far as Clermont Ferrand in France on a forty-seat Viking operated by Autair. Passengers then faced an overnight coach trip to Narbonne in the south of France for an early breakfast, where we met passengers coming home from Spain and swapped over all the luggage. It then took five hours on country roads in a Spanish coach across the border to Calella. The overall journey time from Luton airport to the hotel by plane and coach was not far short of twenty-four hours, but passengers never complained.

Tom Gullick's philosophy was to research what people were prepared to pay, and make the costs fit to offer unbeatable value. He would say to a hotel: "If you give me a low-price deal, I will guarantee that your beds are always full and extend your season as well." Our customers were generally young singles and couples without children, and for many it was their first holiday abroad.

That same year, 1964, Tom sent me on a scouting mission to Mallorca. My job was to see what was going on in Arenal – which tour operators were using which hotels, and how successful they were. I was there the day that Fiesta Tours went bust – people were sitting on their suitcases in their hotel lobby wondering who was going to help them. Package holidays made foreign travel very affordable and brought that experience to the masses at a time when few people spoke a foreign language, and few Europeans spoke English. But there wasn't any protection when a company like Fiesta went bust, and this was the start of legislation and co-operation among tour operators to protect customers' money and safeguard the reputation of the industry.

Companies such as Wings grew rapidly despite the continuing licensing restrictions. In its second season, 1957, Wings had to put a leaflet into its brochure announcing the cancellation of holidays to Portugal because BEA had objected. Wings had planned two-week holidays costing 49 guineas. BEA's return fare to Lisbon, not including any hotels or meals, was £54 18s. Inevitably, however, the scheduled airlines hit back. By 1959 BEA was offering seat prices on less busy Viscount flights that could match charter prices, with none of the risk faced by travel firms chartering their own aircraft. On the other hand, charter flights became more comfortable and reliable as aircraft such as Viscounts, Britannias, DC-6s and DC-7s were retired by national airlines in favour of the latest models, subsequently joining charter fleets. But even aircraft such as these were small and slow compared to what was coming only a decade later. The seventy-five-seat DC-6, for example, took five hours to reach Palma, Mallorca including a technical stop en route.

Spain did not dominate the package holiday business until the 1960s, and charters were hopping all over the Mediterranean to places including Sardinia, Perpignan (South of France) and Tangier in Morocco. The allure of some places was so great that people would travel a long way overland to get there, either all the way from England or from the nearest airport on the Continent. One example was the Istrian coast, now in Croatia but then in Communist Yugoslavia (also see chapter six).

Christopher Lord's first job in travel was as a Wings rep in Lovran, along this coastline, in 1956. He had finished National Service and got the travel bug, while his brother Basil was a rep working for another company, Swans, just up the coast in Opatija. To get there and back involved a three-night train journey in each direction, but the following year, with a third brother called Stephen, they took a holiday in Opatija and planned their own tour operation, Lord Brothers.

'Italy was the major holiday destination at that time, as Spain hadn't got off the ground and France was too expensive,' recalls Christopher Lord. 'Our first customers were professional people, as we advertised exclusively in *The Sunday Times*. Yugoslavia was unbelievably cheap with good food and wine, and interesting excursions. I was dazzled by the place – the sights, the sounds and the smells. It was 1958, and we ran two-week holidays costing 48 guineas from a grand-sounding address at Warwick House, Wimbledon. In fact it was our council flat.'

But, instead of the arduous train journey, Lord Brothers chartered a DC-3 from Blackbushe airport to Graz in Austria, with the final leg by coach still taking twelve hours. 'It was all part of the fun in those days, but of course it wouldn't be acceptable now,' says Lord. 'Even the flight to Graz took five hours, non-stop if you were lucky but depending on tail winds.'

Another boost to tour operators at around this time was an increase in the overseas travel allowance from £10 to £25, with the cost of hotels, meals and resort transfers having to be accounted for on the infamous V Form. Currency restrictions – imposed after the war in a bid to redress the UK's Balance of Payments deficit – lasted until the late 1970s, but were gradually eased. The licensing regime was also eased when the Air Transport Licensing Board started work in 1961, still protecting scheduled airlines, but with a more liberal attitude. Britain was increasingly prosperous, with TVs starting to appear in living rooms and the war becoming a distant memory. In one of the most-quoted political speeches of modern times, Prime Minister Harold Macmillan claimed in 1957 that 'most of our people have never had it so good'.

'Our major competitors were Wings, Horizon and Yugotours, but on a personal level we were all very friendly and often shared charter flights,' continues Lord. 'Vladimir Raitz, and Ernest Welsman of Wings, were honourable men who didn't resent competition, and would even give us advice. There was more than enough demand for all of us to do well. By 1961, when we were also selling holidays to Italy, Spain, France and Greece, Lord Brothers was profitable and people had the impression we were wealthy young men. But when customers started turning up and looking askance at our council flat, we decided we had to open an office and that was in Regent Street.'

By then it was chartering Viscount aircraft from British United Airways, run by Freddie Laker who became a household name in the 1970s when he launched cheap transatlantic flights called Skytrain.

Laker started as an aircraft trader who made money during the Berlin airlift of 1948–49, and also operated the Channel Air Bridge carrying drivers and their cars to the Continent. Eventually Laker was to take over Lord Brothers, but the brothers ran it for ten years.

'By 1960 we had a licence to print money, as we had so much cash on deposit with people paying us twelve weeks in advance, when we didn't have to pay the airline or hotels until close to departure,' says Lord. 'The hotels were glad of our business, and our clients tipped well. Our first flights to Mallorca were in 1960, and word spread quickly that it was an unspoilt holiday paradise. There weren't enough hotels, but as we had so much cash we started paying people up-front to get more hotels built.'

Other tour operators with equally modest beginnings included Gaytours, soon to become big out of Manchester, a Blackpool company whose niche was organising end-of-season holidays for the town's legions of seaside landladies, who were flush with cash by September. The word 'gay' had nothing to do with sexual orientation in those days, and when companies such as Lord Brothers stated in their brochures that 'Opatija is always very gay at night', they meant it was lively.

Some idea of the heady excitement of that era comes in *Unfinished Journey*, the autobiography of another package holiday pioneer, Aubrey Morris (1919–2008), a London taxi driver whose love of travel started when he took his cab on holiday to France and Italy. The man who would become the first boss of Thomson Holidays left school at fourteen and was a lifelong Socialist, witnessing the infamous 'Battle of Cable Street' in London's East End in 1936, when 300,000 protestors turned back a march by Sir Oswald Mosley's British Union of Fascists.

In 1956 he set up Riviera Holidays, offering rail-based packages to the south of France. He knew nothing about the travel business and retained his cab-driver's badge, selling mainly to other drivers and social clubs. But he learned that the vast majority of bookings were taken in the three weeks after Christmas, and one day in late December 1958 he was driving his cab down Piccadilly in London at five in the morning, when he saw a queue outside the Universal Sky Tours office.

'I was amazed; it was just after 5.00 a.m. but already there was a queue of people stretching around the block and further, waiting for the office to open at 9.00 a.m.,' he recalled. 'Excited, I drove down to Wilton Street by Victoria station where I saw a similar group of people waiting for Martin Rooks (another pioneering company) to start taking bookings. Eventually I worked my way back towards our office to find no queue, just one lady with a copy of our leaflet and a deposit. I dealt with the booking and sat there all morning receiving neither a phone call nor a visit. And, into the bargain, I lost a valuable day's work! It was a disaster.'

Little did he know that Riviera would soon become a competitor to Universal Sky Tours, and that the two would become the first tour operators bought by media conglomerate Thomson in 1965. Riviera developed a niche organising trips for fans of Tottenham Hotspur to watch their team play in Europe, but by 1961 it started selling package holidays. It soon abandoned its South of France roots to concentrate on Italy, mainly the Adriatic resorts of Rimini and Cattolica.

Other companies that started packages by air and coach in the early 1960s included Global and Cosmos, while Leroy Tours started in the 1950s. Lewis Leroy, known as 'the man in the beret', owned a hotel in Dover where coach groups would stay before joining a ferry, and the chef knew how to cook only one dish on the menu as no one ever stayed more than one night! But none of these companies was as big as 'Captain' Ted Langton's Universal Sky Tours, which had grown rapidly by 1960, challenging Horizon as market leader.

Morris describes Langton as 'the archetypal buccaneering entrepreneur', the most influential and innovative of his era. In 1962 Langton set up his own charter airline, Euravia, buying ninety-seven-seat Constellation aircraft and basing them at Luton airport, a ground-breaking move at that time. By 1964 he had replaced them with Britannia 102s, known as the 'whispering giants'. Britannias were now being retired by scheduled airlines in favour of jets, and when available to charter airlines they brought further economies of scale to drive down holiday prices. Euravia then took the name Britannia, later becoming the UK's leading charter airline, the name lasting for over forty years. Universal Sky Tours built its own hotels including the Arenal Park in Mallorca, and invested in others such as the 900-bed Taurus Park on the Costa Brava, one of the first giant holiday hotels.

Eyewitness: James McWilliam
He set up Dixon Travel in Glasgow in 1952 and helped create Caledonian Airways. McWilliam turned 100 in 2014.

I grew quickly by arranging coach tours to Blackpool and around Scotland, at a time when no one owned a car. Ostend was considered a faraway place and that was the first foreign holiday I organised. As a travel agent I started booking flights to America and Canada, as people were emigrating from the Greenock and Port Glasgow areas in droves.

By the 1970s package holidays had become very popular and I took over a company called Sunseeker, and I also had a partnership with Vale of Leven Travel Agency for a tour operation called Volta Dixon. We operated some of the first holiday flights to the Mediterranean from Edinburgh and Aberdeen, whereas Thomson Holidays was well established in Glasgow. Edinburgh wasn't interested in holiday flights at first, while Aberdeen, despite the oil boom, didn't even have Customs or security. I was told I was mad to start selling Mallorca from Aberdeen, but it worked.

I also brought people into Scotland from the US on an airline called British Eagle, and in 1961 I met a pilot called Adam Thomson who wanted to set up a Scottish airline with a Scottish bank account. I took him unannounced to the Royal Bank of Scotland and told them we wanted to start an international airline. They looked at us incredulously but told us to draw up a business plan, and we went back later that day where I put in £60 to form the company, and that's how Caledonian Airways started. Lots of local traders chipped in and we soon had £4,000. Our first flight was from Prestwick and I was involved in that airline for more than twenty years.

In 1970 we took over British United to become British Caledonian, the largest independent airline in Britain, and we acquired a tour operation called Blue Sky and some resort hotels including two in Cala Millor, Mallorca. Gatwick became its main base and we fed a lot of traffic into Gatwick from Scotland. British Caledonian retained its Scottish identity right up until 1987 when it was taken over by British Airways.

Despite larger aircraft such as the Britannia, flying was still very expensive – especially at weekends, when most people wanted to travel, as fixed one- or two-week holiday periods used to be the norm in most jobs. As late as 1962, Swans was advertising rail travel to countries as far away as Spain and prices for Mallorca make an interesting comparison. Two-week holidays by air cost from £40 14s, but increased to £43 14s at weekends. The equivalent holiday by rail cost from £30 16s 6d, but you spent only ten rather than fourteen nights in your hotel as it took nearly forty-eight hours in each direction to get to and from Mallorca!

The British weren't the only ones starting to colonise parts of Spain. Even back then some resorts were developed to cater for British tastes while others concentrated on Germans or Scandinavians, who were also keen to escape the northern European climate. But when the British and Germans were mixed up in the same hotel there could be trouble, with memories of the war all too keen for some people.

Vincent Cobb, who worked for Gaytours, witnessed this himself when investigating complaints that the well-organised Germans were 'posting sentries' at the dining room door. 'It did not take long for fights to break out, despite warnings from us to the hoteliers,' he wrote in *The Package Tour Industry*. 'At seven thirty in the evening some half a dozen German men were blocking the doors to the dining room, and were actually manhandling the British clients away. Suddenly the Brits reacted and a fight broke out. It was bloody and quite vicious, and didn't stop until I persuaded the hotel owner to call the Guardia Civil.'

Horizon, meanwhile, was growing rapidly and trying to stay ahead of its increasing number of competitors by finding new destinations. It was the first tour operator to discover Menorca, in 1956, but Ibiza had to wait for the simple reason that it didn't have an airport. Horizon also started to develop the Costa del Sol. Raitz commented that there was no problem getting a licence to fly to Malaga as no one had ever heard of it! Such places could still be considered exotic in the 1950s/ early 1960s, and Raitz liked to be photographed with celebrities or glamour girls. Package holidays were becoming sexy.

But there were rogues around too, and the media began to report cases of people fleeced of their money or left stranded abroad when a company went bust. Although airlines had to apply for licences on tour operators' behalf, there was no requirement for holiday companies to safeguard people's money. The collapse of Fiesta Tours in July 1964 hit the headlines as it happened at the height of the summer season. TV crews turned up outside Fiesta's London headquarters to film its boss being confronted by angry crowds, and the travel industry launched a rescue mission.

ABTA (originally the Association of British Travel Agents, now simply ABTA – The Travel Association) had been set up in 1950, but didn't include any tour operators until 1959. It co-ordinated the rescue, with Travel Club's Harry Chandler persuading other companies to follow his example by giving Fiesta customers any empty seats on his flights, with Fiesta's owner stumping up £7,500 of his own money. The rescue was a success, the reputation of package holiday operators was saved, and thoughts turned to preventing a recurrence of this situation in future.

While all this was happening another tour operator was beginning its rapid growth, which would see it overtake Horizon and Universal Sky Tours to become the biggest kid on the block by the late 1960s. In 1958 it was running day trips to the Dutch bulbfields for £6, and Tom Gullick, its driving force, said: 'My happiest moment was standing at Rotterdam airport at the end of the day, watching the buses return from the bulbfields with the Dakota DC-3s lined up waiting to take our customers home. They were so happy because they had never believed they could afford to go abroad.'

By 1964, Clarksons was operating packages to Spain and gaining a reputation for 'pile them high, sell them cheap' marketing tactics that made a holiday in the sun affordable. A competitor, Ken Swan of Swans Tours, described Clarksons as 'incredibly cheap and cut-throat. Although a lot of people travelled with Clarksons who couldn't otherwise have afforded it, Clarksons cut corners and I'm afraid standards dropped.' Like Fiesta before it, the collapse of Clarksons ten years later was a turning point in consumer protection, but by then the package holiday had truly come of age.

2

Viva España!

By the time the song 'Viva España' became popular in the 1970s, Spain was already the top destination for package holidays, not only from the UK, but also from Germany and Scandinavia. It's still the most popular place today for foreign holidays, but so many people now travel independently or to their own properties that traditional package holidays have slumped, though are possibly poised for a comeback.

Although the south of France and Italy were also ripe for development in the 1950s, Spain soon eclipsed them simply because it was cheap, with its then-exotic appeal being a bonus. But Spain was also a backward country, and one often regarded with animosity as it was ruled by a fascist dictator, General Franco, who won a brutal civil war in the 1930s when many British idealists enlisted to fight with the Socialist opposition. Tourism, however, was identified by Franco as a way of developing and enriching the country. Tour operators jumped at the opportunity, though some needed a little persuading.

Aubrey Morris's Riviera Holidays was one that had misgivings as Morris was a lifelong Socialist, but he was persuaded that tourism would help improve living standards and contact with other nationalities would help marginalise Franco. The dictator's influence (and that of the Catholic Church) waned only slowly and was still being felt at his death in 1975, which paved the way for democracy.

The Costa Brava was the first area to be developed because it was just over the border from France. It could be reached by coach or rail in around twenty-four to thirty hours from the UK, and although Gerona airport didn't open until 1965, people could be bussed across the border from Perpignan in France. Lloret de Mar became the first ugly package holiday resort, although many of the small *calas* (coves) of the Costa Brava remain unspoilt.

Mallorca had the added appeal of being an island, and when Palma's new airport opened in 1960, it was poised to become synonymous with package holidays. Mallorca's ups and downs over more than half a century mirror the fortunes of package holidays generally, and while other places like the Costa Brava have fallen out of favour, it could truly be described as the great survivor. Four of the largest holiday hotel groups in the world all have their roots here, as what was to become the Mallorcan style of package holidays was exported first to other parts of Spain, and then to Latin America, other countries in Europe and around the globe to places as diverse as Cape Verde or Bali.

It might seem that Mallorca (often spelt Majorca in English) developed from nowhere in the 1960s, but a select few started visiting in the nineteenth century including the French writer George Sand and her lover, the composer Frederic Chopin, whose sojourn in 1838 led to Sand's book *A Winter in Mallorca*. The Mallorca Tourist Board started in 1905 promoting the island mainly in winter, especially to French visitors. The Gran Hotel in Palma opened in 1903 and by 1960 there were many small hotels. Many people got rich quickly in the 1960s, and ironically, they were often the youngest sons or daughters of the family who inherited what was considered worthless land by the sea.

One of the small hotels developed in the 1950s was the Bon Sol in Illetas, which has been run by the same family for over sixty years with the same attention to care and detail as the founder. The Bon Sol has not stood still, however. What started as a family home with guest accommodation in 1953 is now a luxury hotel with ninety-two rooms, thirty-seven villas, a spa and its own small beach. It has won the Thomson Gold Award many times over the last thirty years.

Owner Martin Xamena, who runs the hotel with his English wife Lorraine and son Alejandro, grew up in the family home, which stood where the main bar is today. He remembers the film star Errol Flynn, who built his own villa nearby, teaching him how to sword-fight when Martin was a youngster. In those days most visitors arrived by ferry in Palma, five miles away, and taxi drivers would earn a commission by bringing passengers with no hotel bookings to the Bon Sol.

'The people who came from England were cultivated and they always wanted to discover the place where they stayed, and they started coming to Mallorca when the Côte d'Azur in France became very expensive,' recalls Xamena. 'All our guests were educated people and they came mainly in winter, but in the 1960s the building boom started and tour operators started offering farmers money to build hotels on their land. The building boom was so intensive that at times you couldn't get concrete or steel. You needed permission from the town hall to build a hotel, but deals were done. There was no opposition to development, and no green movement – they only happen after a country becomes wealthy, and not when you need the money to live day by day. Rubbish was put in a pile, and sewer pipes emptied directly into the sea.'

The Bon Sol had to expand or be left behind, but when the new hotel was built it was designed in grand classical style, complete with generous lounges and suits of armour, rather than the concrete palaces going up along the more popular beaches around the Bay of Palma. Xamena also bought the land leading down to a small cove where he built villas, swimming pools, a beach bar and restaurant. Throughout its sixty-plus years the Bon Sol has retained a loyal clientele, many of them British, with the third generation of many families taking their holidays there. Loyalty is also shown by the staff with a typical length of service being twenty-five years, which is almost unheard of in the hotel business. Some have worked there for over forty years, with a seventy-five-year-old head waiter only retiring reluctantly due to ill health.

'As people get older and become more experienced travellers, they start to appreciate us more,' says Xamena. 'We didn't want to adapt to mass tourism because this is still our home, and we never reduce our prices because that means reducing quality. Our most regular guests are like our family, because we have known some of them since they were babies.'

The Bon Sol has ridden the ups and downs through decades of huge change, but is very much the exception as a larger hotel owned by a family still living there – with the Xamenas even taking most of their meals in the dining rooms along with guests. But the style of large resort hotel developed in Mallorca and later exported throughout the world is very different, with extensive grounds along the beachfront, children's clubs, plenty of sports and vast buffet-style restaurants. All the facilities you might want are there, but they cannot avoid being impersonal.

Sol Hotels, which bought the Melia group in 1987 and is now known as Melia Hotels International, was one of the Mallorcan companies that designed the new type of hotel with input from major British and German tour operators. Founder Gabriel Escarrer, who is still the company's chairman, opened his first hotel, in Palma, in 1956. In the 1970s he started opening Sol hotels in mainland Spain, with his first hotel outside Spain opening in Bali, Indonesia in 1986. It has grown into one of the world's largest groups with over 350 hotels in thirty-five countries, and is the largest international hotel operator in Cuba.

Barcelo, with over one hundred hotels in nineteen countries, has even older origins, being founded in Mallorca in 1931 transporting goods and passengers. In 1962 it opened its first hotel, with the Pueblo chain developed from 1965 aimed specifically at families. Benidorm was to follow in 1970 and its first hotel outside Spain, in the Dominican Republic, in 1985.

Riu Hotels, which is closely associated with Thomson Holidays and other tour operators in the multi-national TUI group, started in Mallorca in 1953 when the Riu family bought the San Francisco hotel in Palma. It went into partnership with German tour operator Dr Tigges, which became TUI (Touristik Union International) in 1968, and TUI helped Riu build new hotels in the 1970s. Gran Canaria, then relatively unknown, was developed in the 1980s and now has more than twenty Riu hotels. Like Melia and Barcelo it has expanded into cities too, and Riu hotels now operate in countries including Mexico, the Dominican Republic, Jamaica, Aruba, the Bahamas, Cape Verde, Costa Rica, Morocco, Tunisia and the US.

With Iberostar, another Mallorcan company, starting in 1986, the Mallorcan model of resort hotels was exported around the world. But in Mallorca, by necessity, development had slowed down by the mid-1970s. The oil crisis of 1973 led to a major slump in tourism the following year, and controls on new hotels were introduced as Mallorca took stock and started coming to terms with what some people were describing as a tourism monster. The number of hotel beds had increased from 38,000 in 1963 to 164,000 a decade later, and 267,000 by 1993.

A halt to new building was called in the 1980s, but many existing hotels were allowed to get bigger. By the 1980s much of the Bay of Palma was covered in concrete, with the British ensconced around Magalluf on the western side, and the Germans around Arenal and Playa de Palma in the east. The mass-market resorts had become vulgar, and many families moved away to the quieter resorts along the northern and eastern coasts such as Alcudia or Pollensa. Another trend that developed from the 1990s was small-scale, upmarket rural tourism, with many farmhouses being converted into boutique hotels.

Mallorca can still attract the five-star tourist who wants privacy and refinement, and as it is larger than some Spanish islands, it has managed to cope with diverse nationalities as many Russians and

Eastern Europeans joined the mix. It still welcomes diverse customers ranging from the young and rowdy to the cultural visitor keen to explore the history and chic hotels of Palma's old town, but there has been reputational damage along the way, especially in Magalluf.

Young, drunken Brits had trashed its image by 2014, when a clampdown on bar crawls was belatedly announced as the authorities tried to stop Mallorca's whole image being sullied. A British resident of Magalluf wrote to the *Majorca Daily Bulletin* to complain that three-thirty in the morning was as rowdy as three-thirty in the afternoon, with young people 'shouting, drinking, eating takeaway food, cavorting naked in the sea and openly having sex in front of anyone who wanted to watch, which they did'. The debauchery plumbed new depths in July 2014 when a young British woman was filmed performing sex acts on twenty-four men in a Magalluf bar, the online footage going viral.

Since then, it is claimed, Magalluf has quietened down – with British police having a token presence and a determined effort by local police to stop the worst excesses. Hotel group Melia claims that families are returning to Magalluf, and that its hotels in the area, which have benefited from investment of €130 million, offer a 'peaceful and idyllic' holiday experience. But, if 2015 was indeed a turning point, it may take some years for improved public perceptions to follow – while the young drunks and fornicators will move on somewhere else.

Andrew Ede, editor of the *Majorca Daily Bulletin*, says:

> Whether Magalluf can eliminate its problems is a key issue in the island. Melia has a long-term strategy but bars, clubs and restaurants have a short-term view. There are many sceptics who say Magalluf is Magalluf, but it can change, and some of the media who came looking for stories in 2015 left disappointed.
>
> Another issue is the all-inclusive hotels which started in the 1990s, and some mayors describe it as a complete disaster as visitors don't go out of the hotels to spend money. All-inclusive probably represents about 35 per cent of all hotel rooms, but in areas like Alcudia it is being cut back. Another problem is a lack of flights in winter, with many hotels wanting to stay open having to close.

The British tabloid press, which feasted off Magalluf, has often been responsible for some of the misconceptions about package holidays. This is particularly true of Benidorm on the Costa Blanca, which developed so rapidly from the mid-1960s that it became synonymous with cheap package holidays. British beer, fish and chips, steak and kidney pie and people singing God Save the Queen in the sun became the stock images, gleefully seized upon by the ITV comedy drama *Benidorm*, which started its eighth series in 2016.

With two beautiful but busy south-facing beaches and over one hundred mainly high-rise hotels (the 776-room Hotel Bali being the tallest hotel in Europe), Benidorm clearly won't appeal to anyone who wants a quiet time. But it is still bad-mouthed by some people who have never been there, and the tabloid press is largely responsible for that.

Clarksons played a key role in Benidorm's development in the late 1960s and early 1970s, funding the building of many hotels. The airport that opened in nearby Alicante in 1967 made Benidorm much more accessible, as previously visitors had faced a three-hour coach journey from Valencia airport. Another ninety-five hotels were completed by 1972 and, with hundreds of bars, restaurants and night-clubs, Benidorm soon claimed to be the biggest single holiday resort in Europe.

Christopher Lord, who ran Lord Brothers in the late 1950s and 1960s, says there was a serious lack of control as Spain developed. 'We were as guilty as any other tour operator, getting people to build hotels,' he adds. 'That's when it became a rat race, with Clarksons lowering the tone of people who went to Spain and leading to the kind of behaviour we see today in Magalluf. When we started, a third of our clients were titled – Lord This and Lady That. Within a few years it changed to "we just come here to get drunk".'

A long-time British resident, Charles Wilson, set out to debunk the myths in his book *Benidorm: The Truth*, published in 1999. By that time Benidorm had already run publicity campaigns trying to change its image, which had been partially successful. According to Wilson the smear campaign started as early as 1971, based on 'trivial' complaints by some holidaymakers. Although figures in 1990 showed that only two hundred of over one thousand bars and restaurants were British-owned, and only two of these were fish-and-chip shops, the tabloids persisted with their portrayal of Blackpool in the sun with headlines proclaiming that 'you've had your chips in Benidorm' and 'Benidorm has other fat to fry'. By the 1980s it was being portrayed as the playground of lager louts, but although three hundred British people were arrested and fined for drunkenness and vandalism in 1983, they represented a tiny minority of the 700,000 British visitors.

Vexing though its reputation might be, the Benidorm presented in the media does not put off visitors and summer 2015 was claimed to be its best ever season. Maria Jose Montiel, who worked for Thomson Holidays from 1975 and was director of the Benidorm Tourist Board from 1999 to 2009, recalls a surge of bookings when the ITV comedy series first aired.

'At the end of the day, programmes like this are about the British making fun of themselves,' she says. 'We do have one area that is full of pubs and British-style entertainment, but we also have lots of typical tapas bars and good restaurants. It is true that Benidorm is a mass tourism resort for the British lower and middle classes, but it is also very popular with the Spanish.'

Nearly half Benidorm's visitors are still British (the other half are Spanish), and the problems facing tourism in North Africa mean that many are now going back to the familiar resorts in Spain that offer great value. But with many low-cost airlines now flying to Alicante and all the other main resort gateways, fewer people now choose a traditional package.

'Thomson used to contract forty hotels in Benidorm that worked with it exclusively, but now it is completely different,' says Montiel. 'All hotels now sell online to the general public, and of course there are now a lot of all-inclusive hotels that I don't agree with, as there are so many places to eat and enjoy entertainment. It's not like parts of the Caribbean where people don't feel safe and there's nowhere else to go.'

Quality has definitely improved, as online reviews would soon name and shame hotels with low standards and gone are the days when tour operators would pay hotels a pittance. Montiel remembers that, as a Thomson rep, she would take tourists on barbecue excursions and tell them to eat all they could during their escape from the dreary fare in hotel restaurants, but now the buffet tables groan with a huge choice of dishes. Benidorm has diversified by opening the Terra Mitica theme park and five-star hotels with golf courses, and yet some of the old myths live on.

Many more people now appreciate Spain's history, culture and gastronomy as they explore by car, or on coach tours or city breaks. But Benidorm and Mallorca will always mean cheap and not necessarily cheerful for many people, and now there is a far greater choice of holiday destinations both in Europe and further afield.

Menorca and Ibiza, the other main islands in the same Balearics group as Mallorca, have had varying fortunes. Menorca has always appealed to families and has avoided the excesses of its neighbours, with a greater proportion of apartments. Ibiza, being much smaller than Mallorca, has struggled to hang on to families while gaining a reputation as Europe's top party island. Fortunately for the island's image, the higher prices charged by its huge night-clubs and general air of hip-ness have kept Ibiza a lot more select than Magalluf.

The Costa del Sol was unknown when Horizon Holidays discovered it in the mid-1950s, when Torremolinos, which became the biggest resort, had only two hotels. But by the 1960s the Costa del Sol was built up all the way from Malaga to Marbella, with Marbella cultivating its exclusive image even after the film stars had moved on. Like many parts of Spain, Marbella gained a reputation for corrupt local politicians, leading to the local council being dissolved. Many years after their construction it emerged that some hotels all over Spain had been built illegally, but despite some posturing it was too late to do anything about it.

Parts of the Spanish coast that developed later, such as Murcia and Almeria in the south-east, generally avoided high-rise development. Tastes changed and resorts were developed as much for long-term residents as package holidays. Large expatriate ghettoes, especially along the Costa del Sol, fuelled demand for cheap flights without a hotel thrown in.

Some resorts actually went into decline, especially along the Costa Brava, with tour operators complaining about lack of investment. The Costa Brava was rescued by Ryanair's decision to base a fleet of aircraft at Gerona airport, but few visitors nowadays come on package holidays and many come from Eastern Europe as well as the UK or Germany. The Costa Dorada, slightly to the south, started extending the summer season when the Port Aventura theme park opened in Salou.

One part of Spain that has tourists year-round is the Canary Islands, hundreds of miles south of the mainland in the Atlantic Ocean, which have steady temperatures of around 20–22 degrees centigrade all winter. Tenerife, Gran Canaria, Lanzarote, Fuerteventura and the lesser-known islands were originally winter sun destinations for a select few, and did not start to develop mass tourism until the 1980s. That meant they could learn from the experiences of mainland Spain and the Balearics, but this did not prevent high-density resorts such as Playa de las Americas (Tenerife) from opening up. Tenerife used to be a stop-over point for British people returning by sea from the colonies in Africa or India, and had a following before the era of air travel. Most people headed for Puerto de la Cruz in the north with its warm and often damp climate, and no one ever went to the hot, arid south.

All that began to change in 1978 when Tenerife South airport opened and the coastline was built up, but many of the hotels are five-star, in substantial grounds, some with golf courses despite the shortage of water. Wings was one of the first tour operators to fly people to Puerto de la Cruz, but aircraft had to stop and refuel in Gibraltar before the jet age. Longer-range aircraft such as the Boeing 707 cut the journey time to the Canary Islands to about four hours by the late 1960s, bringing guaranteed winter sunshine closer than ever.

Spain is still the number one choice for many sun seekers, sixty years after it was first discovered. That says a lot about its appeal, but only a minority now takes package holidays. It has gone in and out of favour as the Greek Islands, Turkey and Egypt emerged, but found new sources of tourists such as Russians, who were free to travel after the Soviet Union broke apart. As North Africa and possibly Turkey now face serious problems, another golden age for Spain might be coming.

3

1965–1974: From Boom to Bust

1965 marked a major turning point for the young, upstart package holiday business when media conglomerate the Thomson Organisation bought its way in – leading within a few years to the establishment of Thomson Holidays as the best-known name. It was to become the biggest package holiday company within a decade and still holds that position over fifty years later, an achievement few market leaders in any business can claim. How sad, then, that the Thomson name will soon be swallowed up by its German owner TUI, the latest of many famous names to disappear.

The Thomson Organisation was a Canadian company that owned *The Scotsman*, *The Sunday Times* and a large number of regional newspapers, plus Scottish Television. Starting in 1965 it bought Universal Sky Tours, Britannia Airways, Riviera Holidays and Gaytours in quick succession, and set about transforming them into a professionally run, quality company with its own charter airline. By 1972 it had added Lunn Poly, which became the name of its travel agency chain. All the pieces were in place to launch a bid for the number one spot then occupied by Clarksons.

What attracted big business to package holidays? It was simple – cash flow – and the opportunity to be involved at an early stage in a sector ready for enormous growth. Tour operators took in a lot of cash during the winter, when newspapers were struggling, and those same newspapers could be used for low-cost advertising. Package holidays appeared to require little expertise, and people such as Riviera's Aubrey Morris were persuaded to stay on to smooth the transition.

Thomson's first target was Horizon, but Vladimir Raitz didn't want to sell. So it turned instead to Ted Langton of Universal Sky Tours, who was past sixty and, by all accounts, somewhat eccentric. Jed Williams, whom Langton had recruited to run Britannia, remembered him as a 'one-man Mafia with no management skills whatsoever', adding: 'The airline could go bankrupt because Ted could have left a nought off one of those sums he worked out on the back of an envelope'.

Langton is remembered more fondly by Philip Morrell, who became a rep in Benidorm around the time of the purchase, working for Thomson until 1978. Morrell says his passion was to build things rather than to actually run them, and like other entrepreneurs he gathered the right people to manage for him. Thomson's purchase was for about £900,000, but Langton felt he had sold too cheaply. He returned to his office one day to find the locks had been changed.

Bryan Llewelyn, who was brought in from the newspaper side to run Thomson's new acquisitions, says: 'It made sense to destroy those brands and create a new one, as customer loyalty lasts only as long as your prices are right and sentimentality lasts for only a few minutes. Our main thrust was to ensure we could run charter flights despite British European Airways fighting to stop us, and to ensure we had enough hotel beds in the resorts. Our ability to finance the building of hotels was very important.

'We developed the concept of children's clubs at hotels, so parents could enjoy some time on their own. Prices were always competitive, but we promised more than a seat on a plane and a hotel bed. We dropped the names of Universal Sky Tours, Gaytours, Luxitours and Riviera but we did it for good reason. Sentiment for old names lasts for only a few minutes.'

Roger Lambert, who joined Riviera in 1965 and stayed with Thomson for more than twenty years, remembers that period of frenetic hotel building with mixed feelings. 'We had a bad case in Cala Millor, Mallorca – a large hotel that didn't open in time for the 1967 season,' he says. 'It looked good as an artist's impression, but it was nowhere near finished and we had to put customers wherever we could find them beds. One of the tabloids ran a spread about the "heartbreak hotel", but that hotel sold out completely when it did open in 1968.'

With incentives from the Spanish government to build hotels and plenty of tour operators offering cash up-front, many local people saw the opportunity to get rich quickly. David Harrold, who also worked for Thomson, says: 'Hotels were being built so quickly that, one year, we had twenty-seven artists' impressions in our brochure. A kitchen porter could end up running a hotel, but he ran it like a kitchen porter.

'Thomson was determined to become the top tour operator, but we had six bosses in the first couple of years after the takeover and the instability affected us. Bryan Llewellyn was the one who brought in modern management techniques, a proper sales force and a marketing department. Thomson became a marketing-driven organisation, rather than an entrepreneurial one.'

Most people were happy with even basic hotel standards, which were better than in a British hotel or guest house, and sometimes better than they had at home. 'A lot of people had never been abroad before and were very naïve,' says Harrold. 'They would wake up in Benidorm and find they had not only a private bathroom but also a balcony, when they were used to a boarding house in Morecambe or Blackpool, which had neither.' And, of course, there was nearly always sun.

Michael East, who worked in Clarksons' hotels division, says: 'In 1972 we did a survey of customers who flew mainly from Glasgow and Manchester, and 15 per cent came from homes with no bathroom, but an outside toilet and a tin bath. They were used to holidays in Britain, in a caravan or bed-and-breakfast.'

Also involved at the sharp end was Hugh Morgan, whose career in tour operating has lasted half a century. In 1966 he joined a cheap start-up company called Sunair whose boss, Harry Goodman, would later be acclaimed as the greatest entrepreneur the package holiday business had ever seen. In those early days, the problems were rife.

'Sometimes a plane would arrive in Mallorca and there were just no beds for the customers, and one day we put them straight back on the plane and flew them on to the Canary Islands,' he recalls. 'Communications were very bad, and if a flight didn't turn up for some reason, no one told us. The Costa Brava was a big destination, but before Gerona airport opened we had to fly people to Perpignan and bus them across the border. The trip took several hours and my job as a rep was to keep the coach driver awake. Accommodation was basic, but customers booked lots of excursions and no one sat around in their hotels looking at the cracks in the ceiling. As long as the sun shone and they had plenty of sangria and things to do, people were happy.

'We had five hundred customers at a hotel in Palma Nova, Mallorca, where a huge crack developed down the side. The *Daily Mail* revealed that it was officially closed due to faulty foundations, and I had to go out and face the press, at a very young age, and say, "what crack?" Someone must have bunged the mayor some money.

'Some hoteliers were very unscrupulous, taking bookings from lots of different tour operators and selling twice as many rooms as they actually had. Then they would put people in what they called annexes two streets away, and the dining room, which seated one hundred people, would have three sittings with awful food, and waiters rushed off their feet. People would arrive at hotels that were only half built – they would look out of their windows and see a forest of cranes. It got worse – there were people dying of legionnaire's disease in Benidorm. The media turned up, but reporting wasn't in depth. This was long before programmes like *Holidays from Hell*.'

Horizon managed to steer a steady course through the 1960s, growing cautiously while some of its newer rivals were going full-tilt for expansion. Regional tour operations were starting to grow, and in 1965 it took a 25 per cent shareholding in a new Birmingham company called Horizon Midlands, which would outlast its parent and become a major player in the 1970s and 1980s. An established company in Birmingham at that time was Sunflight, set up by Doug Ellis who became long-standing chairman of Aston Villa Football Club.

Another development by Horizon was setting up one of the most famous, or infamous, names in package holidays – Club 18-30. The name that would become synonymous with sun, sea, sand and plenty of sex – not to mention plenty of booze – was rather more innocent at the start, as indeed were its customers. David Heard was a music student when he got a part-time job working for Horizon in 1963, but then he damaged his hand badly in an accident and realised his dreams of becoming a guitarist were in tatters. Instead he took a full-time job working for Lenny Koven, Vladimir Raitz's partner at Horizon.

'Lenny was like a mentor to me, and I used to bring him ideas in the afternoon, when he was relaxed,' says Heard. 'There had been an organisation called the Under Thirties Travel Club that had gone bust, and Horizon's advertising agency came up with the idea of a new operation called Club 18–30. Horizon had gone into time charters, which were revolutionary. It would say to an airline, "We will buy seven hundred hours of flying from you – how much? And if we bought one thousand hours, what discount can you give us?" Young people didn't mind flying at night, so the idea behind Club 18–30 wasn't to tap into a new market, but to take advantage of night flying and fulfil our commitments to airlines.'

Club 18–30 made its debut in 1965 with a small programme to Playa de Aro, Cadaques and Estartit on the Costa Brava, with two-week holidays costing from £34 (£616 in today's money) including meals with wine – 'about what you'd spend in Margate in a wet October'. Its first brochure promised:

Nobody is in charge of a Club 18–30 holiday, but at each hotel there is a resident Horizon layabout. He knows where the music is coolest, the sand softest, the brandy cheapest. He knows the best clubs, bars and dives. If he doesn't know it – it doesn't exist.

The brochure added, 'It's no use bringing Mother, she wouldn't like it.' Sometimes, recalls Heard, mother would pack off her son or daughter hoping they'd 'grow up a bit' on their first solo holiday, which they very often did! But sometimes the weight of expectation hung heavily on these young people, who right from the start were predominantly in their late teens or early twenties. Heard recalls one case where a young man threw himself off a balcony but survived, and when Heard rang up his mother her response was, 'It's the sex, dear, I thought a holiday would do him good as he wasn't getting any.'

Club 18–30's 'layabout' was in fact a dedicated rep living and working in one hotel rather than covering several hotels, as most reps did. 'We realised very soon that young people spent as much while away on holiday as they did on the package,' explains Heard. 'Our objective was to get that spend by organising lots of our own excursions, separate from Horizon's excursions as their people wouldn't want to mix with us. These included horse-riding and barbecue beach parties, and we used to incentivise our reps not to run their own private excursions that they didn't tell us about. This was common practice at the time, and why tour operators could get away with paying their reps peanuts.'

John Bond, now chairman of Jetset Tours, started as a Club 18–30 rep in 1970 and met his wife, Hilary, when she was one of the customers. 'We did things you just couldn't do now because of health and safety, such as boozy horse-riding trips and cooking our own food on the beach,' he recalls. 'You could usually tell Club 18–30 customers at the airport because they were shy and had heavy sweaters and overcoats – their parents had probably sent them away. I had to try and integrate them, and in those days we had cultural excursions too. In the more expensive hotels, there were usually more girls. If a girl was getting too much attention or was a bit shy, the rest of the group would try to protect her – it was quite extraordinary to watch. Of course there was sex, but the guys who came out looking for it often didn't succeed. There were usually one or two crazies that we had to babysit.'

Heard was to buy Club 18–30 from Horizon in 1972, and build it up into a household name. But the days when this type of holiday became truly infamous were still in the future.

Eyewitness: Christine Blocksidge
She worked for nearly fifty years as a travel agent in and around Preston, Lancashire.

In the early 1960s, package holidays did not really exist. Sophisticated and experienced travellers would visit a travel agency and select a destination, and we would find flights from scheduled airlines and show them the black-and-white photo book produced by Swans with "touristy" hotels throughout the Mediterranean. In the North there were no charter flights, no holiday brochures and no package holiday companies, but there were tour operators offering coach tours and holidays by rail. Invention of the charter flight was long overdue, and, when it happened, it was a brave move that catapulted the travel industry into the future.

The company which first produced a brochure and a reservation system was Horizon, and brochures for the following summer were issued in November. This became party time for travel agents as each tour operator held long and lavish parties to celebrate. Making a booking involved telephoning the tour operator and telling them what the client had selected, and STD (Subscriber Trunk Dialling) had only just been introduced. One year, just after the launch of the Horizon summer brochure, it took one dedicated member of staff in my agency twenty-one days' continuous dialling to get through to Horizon and ask for the reservations we had spent this time collecting! When she did get through, she was on the phone for nine hours.

It was a fantastic breakthrough when computerised reservations arrived in the 1980s. Good old Thomson Holidays was the first tour operator to bring computerisation into the package holiday industry, and Skytrak followed soon after, which allowed us access to airline reservation systems. What followed was a glorious time for the travel industry as taking a holiday, especially a foreign holiday, became almost standard for the average family. Specialist tour operators began to emerge, concentrating on a smaller section of the emerging holiday world, and the whole travel industry developed and matured into a multi-million-pound business.

Tour operators employed huge teams of resort representatives to look after the arriving holidaymakers. Many of today's great movers and shakers in the travel business started their careers in overseas locations, welcoming tired and emotional Brits arriving at Gerona Airport at some unearthly hour of the morning. Happy Days!

Although the airlines that flew their customers had to be licensed, tour operators faced no regulations at all. Harry Goodman, who left school at sixteen to work in a travel agency, learned tour operating the hard way by selling from door-to-door in south-east London. 'It was cowboy country, and like the beginning of a gold rush,' he recalls. 'Package holidays were driven by two things – where the hotels were cheap, and the exchange rate favourable. There weren't any consumer protection rules, and you could get away with things that you'd go to jail for now. At Sunair we were small, off the radar of the big companies. I didn't want to emulate Clarksons, which was the number one operator in the 1960s. But, like me later on, Clarksons was ahead of its time.'

Clarksons was run by the mercurial Tom Gullick, and was the first tour operator to see the benefits of piling holidays high and selling them cheap while more established companies – especially Horizon, Wings and Lord Brothers – guarded their quality reputation. The Thomson-owned companies stood somewhere in between but didn't indulge in a price war until the early 1970s. Clarksons started to build up Spain in a big way from 1965 and once again the artist's impression and the unfinished hotel would loom large.

'There was a huge press campaign against us, and the media were moving cement mixers from one hotel to another to make a better story,' Gullick would recall later. 'Right from the start, Clarksons was never a very commercial operation. But we were providing a social service, making holidays available to people who could never otherwise have afforded them. The thing to remember is that 95 per cent of our customers were totally happy, but to make the other 5 per cent happy we would have to raise prices when a lot of their grievances were not genuine. The price of perfection was simply not attainable.'

The first package holidays had operated only from major airports such as Gatwick and Manchester, and put others such as Luton and Southend on the map. But other regional airports, mostly owned by local authorities at this time, were clamouring for a slice of the action. To base aircraft at smaller airports would not have been economic, and using foreign airlines was expensive. Stewart Wild, who ran the Clarksons tours programme, remembers his boss Tom Gullick coming up with the idea of basing an aircraft at Luton, flying it to a holiday resort, then back to a smaller airport such as Cardiff or Newcastle. It would then return to the resort and back to Luton, all the while using just one crew: what became known as the W pattern.

'This was very efficient and really drove down costs,' says Wild. 'We were able to achieve even greater economies of scale by the late 1960s when jets became available. Jets offered faster journey times and were also more comfortable and offered a quieter ride. Dan-Air was a leading charter airline and it operated Comet jets, which really came into their own on longer routes such as Tenerife. There were several accidents involving Comets in the 1950s, but no one remembered them. People just felt privileged to be riding on a jet, which was something new. Tom Gullick always wanted to stay ahead of the competition, and he usually succeeded,' adds Wild. 'Thomson was more conservative and sensible, and made more money. We took more risks.'

Philip Morrell, at Thomson from 1965 to 1978, remembers Clarksons as a formidable competitor that also sold a broader range of holidays including cruises, ski breaks, lakes and mountains resorts, city breaks and the Dutch bulbfields. Thomson looked 'tired and unimaginative in comparison', he adds.

The British-made BAC 1-11 jet made its debut in 1965, and by the late 1960s was widely deployed by airlines including British United, Laker and Autair, which was acquired and absorbed by a conglomerate called Court Line. These new jets could fly at 550 mph from London to Palma, Mallorca in just two hours – a flying time that remains the same today and a far cry from the 48-hour overland journey that people had faced just a decade earlier. They shaved an hour off the typical journey time to the Mediterranean by a turboprop aircraft, and allowed more tour operators to plan the intensive schedules introduced by Clarksons. But these new toys were expensive. They had to be kept flying and earning their keep at all costs, and this was to cause the collapse of tour operators who were over-committed.

The need to fill his new jets was uppermost in Freddie Laker's mind when he bought two tour operators, Lord Brothers and Northern-based Arrowsmith, in the late 1960s. 'Freddie Laker wanted to have a package holiday business to keep his three 1-11 jets flying,' says Christopher Lord. 'He needed 2,200 flying hours per year guaranteed for each aircraft, and these companies were able to keep two of them busy while Wings chartered the third. Jets made a huge difference. They may not have saved a lot of time on shorter routes, but on longer routes such as the Canary Islands they made non-stop flights possible in under four hours.' The Lord Brothers name was not kept on, as Laker Holidays took over. But the Arrowsmith name, which had huge recognition in the North, lasted into the 1980s.

The introduction of jets was high on Thomson's agenda too, and after much wrangling it finally decided on the American Boeing 737 rather than the home-made 1-11. This proved to be a master stroke as the 737 was much more efficient than the British model and became the workhorse of charter airline fleets for a generation. Even today, the latest versions of the Boeing 737 are used throughout the world by airlines including Ryanair, although its main rival, the Airbus A320, is now in the ascendancy throughout Europe.

Derek Davison, in charge of Britannia when the decision was made, recalled: 'For us, it was all about productivity. From the days of the Constellations with eighty-two passengers, taking eight hours to Palma and back, we moved to Britannias with 112 passengers taking six hours, to what now became possible – carrying 117 passengers in just four hours. It made jolly good economic sense.'

Thomson had already ordered the Boeing 737 when one of its Britannia aircraft, carrying 110 passengers and seven crew, crashed in Yugoslavia in 1966 with the loss of ninety-five lives. The feeling was growing that older turbo-prop aircraft needed to be phased out, and the first 737 duly arrived in July 1968. Eventually Thomson was to order thirty-one of these aircraft for Britannia, later models carrying 130 passengers with a range of nearly 2,000 miles, making many more resorts viable for package holidays. The 737 was also slightly larger than the 1-11, and this was a crucial advantage. At a time when most charter airlines had hand-me-down aircraft that had seen better days, Thomson had a brand new proposition.

'Thomson's genius was opting for the Boeing 737 rather than the 1-11,' says Clarksons' Stewart Wild. 'With bigger and more efficient aircraft than us, Thomson had an edge and kept prices down.' Thomson hadn't yet entered a price war with Clarksons, which seemed intent on building volume at all costs. That was to come in 1970, but in the meantime Clarksons was wringing the best possible productivity out of the 1-11s it chartered from Autair, which was renamed Court Line Aviation in 1970. One innovation was to squeeze in three more seats by reducing the size of the galley used to serve on-board meals. Seat-back catering was introduced, loading sandwiches into a cavity in the back of the seat in front for passengers to eat after take-off. A second sandwich dispenser would be locked out of use for passengers on the return journey.

This was a real age of adventure when it seemed anyone could start a tour operation, including a Greek called Basil Mantzos who ran the Olympic Electronics shop in west London. Olympic Holidays started in 1967 and Mantzos soon gained a reputation for enthusiastically 'talking up' his country and persuading both the media and travel agents that Olympic was much bigger than it really was. 'Basil hated the colonels who ran Greece as a military dictatorship from 1967 to

1974, and he wanted to show people what his country was really like,'
says Colin Brain, who was recruited to run the tour operation. 'He
was fantastic to work for and we did some amazing deals, including
chartering an Olympic Airways [no connection] Boeing 727 for weekly
flights to Corfu and Athens. He persuaded the Duke of St Albans to act
as chairman to give us some credibility.' Olympic Holidays survives to
this day under different ownership, but came close to collapse a couple
of the times in the 1970s and 1980s.

In winter 1971, the licensing authorities abolished the 'Provision
One' restriction requiring package holiday prices not to undercut the
lowest scheduled air fare, but only for winter holidays of less than
seven nights at first. Clarksons' Tom Gullick welcomed this as 'the
most momentous breakthrough in the holiday industry of all time',
but tour operators had already found ways of getting around the rules,
as they would later get around the rule that passengers on European
charter flights must have a hotel included in their package. John
Harding, who worked for Global, recalls: 'The return scheduled air
fare to Palma was £29, so all our holidays cost £29. But we included
£5 credit vouchers to spend on excursions or your bar bill at the hotel,
and eventually we were able to persuade the Air Travel Licensing
Board that maintaining artificially high prices was just not logical.'

Abolition of price controls and the efficiency of the new jets led to
a rash of cheap long weekend offers to Spanish resorts from as little
as £10. But in one of those flashes of brilliance that everyone would
remember for many years to come, Thomson – which had by now
superseded the names of its acquisitions – did something which really
captured the imagination. In 1972 it introduced £29 weekends to
Moscow!

Media interest was unprecedented, as the Cold War was at its
height. But the Soviet Union, like all of Eastern Europe, needed foreign
currency and a deal was done behind the scenes to make it possible
(see chapter six). From an airline point of view, it also made perfect
sense. The Moscow weekends – which laid the foundations for twenty
years of Thomson invading the Soviet Union – were available only in
winter, when Britannia's 737s needed the work.

For the vast majority of people, however, a package holiday meant
a week or two in the sun, usually in Spain or another Mediterranean
country. As the 1960s wore on people became more experienced and
worldly, and by 1968 a book called *A Truthful Guide to Package
Holiday Resorts* was published. The BBC's *Holiday* programme
made its debut in 1969 as the media began to take package holidays

seriously, and yet many of the myths that grew up in the early 1960s persisted.

The long-running series of Carry On... films were often rather behind the times in any case, and in the 1972 release *Carry On Abroad* Sidney James, Kenneth Williams, Barbara Windsor, Hattie Jacques et al fly to the fictitious island of Elsbels for a long weekend costing £17 all-in. 'You're always the same when you go abroad – you become an animal!', Sid's wife cautions. The Elsbels Palace Hotel is not only unfinished, but has dodgy electrics, a dubious water supply and swarms of mosquitoes. The incompetent manager and lecherous waiter serving 'sausage, beans and chippings' add to the fun, before the whole party is locked up after a riot at a strip club and the hotel is washed away in a flood. *Carry On Abroad* was filmed not in Spain or Italy, but at Pinewood Studios near London and in Slough.

A boost for package holidays came from the unlikely source of drinks brand Campari, which employed famous actress Lorraine Chase in 1974 for a TV advertisement, available to view on Youtube. 'Were you truly wafted here from paradise?' asks her admirer, as they drink. 'No,' she replies, in a broad Cockney accent, 'Luton airport!'

Despite the image that many people still had of package holidays, the industry was growing up and that included a drive to protect the public's money when a tour operator went out of business. Fiesta's collapse in 1964 had led to a warning from the government that it would consider a licensing system for tour operators if they didn't come up with an alternative plan, and in 1965 ABTA set up a fund to protect people left stranded. It also introduced the 'Stabiliser' closed-shop rule meaning that travel agents could only sell holidays by ABTA member tour operators, who in turn would only sell through ABTA agents. ABTA effectively became a licence to trade and membership grew rapidly, and as it imposed strict financial standards there was no repetition of the Fiesta collapse with customers stranded abroad.

But apart from the limited fund set up by ABTA, customers could still lose their money as there was no safety net if a company went to the wall. This was seen as an increasing risk as package holiday companies grew rapidly, and the devaluation of the pound in 1967 – which meant heavy losses for companies afraid to increase their prices – made that even more likely. Many tour operators were walking a financial tightrope and in 1970 the top companies, which had set up Tour Operators Study Group three years earlier, came up with a bonding scheme underwritten by a bank.

Now there was a fund worth over £5 million to draw upon if one of its twenty-two members went down, and in 1972 ABTA followed by introducing bonding for all its tour operator members. Companies not belonging to ABTA or Tour Operators Study Group were still outside the safety net, however, and after the Civil Aviation Authority was set up in 1972, the Air Travel Organisers Licence (ATOL) scheme was started. By the 1990s, the CAA had taken over responsibility for licensing all holidays by air.

It might seem that ABTA and Tour Operators Study Group were operating a club that outsiders found hard to join, but the whole purpose was to protect the public, and the travel industry was making a better job of this than most other sectors. If you paid for almost any kind of goods and the company you bought from went bust before they were delivered, you lost your money. The 1974 Consumer Credit Act protected people paying by credit cards, but these were in their infancy as the 1970s dawned.

Global's Sidney Perez, who with Travel Club's Harry Chandler, was instrumental in setting up financial protection, recalls: 'Any damage to consumer confidence hit the whole industry, and after Fiesta we couldn't let that happen again. Tour operators also came together to discuss all sorts of other problems, and although there was self-interest, it was balanced. Having seen the progress we made protecting customers' money, the CAA decided to broaden this to cover the whole of the industry.'

By 1972 the travel industry seemed to have solved its own problems. All looked set fair, but a crisis was brewing that no one could have foreseen. Clarksons continued its phenomenal growth, but started running into trouble as its profit margins were wafer-thin and Thomson, its main rival, slashed prices. In 1970 Clarksons notched up its one-millionth customer, only a few years after starting mass-market holidays to Spain. Most of its flights were operated by Court Line Aviation, and Court Line became so concerned about Clarksons, its main customer, that it bought an 85 per cent stake in it for a nominal £1 in 1973, taking on its debts. Tom Gullick, Clarksons' driving force, had left the previous year after a disagreement with the owners, Shipping and Industrial Holdings. In 1973, Clarksons lost over £3 million – an enormous amount.

Court Line was a highly ambitious organisation, which had a fleet of oil tankers, a shipyard and other tourism interests, including hotels and a regional airline in the Caribbean. In 1973 it introduced two wide-bodied, twin-aisle aircraft, Lockheed TriStars, which could carry nearly four hundred passengers each. Clarksons, seeing the opportunity to slash holiday prices because of economies of scale, signed a five-year deal to take them on.

Stewart Wild remembers: 'On routes such as Palma and Alicante in Spain, one TriStar could replace three 1-11s and the price we paid per seat was halved. But no one had considered what to do with the TriStars in the off-season, as you couldn't cut a TriStar in half. Cancelling TriStar flights and putting passengers onto 1-11s was a messy business.'

Clarksons' costings were based on selling 95 per cent of seats on a charter aircraft before it started making money, whereas most tour operators started making money when they had sold 85–90 per cent of seats. The price war with Thomson drew in other companies too, including Horizon, as Vladimir Raitz recalled. 'We had to cut margins drastically in order to compete,' he wrote. 'Horizon Holidays was to learn the bitter lesson that, by and large, the travelling public was not interested in brand loyalty. A holiday from a competing firm that was just a few pounds cheaper was all it took for a client to switch.'

Most tour operators, Horizon included, were racking up big losses by 1973. Then, in October that year, fuel prices suddenly rocketed. In response to American support for Israel in the Yom Kippur war, Arab members of the Organisation of Petroleum Exporting Countries announced an embargo on selling oil to the US and its allies, which had the effect of raising oil prices from $3 a barrel to $12, with catastrophic effects on Western economies. Oil had been cheap up till then – now all nations discovered how much they depended on it. Further economic difficulties were caused by a coal miners' work-to-rule, leading to the imposition of a three-day working week at the start of 1974 to conserve electricity. The economy was in crisis, and holiday bookings dried up.

Horizon was pushed to the edge of collapse despite Raitz putting up everything he owned as surety to his bank. 'All I wanted was Horizon's survival, and everything was expendable,' he wrote. '"Would you like me to place my children in your vaults?" I asked the bank manager on one occasion. He didn't seem to find this funny.' Court Line took over Horizon in February 1974 but Raitz lost almost everything and was out of a job. 'I could not possibly consider working in tandem with Clarksons, even though by that time Tom Gullick had been dismissed by his board who had finally realised that his price-war tactics had brought their own organisation to the brink of ruin,' he wrote. Although Raitz went on to find other roles in the travel industry, mainly with Air Malta, he remained bitter about Horizon's demise until his death in 2010.

It was just as well that Raitz didn't join Court Line, as that company and all its offshoots, including Clarksons and Horizon, went spectacularly bust only a few months later in August 1974. All the financial safeguards that the travel industry and the government had put in place were not sufficient to protect everyone in a collapse of this magnitude, but the winners were Thomson and a small company called Intasun, that Harry Goodman had set up as a successor to Sunair. On that August day Thomson became the top package holiday company in the UK, a position it has held on to ever since.

4

To the Med and Beyond

Spain may have dominated package holidays since the early days, but of course many other countries saw the opportunity to develop mass tourism in their own way, or try to imitate what Spain was doing. Many people are loyal to one country while others want to broaden their horizons, but, because Spain is so familiar, other countries are often judged – unfairly – by how they match up.

In the early days of mass tourism it was sometimes one tour operator, or even one person, who blazed a trail and put a country or resort area on the international tourist map. So it was with the Algarve, in southern Portugal. When the Algarve was a wild and mainly uninhabited coastline, tourism to Portugal was concentrated on the Lisbon area and around Porto in the cooler north. Harry and Rene Chandler of Travel Club of Upminster, who were pioneers of package holidays and tours, first discovered it in the early 1960s when Rene described it as 'like Ireland, but with sunshine'. But Harry ruled out starting a holiday programme to the Algarve because it had no airport, and the 200-mile trip by road or rail from Lisbon made it unattractive for package holidays. That soon changed with opening of Faro airport, and Travel Club joined Lord Brothers to offer charter flights despite the small number of hotels. But it did have a growing number of villas, including a complex built by Sidney de Haan, the founder of Saga.

Throughout the 1960s tourism development took off along most of the Algarve coast, continuing when the military dictatorship was overthrown in 1974 and Portugal briefly descended into chaos. Not for the first time and certainly not for the last, British tourists demonstrated a determination to carry on and not be put off by political events. Chandler later reflected on how the Algarve developed, musing: 'People are always contending that places have been spoiled, and blaming tour companies and travel writers who encourage people to visit certain resorts and bring about pressure for change. But for every person who objects, there is one who will welcome it – usually because he or she is on the receiving end of the benefits. As for the Algarve, the change wrought by tourism has been overwhelmingly for the better.'

The Algarve soon developed into one of the big tourist destinations of southern Europe. But far greater scope existed in Greece, with not only a long coastline but hundreds of islands offering the possibility of escape on the one hand, and tourism development to alleviate poverty on the other. Like Italy, Greece was thought of only as a cultural tourism destination until the 1960s. Wealthy and idealistic British visitors had been coming since the poet Lord Byron arrived in 1823 to help the struggle for independence from the Ottomans, dying there the following year. People came to Greece to see the classical ruins and celebrate the cradle of democracy, but when jets started flying non-stop to Athens, beach lovers and island hoppers started coming too. Greece was undeveloped compared to Spain, and *A Truthful Guide to Package Holiday Resorts*, published in 1968, was guarded. 'For the archaeological enthusiast, yes,' it remarked. 'For the adventurous, unconventional beach fan, yes. Sophisticates and luxury lovers, choose with care. On the whole we think not a country for families with young children.'

The first islands to be developed were Crete (which is big enough to offer many kinds of tourist experience), Rhodes and Corfu. Large hotels were built on these islands, as they were on the Halkidiki peninsula in the north of the mainland where the Spanish pattern was followed, and along the coastline near Athens. But for the most part, Greece relied on small hotels, tavernas, simple villas and apartments right through the 1970s and 1980s, and that was (and still is, in many places) its charm. Greece attracted package holidaymakers who didn't like the idea of packages, plus backpackers and island hoppers who arrived in their thousands at Athens, went down to the port at Piraeus, and hopped on a ferry. People often felt closer to the country than they did in Spain, and were happy with lower standards. Sunmed, a Greece specialist, became famous for 'tell it like it is' brochures.

The romance of Greece was enhanced by various films, starting with *Zorba the Greek* in 1964 starring Anthony Quinn and Alan Bates, set in western Crete. Greek restaurants started to appear all over the UK, although many of these were in fact owned by Greek Cypriots. In 1989 came *Shirley Valentine*, a film based on the Willy Russell play of the same name, about a bored housewife (Pauline Collins) who finds sex, romance and a huge boost to her self-esteem with taverna owner Costas (Tom Conti) on the island of Mykonos. In 1999 came the musical *Mamma Mia!*, also set on the Greek islands, with *Captain Corelli's Mandolin*, set in the island of Kefalonia, following in 2001.

Many of the islands remained unchanged and the preserve of visitors happy to rough it on long trips by ferry, or pay the high prices of flights from Athens. But by the 1980s islands including Kefalonia, Zante, Kos, Mykonos, Santorini and Samos all had direct flights from the UK and other countries, and when a small island has direct flights, the chances of retaining its character are much diminished. By the 1990s Greece was attracting up to three million British tourists a year, with major hotel developments on many more islands and luxury boutique hotels also appearing on islands such as Mykonos and Santorini. Some parts of the mainland remain undeveloped by comparison.

Few Greek resorts gained the (often undeserved) reputation for steak and kidney pie with pints of bitter as in parts of Spain, but some of the evils of tourism did arrive. Resorts including Faliraki in Rhodes, Malia in Crete and Laganas in Zante became notorious for drugs- and booze-fuelled young Brits, and by 2002 Faliraki's dire reputation was affecting the whole of Rhodes. It largely got over that as the lurid headlines moved on elsewhere, but for some potential visitors to Rhodes, the damage was done. In contrast, all the negative headlines about Greece's financial crisis have not affected tourism at all, with many visitors aware how much Greece relies on visitors, and returning out of loyalty to find that everything in the resorts functions normally, with prices keener than ever.

Cyprus was little developed for tourism by the time of the Turkish invasion in 1974, which led to partition and one of the most intractable political stand-offs in Europe. The Varosha area of Famagusta was developed as a major resort in the late 1960s, and found itself on the Turkish side after the invasion when hotels, homes and all kinds of businesses were suddenly abandoned in what became a ghost town. The Turkish army sealed off the resort and it has remained so ever since, its derelict hotels a potent symbol of the conflict and the stand-off that followed. The Greek-owned south of Cyprus became a major package holiday destination especially around Paphos and Larnaca, whereas Northern Cyprus – recognised only by Turkey and with no direct flights – remains little-known.

Britain granted independence to Cyprus in 1960 and Malta in 1964, but those countries remained in the sterling area for many years. That gave them an advantage in the 1960s and 1970s when currency restrictions were imposed on British people travelling abroad. These restrictions did not apply to Cyprus, Malta and also tiny Gibraltar, which remains a British Overseas Territory today. One tour operator, Exchange Travel, specialised in these sterling areas and had its brochures emblazoned with the Union Jack. After Spain unilaterally closed the border with Gibraltar, Exchange boss Gordon McNally was pictured sitting on his suitcase at the border demanding its re-opening.

Eyewitness: Noel Josephides
He started Sunvil Holidays in 1974 with Cyprus being his first destination, but this was the year the island was torn apart by war.

I come from a Cypriot-Italian family and we settled in Britain in 1960, after Cyprus became independent. I had started as Cyprus Property Tours a few years earlier, selling as well as renting villas, when the idea of a self-catering villa holiday in Cyprus was as exotic as going to India.

Our villas were in the mountains around Kyrenia and mainly owned by British people, but after the Turkish invasion in July 1974 everyone fled and they went so suddenly that radios were left on. We had three hundred customers in villas around the Kyrenia mountain range, but fortunately our English resort rep was married to a Turk and she was able to gather them. The next thing they knew was being surrounded by paratroopers, and one family decided to stay put so that they could watch the fighting.

There were only two large hotels in the Greek part of Cyprus at this time, and the others were around the Famagusta and Kyrenia areas which fell under Turkish control. The Greeks were moved out and very poor people from near the Syrian border in Turkey came to Cyprus to replace them. All the villas were looted, and people who owned villas in the Turkish zone never recovered them and I don't know what happened to their properties. We had to refund everyone and came close to going into liquidation.

It took a long time for the Greeks to establish a tourism industry in Cyprus, and you had to get there by sea until Larnaca airport opened. The demand was there so it was a good time for us, but there were very few hotels. We started offering holidays to Greece too, starting with Corfu and Crete. Our clients were well educated and interested in culture, and we have had the same type of clientele ever since.

Sicily was our next destination, and although Sunvil has added many countries since, we have done it very slowly. We have never gone for countries just because they are flavour of the month, or abandoned places because people stopped going, because everywhere has ups and downs.

Another advantage of visiting these three places – for some – was that many people spoke English, and visitors could eat British-style food. *A Truthful Guide to Package Holiday Resorts*, from 1968, lamented about Malta: 'The food can be distressingly British, and the gaiety lacks continental abandon'. It advised tourists to cover their head and shoulders when visiting churches, and to use one-piece swimsuits on public beaches. Malta became a love-it-or-hate-it destination, with some ugly tourism complexes. A big increase in hotel capacity in the 1980s included converted barracks being used as tourist accommodation, and complaints soared. Belatedly it cut back on volume and increased quality, with the converted farmhouses of Gozo, the neighbouring island, becoming popular with higher-spending tourists.

Italy, one of the first package holiday destinations, failed to live up to expectations as prices went up and quality became an issue. *A Truthful Guide* remarked: 'We have the impression in Italy – unlike Spain, for example – of always paying out for something, however small. Beach charges are the tourist's nightmare, and many of the best beaches are private.' You can still find the Neapolitan Riviera and Sicily in mainstream brochures, but Italy has been left to the Italians far more than Spain or Greece, and is the better for it. Cultural tourism to Italy remains very strong but few British people by comparison head for the beach.

France, also a front runner in early package holidays, failed to take off due to higher prices than Spain, but is of course hugely popular for touring, rural holidays in gites, city breaks and skiing. *A Truthful Guide,* again in 1968, wrote: 'Crippling prices and off-hand treatment are often justifiably cited. Prices are high and still rising; while you can with care keep costs down, the constant financial vigil may spoil a holiday.'

But people didn't have to go far for a package holiday, as Ostend in Belgium, and also the British-owned Channel Islands of Jersey and Guernsey, became popular. Visiting these islands was rather like going abroad as you had to fly or sail, duty-free was available, and many of the place names (though not the food) sounded foreign. But Spain became cheaper, the sunshine here was a lot more reliable, and tourist numbers declined. Jersey and Guernsey now have only a fraction of the tourists and hotel or guest-house beds they had in the 1970s, but have re-invented themselves as up-market islands for a short break, with a strong emphasis on fine food.

North Africa started to appear in package holiday brochures in the late 1960s, with Tunisia developing a string of Mediterranean beach resorts which were well planned, low-rise and spread out. As *A Truthful Guide* pointed out, it had started from scratch and now offered 'the best of both worlds: you can sample the mysteries of Arab life from the comforts of a fine modern hotel built on a dream beach'. Morocco, in contrast, had more of an exotic appeal and retains that today, with the city of Marrakech now being more popular for the British than the beach resorts of Agadir or Tangier, although the latter's risqué reputation continued to underpin its popularity for many years.

As the flying range of charter aircraft improved and people became more adventurous, tour operators started looking further afield especially in winter, when sunshine can't be guaranteed anywhere in the Mediterranean. Israel created a purpose-built beach resort at Eilat on the Red Sea, which reached the height of popularity for the British in the 1980s when the big tour operators flew in their own aircraft alongside the jumbo jets of national carrier El Al. Then came the first Palestinian intifada, widespread unease at the actions of Israel, and the rise of new and cheaper destinations. Hardly any British people now go to Eilat.

The new destinations that started coming up in the 1990s were Turkey and Egypt, both known only as cultural destinations but with big ambitions to attract the 'fly and flop' holidaymaker. Turkey took advantage of the latest trends by developing all-inclusive hotels from scratch along its Mediterranean coast, becoming so successful that Thomas Cook was selling more holidays there than to any other country by the mid-2000s. Prices were keen, quality was good and it soon came to rival Greece, while the rise of Egypt was equally striking. While continuing to develop cultural tourism and Nile cruises, Egypt opted for purpose-built Red Sea resorts such as Sharm El Sheikh, Hurghada and Taba. Here tourists staying in the mainly all-inclusive hotels could sunbathe, scuba-dive and indulge themselves at a wide choice of themed restaurants while being totally cut off from Egyptian life. The formula seemed to work, until terrorists attacked tourists in Luxor and around Cairo.

Whether the events of 2015 prove to be a tragic but temporary blip, or the start of a long-term trend, will not be known for years. But the terrorist attack which took the lives of thirty-eight people (thirty of them British and three Irish) at Port El-Kantaoui, Tunisia in June 2015 was the most shocking attack ever aimed directly at British package tourists. This was followed by the mass evacuation of holidaymakers of all nationalities from Sharm El Sheikh in Egypt in November 2015 after a Russian jet was apparently brought down by a bomb just after departure, with the loss of all 224 lives on board.

Holidaymakers of many nationalities, but especially the British, have proved extremely resilient to terrorist attacks, natural disasters, strikes and many other problems that have afflicted resorts over the years. But whether or not package holiday operators show faith in Tunisia and Egypt in the long-term, and whether or not further atrocities follow, tour operators are facing a huge potential problem with so many of their holidays programmed to these destinations. The consequences of further Islamist-inspired terrorist attacks on resorts could be drastic, especially in Turkey, which shares a border with war-wracked Syria, despite the resorts being hundreds of miles away.

A move back to the familiar destinations of Spain and Greece is being seen, but extra quality accommodation is in short supply and many more nationalities now want it, especially the Russians. Tour operators face anxious times ahead to provide their customers with safe, quality, good-value beach holidays.

5

1974–1982: Battle Lines are Drawn

If anyone thought that the collapse of Clarksons showed that price cutting can only lead to ruin, they would soon be proved wrong as the collapse became a major opportunity for some to fill the gap. But the priority, for one quick-witted entrepreneur, was to rescue people stranded abroad and those booked to travel with Clarksons. The financial safety net put in place to protect people's money was torn apart by the scale of the collapse and was nowhere near sufficient.

Clarksons was effectively bankrupt when taken over by Court Line in 1973, as official enquiries into the Court Line failure were later to prove. Clarksons lost over £3 million in 1972–73 and was expected to lose over £5 million in 1973–74. Court Line was brought down not only by the problems of Clarksons and its airline, but the global economic crisis that hit its oil tankers, shipbuilding interests and Caribbean tourism businesses.

'In a period of about six months, everything Court Line had invested in went wrong for reasons which were outside its control,' says Stewart Wild, Clarksons' tour operations director. 'We knew Clarksons had its problems, but by early 1974 with the oil crisis and three-day week, nearly all British companies were having problems and companies were going bust across the board. We didn't think that would happen, but we knew only bits of what we know now – that nearly every part of Court Line was losing money. We were all so wrapped up in the present that we didn't look ahead. The public eventually got their money back, but the staff, the shareholders and the creditors all suffered. I still have a cheque for £10 that was sent eight years after the crash by the liquidators, which paid us 2½p in the pound.'

Behind the scenes, trade leaders including Travel Club's Harry Chandler worked with the Government's Board of Trade to try to keep Clarksons and Horizon afloat, at least until the end of the peak summer season. But lawyers ruled this was illegal, and Tour Operators Study Group called in the £3.3 million bankers' bond and started to organise rescue flights. There's something emotive about images of 'innocent' Brits stranded abroad, which returned to our screens in 2015 with the evacuation of tourists from Egypt and Tunisia. Less innocent were the hordes of angry people besieging Clarksons' London office. During the next ten days about 35,000 people were brought home, with many others anxious as they had yet to travel. There were huge problems in resorts too, with some hoteliers owed money by Clarksons threatening to seize customers' luggage and refusing to let them leave.

The government, facing a general election a few weeks later, wanted to appear on the side of the consumer – a position made more pressing by a House of Commons statement by Industry Secretary Tony Benn. He announced in June 1974 that the government would secure jobs by taking over Court Line's shipyards and that this would protect holiday bookings, reassuring travel agents who had held off booking Clarksons. After the collapse, the government decided to indemnify other tour operators for paying off hotel debts and bringing stranded holidaymakers home, as it became clear that the £3.3 million in bond money wouldn't be enough.

But it wasn't long before the consumer started paying to clear up the mess. In 1975 the re-elected Labour government introduced the Air Travel Reserve Fund, started with a £15 million loan but then funded by a levy of 1 per cent or 2 per cent on everyone taking a package holiday. The levy continued for many years and the safety net, now called the Air Travel Trust Fund, still exists today. A legacy of the Court Line failure is that never again have the customers of a failed package holiday operator been left out of pocket.

Eyewitness: Sidney Perez
He was called on to lead the rescue mission when 35,000 people were stranded abroad by the collapse of Court Line at the height of the summer 1974 season.

Court Line was put into liquidation on 15 August 1974 after the government decreed it was insolvent and that a plan to rescue it as a growing concern could not go ahead. The following days were perhaps the most dramatic in the history of package holidays as people who had travelled with Court Line companies such as Clarksons and Horizon were stuck abroad. The rescue was carried out by the Tour Operators Study Group (TOSG) Trust Fund, which held Court Line's £3.3 million bank bond.

On 16 August, at the request of the Civil Aviation Authority and TOSG, I established an office in Sun Street (Clarksons' headquarters) and with the help of Clarksons staff, we efficiently carried out the repatriation of the holidaymakers. With the Court Line Aviation fleet grounded the search for available aircraft was not easy, but we were greatly assisted by Dan-Air and another charter airline which set up desks at the same offices. Over the next six days, over 21,000 people were brought home.

The cost of the rescue flights reached £1.3 million, but the £2 million we also had available from the bond wasn't enough to reimburse people who had booked holidays but hadn't yet travelled. The government agreed to loan the money, which it recouped through a levy. That money couldn't be used to pay Court Line's debts to hotels and other service providers, so at the request of the British government I led a delegation to the Spanish Ministry of Tourism in Madrid. Hoteliers were arguing that the bond money we held should be used to pay them for services provided to holidaymakers for their entire stay, and not just from 16 August onwards. They felt it was unfair for them to suffer loss and were reluctant to accept that the conditions of the bonds did not permit us to do this.

At times the discussions became heated, during which we managed to persuade them that any action taken against holidaymakers would do long-term damage to them and the holiday industry in general. Having resolved the matter after many hours of discussion, the hoteliers reluctantly accepted the situation. We returned home to waiting TV cameras and press to assure people that a deal had been done that meant people's holidays were safe. The reputation of tour operators was not only preserved but enhanced, and the following year the Government created a safety net so that nothing like this could happen again.

While the travel industry was busy bringing home the customers of Clarksons, Horizon and other companies owned by Court Line, and transferring bookings to other tour operators, the collapse suddenly opened up opportunities for a company that could move fast. That company was Harry Goodman's Intasun, formed just one year earlier as the successor to his first tour operating venture, Sunair, which had grown quickly to take over Lunn Poly. Sunair sold holidays cheaply but got into financial trouble, being taken over by Cunard then sold on to Thomson. There was no denying that Intasun was Sunair Mark 2, with its brochures – showing a cartoon-like figure of a sun-bronzed, bikini-clad girl – looking remarkably similar.

'It's a bit of a myth that I had private jets on standby, but we were ready for Court Line to go bust and this was a defining moment for us,' says Goodman. 'We were ready to pick up their hotel beds and had people out in the resorts within hours, putting cash on the table. We bought all the flight capacity we could get and took 18,000 on holiday in 1974, then 150,000 in 1975. There was a shortage of holidays on offer, and we cleaned up. Our profit margins on Court Line passengers rebooked with us were astronomical.'

Hugh Morgan, who had worked for Goodman since 1966 and became Intasun's overseas director, also sees 1974 as the great turning point for Goodman. 'After the Court Line collapse, Harry felt he could be as big as Thomson,' he says. 'I remember going to the Pollensa Park hotel in Mallorca where Clarksons had contracted every bed, but after Clarksons went down the hotel was desperate and signed a contract giving us a rate per person of just over £1 a day, including breakfast and dinner. We filled that hotel and others like it. Within a few years we were putting 400,000 people a year into Mallorca alone, and Harry became rich. But it wasn't all plain sailing. We had to buy most of our seats off Dan-Air, who were also known as Dan Dare. We were being squeezed so it wasn't long before we started thinking of setting up our own airline.

'Harry was a risk taker, but he was very, very successful. He was miles ahead of the game, and before long he had a yellow Rolls-Royce convertible. He made and spent a fortune, living a very expensive lifestyle.'

But behind the wheeler-dealer image and risk taking was a recognition that Goodman needed the right people around him to make the business work. He took on former Global chief Sidney Perez to run the tour operations, and set up Intasun North to sell holidays in northern England in an unlikely partnership with Sir James Hill, a textiles manufacturer, who was attracted by the cash flow benefits.

'I had always looked up to Sidney, and to have him working for us was one of the best things that ever happened,' says Goodman. 'We were still looked on as the fly boys, out on the edge. I had a white suit and tousled hair, I was outrageous. We needed a wise old head and a trusted name in the industry.'

Intasun might have grown quickly, but Thomson became the biggest package holiday operator after Court Line's demise. The next thirty years would see a pattern repeated as an upstart operator – first Intasun and later Airtours – would try to become top dog, until the whole outlook changed in the twenty-first century.

Dermot Blastland, who joined Thomson in 1970, recalls one way that Intasun tried to steal a march on its bigger rival. 'It would take an allocation of only two rooms in a hotel where Thomson had 200, and undercut Thomson by £10 claiming its prices were cheaper,' he says. 'Another question was whether to include airport taxes – Thomson did, Intasun didn't.

'But Harry Goodman did tweak Thomson's tail. I remember the day when Ken Thomson, son of Thomson Organisation founder Roy Thomson, came over from Canada to discuss the situation. He said, "Harry Goodman might be a millionaire, but I'm a billionaire. So we're starting a price war to take him out."' Thomson was true to his word, but as a consequence it too lost money.

'When Court Line went down, our phone lines lit up,' says Roger Lambert, a Thomson employee from 1965 to 1986. 'We didn't have a lot of time for Intasun, which grew through low prices and paying travel agents 12½ per cent commission when we would pay only 10 per cent. Thomson did a remarkable job in improving standards, introducing the customer service questionnaire and our own "T" ratings for hotels. It was a real premier league operator, the Manchester United of the travel industry.'

But Thomson and Intasun didn't have things all their own way. Other established companies such as Cosmos and Global continued to grow, while the Horizon name lived on in a separate company with a similar focus on quality to Thomson.

Horizon Midlands was set up in 1965 with a 25 per cent shareholding by Horizon Holidays, which was later increased to 58 per cent. At first it operated only out of Birmingham, later adding East Midlands airport, and had complete autonomy under its boss, Bruce Tanner. It did so well that part of it was floated off as a public company in 1972, the first tour operator to do so. When Horizon Holidays went into liquidation along with Court Line in 1974, Tanner secured the future of Horizon Midlands with local authorities owning some of the shares. They bought into Horizon Midlands to protect the airports they owned, which were highly dependent on package holidays.

Ken Franklin, who joined in 1968 and later became managing director, says: 'Our number one priority was to get a reputation for quality, and we would often sell holidays to the same hotel for £5 a fortnight more than Thomson or Intasun, which was a lot of money then. We never sold holidays at a discount, and as our profits swelled we got people coming back year after year. They were halcyon days, and we piled up so much cash that we decided to set up our own charter airline, Orion, to take away the risk of flying with Britannia, which was owned by Thomson. With Thomson battling it out against Intasun, we were very happy to be number three. We saw no point in chasing numbers, but we grew by expanding to Manchester, Gatwick and then nationwide, and became simply Horizon.'

These were exciting times, as package holidays had survived the bad publicity of 1974 and were regarded as highly desirable and aspirational. Michael Knowles, who joined in 1973 and stayed almost to the end of the company's existence, recalls: 'It sounded like a very dynamic business for a young university graduate to go into, but it was also quite basic in some ways. On my first day I was taken into the reservations room which was full of young ladies writing passengers' names on wall charts. If someone cancelled or changed a booking, they would put a piece of sticky paper over the name But these would fall on the floor in hot weather, and you sometimes didn't know where they were going.

'Horizon Midlands stood almost aloof from the other big tour operators, but it was a tricky time to build confidence after 1974 and persuade travel agents that we were secure. By the early 1980s there were three big companies driving forward – ourselves, Thomson with its corporate structure, and Intasun which was shooting from the hip. Being a public company, we had to be very mindful of the bottom line. Our shareholders were often our customers, and we had to educate financial institutions about our industry's ups and downs. We were literally in the public eye during our heyday from the mid-1970s to mid-1980s.'

Although tour operators no longer faced price controls, they were still not allowed to sell charter flights without a hotel or some other kind of accommodation, such as self-catering. They wanted to sell packages first and foremost, but demand for what became known as 'seat-only' was growing in the 1970s. Selling seats could also be profitable, especially in high season when hotel beds were sometimes sold out. People were becoming more independent and adventurous after years of taking package holidays, and were buying property in Spain in large numbers. Canny tour operators began to find ways around the package-only rule on charter flights. They started offering vouchers for accommodation which, while it might exist, could be in a shared dormitory or, in one case, a cave. Cosmos sold these seats as 'Cheapies' while Thomson called them 'Wanderers'. Despite objections from airlines it became easy to buy seats on charter flights, leading former Intasun man Sidney Perez to comment: 'The idea that Ryanair and EasyJet were the creators of cheap flying is a fallacy.'

Intasun grew partly by acquisition, taking over regional package holiday operators such as Cambrian which flew out of Cardiff, and Airways which flew out of Newcastle. By the late 1970s Intasun had become a serious irritant to Thomson, and this era was marked by two ventures which paved the way for its huge growth in the following decade – setting-up its own airline, Air Europe, and the highly audacious launch of cut-price holidays to Florida.

Only two tour operators had their own airlines – Thomson, which acquired Britannia in 1965; and Cosmos, whose owners set up Monarch Airlines in 1968, although Horizon would form Orion Airways in 1980. Having your own airline was both a blessing and a curse – you could control your own holiday programme, but you also had to fill your planes at any cost, often with the help of rival tour operators. By the mid-1970s all tour operators were using jets, and Britannia had set a high standard with its Boeing 737s. Dan-Air, Intasun's biggest supplier, was still using second-hand Comets along with BAC 1-11s and larger Boeing 727s, but Harry Goodman craved something more modern.

Sidney Perez, his number two, remembers: 'It was a Friday afternoon and whilst I was sitting in Harry's office he told me that Intasun needed its own airline as the future of the business was to purchase more cost-efficient aircraft. There and then, he picked up the telephone to Boeing and McDonnell Douglas and explained he wanted to purchase three new jets. Boeing was the quickest to respond and within a week a Boeing team came to London and a contract was signed for the purchase of three 737-200s.'

Goodman remembers the day that his first aircraft was delivered as one of the proudest in his life. 'Amazingly, no one had registered the Air Europe name, and to take delivery of a brand new aircraft from Boeing was a dream for me,' he says. 'I was in the cockpit on the delivery flight from Seattle in 1978, and when I heard that Air Europe flight one was cleared to land at Gatwick, it was fantastic. We had a golden rule to treat Intasun and Air Europe as stand-alone companies, unlike Court Line.'

Air Europe's travails would eventually be critical in bringing down Harry Goodman's empire, but that was far in the future and optimism was sky-high when Air Europe made its first commercial flight. But Air Europe was not involved when Goodman made his boldest move yet, which made him a household name. In 1979, angered by price rises at Spanish hotels, he announced charter flights to Miami in Florida using

Laker Airways DC-10s, to start in summer 1980. The author wrote a story for travel industry newspaper TTG, proclaiming: 'US package holidays for the masses' (see centre pages).

These were the first charters to the US designed for package holidays rather than the independent holidaymaker, and Intasun's customers were sent to Miami Beach, when summer temperatures were so unpleasantly humid that most hotels closed down until the autumn. Why did they go? Because a week in America cost only £139 – and two weeks from £199. These prices were a come-on, of course, as were the starting prices advertised by all holiday firms. They didn't include any meals, and four adults had to share a room to get that price. But even if you paid £250 or £300, the holidays were an absolute bargain.

'I told a conference of Spanish hoteliers that I was sick to death of their price rises and that I would take my people somewhere else, and when I came out of that conference I wondered where that somewhere else was,' recalls Goodman. 'Most Miami hotels were being run by a kind of Jewish mafia, and despite being Jewish myself they weren't prepared to offer room rates that were low enough even if I promised to fill their hotels. During four days in Miami, I got nowhere. Then a hotel called the Shelborne told me I was mad, but they would give me the rooms at $10 a night. I knew Laker had DC-10s spare, and I chartered ten flights a week at a seat rate of just £79 return, which was cheaper than the seat rate to Tenerife.

'It was my greatest coup, and I kept even my top people out of the loop. They were expecting me to get thirty seats a week on British Airways to Miami but then I told them I had ten flights a week on DC-10s, about 3,500 seats. The BBC Holiday programme got wind of it, and everything went mad. So many people were trying to book these holidays that it brought down the Bromley telephone exchange, where we were based. One day there were twelve people surrounding my car, who wouldn't let me move until I sold them a holiday in Florida. But we weren't ready to go on sale for another week. We sold out the Florida holidays in only three weeks and were soon selling Miami Beach all year round.'

Eyewitness: Cliff Jones
In 1959 he set up the travel agency C. & V. Jones in Eccles, near Manchester, becoming a leading voice in ABTA and later championing environmental causes.

I was fortunate to be in the vanguard of the package holiday explosion in the early 1960s when many of the operators were small and independent, like the agents they dealt with. Owners or directors of these companies, instead of sending out sales reps to cavass for business, did this themselves and it was not unusual to receive a personal telephone call from the managing director or owner.

I well remember receiving such a call from Norman Corkhill of Luxitours in Blackpool, who had just formed a new company called Gaytours, inviting myself and my wife Val and two children to join him on a week's holiday to Mallorca. Val's comment when meeting Norman was, "Why us – we don't do much trade with you?" His response, in typical laconic Norman style, was "That's why you are here!" I and others responded by remaining loyal supporters of Gaytours for the remainder of their existence.

His example was soon followed by other operators. The partnership atmosphere that existed gave rise to many innovations, and Ronnie Booth of Aintree Travel and I established the very first door-to-airport transfers for our clients, in VW Combis bearing boldly the operators' (and airlines') logos.

In the 1970 things began to change with the emergence of the so-called big boys and I well recall a somewhat aggressive presentation by Global at the Grand Hotel in Manchester, where the stick to replace the carrot was strongly in evidence. This attitude was soon copied by the likes of Clarksons, Intasun, Horizon and others. This was the advent of a new and unwelcome era and the beginning of a more hostile relationship between tour operator and travel agent which led to the fragmentation of ABTA.

In this changed environment an element of arrogance prevailed which inevitably led some tour operators to move towards eliminating the agent by selling direct to the public. Tour operators were setting up their own retail offices and became less and less reliant upon agents. The 1970s will be remembered by me as the "writing on the wall" period when arrogance was translated into obvious antagonism by the likes of Clarksons, which bordered on triumphalism at their perceived domination.

The Walt Disney World theme park in Orlando – despite being a four-hour drive from Miami Beach – was a major attraction, but Goodman remembers that Disney was very dismissive. 'They were totally arrogant – they even charged me an entrance fee when I went to negotiate,' he says. 'But when they saw how popular our holidays were, they sent a cast of Disney characters down to Miami to meet the first flight.

'There were some problems, of course, and it wasn't like Spain. People didn't mind the heat, but a coachload of people would arrive at a Miami Beach hotel and there would be only one barman on duty. You needed a car to go anywhere, when our customers were used to bars and restaurants all over the place in Spain. In the first three months we upset maybe 10 per cent of customers, but we got that down to zero. But Miami Beach was always going to be short-term for us. It lasted for a couple of years but by then the exchange rate had gone down from $2.40 to the pound, to $1.80. In any case, people were more interested in Orlando and that's where we started putting in flights. It would be unrepeatable now, but in 1980 America was a magical destination, so glamorous. We made £5 million in one year and every travel agent wanted to sell Intasun. It laid the foundations for floating as a public company.'

Intasun didn't abandon Spain, of course – but with other tour operators also attacking its higher prices, hoteliers there had to learn not to take the British tourist for granted. Thomson, which had scored major publicity coups itself such as £29 weekends in Moscow, realised it couldn't be complacent about Harry Goodman. 'To make any decision, Thomson had to wait for a board meeting,' he says. 'We could have a board meeting every day, and we were really twisting their tail with Florida. They were big, but clumsy. We were like a Jack Russell snapping at a big dog's heels.'

'Harry Goodman did not claim to be an academic – he was an entrepreneur and shrewd businessman,' says Sidney Perez, his number two. 'He knew how to recruit the right people with the right talents to help him to develop his growing and profitable business.'

Horizon's Michael Knowles adds: 'Miami Beach was a classic example of a tour operator moving in quickly on a destination that was cheap and had huge appeal for British tourists. We dismissed it as very short-term because of the oppressive summer heat, but we were wrong. It was marvellous for people to have a holiday in America at that price.'

Intasun was floated on the Stock Exchange in 1981, valued at £44 million, setting the scene for its phenomenal growth in the mid-1980s. By the start of that decade the Court Line collapse was a distant memory, and package holidays were set for a golden era. Intasun was renamed International Leisure Group (ILG) in 1985, acquiring tour operators including Global, Club 18–30 and Lancaster.

By the late 1980s it was taking over two million people a year on holiday, adding a coach holiday operator called NAT.

Almost un-noticed, except in one small corner of northern England, a company started operating package holidays that would eventually become Intasun's successor as the main rival to Thomson. Pendle Airtours, part of a small chain of travel agents in east Lancashire, was a major supporter of Intasun but thought it could offer holidays at an even lower price. It started doing that in 1980, with flights to Malta from Manchester.

Before long there was another major casualty in the travel business, but this time selling cheap package holidays was not the cause of its demise. Laker Airways, which owned the Laker Holidays and Arrowsmith package holiday brands, went down in February 1982 after a last-ditch attempt to sell its tour operations to Intasun. The company that had chartered its DC-10s to Intasun to make Miami Beach so cheap had been started by Freddie Laker as a European charter airline in 1966. But his dream was to offer a low-cost transatlantic service called Skytrain which finally got off the ground in 1977, from Gatwick to New York.

Skytrain was first proposed in 1971 with one-way fares of only £32.50, but opposition from established airlines was immense. It started offering charter flights across 'The Pond' in 1973 but these were subject to all kinds of restrictions, including the need to book at least four weeks in advance, unlike the 'turn up and go' concept of Skytrain. When Skytrain finally started, first to New York (one-way from £59) and later to Los Angeles and Miami, established airlines became very worried. Pan American, in 1981, was the first to cut fares to compete with Skytrain, followed by TWA and British Airways. Laker later sued several airlines for conspiring to put him out of business, winning an out-of-court settlement for $50 million.

Intasun, and others, moved quickly to contract Laker and Arrowsmith hotels. Laker's tour operations survived the collapse, the Laker Holidays brand being bought by Saga and Arrowsmith by the brewer Greenall Whitley, but they would disappear within a few years. Meanwhile, also in 1982, Thomson Holidays introduced a new computerised reservations system for travel agents called TOP. It didn't seem likely at the time, but computerised reservations made possible the phenomenal growth of package holidays in the 1980s.

6

Holidays Behind the Iron Curtain

Anyone born after about 1980 will have no memories of an era, lasting nearly half a century, when Europe was divided by two opposing political ideologies which at times of crisis brought threats of a Third World War. After the Second World War the Soviet Union extended its influence throughout Eastern Europe and created what soon became known as the Iron Curtain, ushering in the Cold War when hostilities were limited to the odd border skirmish, but isolation set in and few contacts were made with the West. The tearing down of the Berlin Wall in 1989 was one of the most momentous but unexpected events in twentieth-century history, followed by many countries embracing democracy very quickly and looking to the West.

It might seem surprising that these isolated Eastern Bloc countries not only wanted tourism but actively promoted it. From the sunshine beaches of the Adriatic or Black Sea to the frozen wastes of Siberia or the Russian Arctic, tourists were welcomed for the very good reason that they brought in much needed hard currency. A secondary reason, especially in the Soviet Union, was the opportunity to spread propaganda.

Many British tour operators organised both package holidays and escorted tours to Eastern Europe, although there were major obstacles. The first was public ignorance about what these countries were like, and the limited funds available to promote them in comparison with France, Italy or Spain. Despite the Cold War mentality on both sides and a British media generally hostile towards the East, countries such as Yugoslavia and Bulgaria attracted big volumes of package holidaymakers who might otherwise have gone to Spain or Greece.

For the more enquiring person who wanted to explore Eastern Europe on a tour, there was the added thrill of visiting somewhere unknown, or even forbidden. Everything about a holiday here was different – even the Soviet-made aircraft you travelled in – and familiar hotel names absent. You couldn't find British cuisine or fast food chains, and more serious barriers had to be faced. Most countries demanded visas, which ruled out going at short notice. Prices could be high, and when changing money you got a punitive rate. When you did get there, your freedom of movement might be limited.

Looking at package holidays first, Yugoslavia got in early for two main reasons – it was relatively liberal, and already had a developing tourism industry before the Cold War began. Under President Tito, in power from 1953–1980, Yugoslavia developed as a cohesive country with few signs to the visitor of the conflicts that would erupt as it fell apart in the 1990s. Although there was state control of the economy an element of private enterprise was allowed, with hotels and other tourist services developing away from the gaze of faraway Russia. And, crucially, it had sunshine and a very beautiful coastline dotted with islands.

Lord Brothers, one of the package holiday pioneers, chose Yugoslavia as its first destination as the brothers had fallen in love with the Istrian peninsula, close to Italy. At about the same time, in 1957, Anglo-Yugoslav Travel was set up in London by Generalexport, a state-owned company in Yugoslavia's capital, Belgrade. That company soon became Yugotours, which grew rapidly to become one of Britain's top ten package holiday operators by the 1980s.

The Adriatic coast became a playground for the British, Germans, Italians and others, with the coastline of Istria and, further south, around the ancient city of Dubrovnik being especially popular. Yugotours – which had British 'front men' but always a Yugoslav boss – knew how to entertain, bringing planeloads of travel agents to be wined and dined and 'educated' about the country. Their reaction to Yugoslavia was generally very favourable, and with plenty of charter flights and no visa requirement, holidays were cheap. There were also mountains, national parks, more historic cities and lots of history and culture to explore. Few tourists would know they were in Croatia, Montenegro, Slovenia or Serbia, which would become independent countries at war with each other in the 1990s. Yugoslavia could be quirky, too. It was one of the few countries in Europe where nudist resorts were developed, and a niche market developed for package holidays in the buff.

If Yugoslavia was liberal, the same could not be said of Bulgaria or Romania, countries which shared a Black Sea coastline with miles of sandy beaches, something lacking in Yugoslavia where most of the beaches were rocky. These countries were rigidly controlled, but in the early 1960s they started building beach hotels, some aimed at providing basic standards for deserving Communist party members and model workers from throughout the Eastern Bloc.

A controversial British businessman, John Bloom – whose Rolls Razor washing machine empire went bust in 1964 – made a surprise move into Bulgaria that same year, launching holidays as English and Overseas Tours with a picture on the cover not of a beach, but of Bloom shaking hands with Prime Minister Todor Zhivhov. Holidays were either by air (from about fifty guineas for two weeks) or by air across the Channel and then by coach (from thirty-two guineas), not arriving until the fourth day and spending only seven of the fourteen days actually in Bulgaria. All meals were included, and you could eat at a wide range of hotels and restaurants as all were under the same management, an arrangement that continued into the 1980s.

Bloom asked Lord Brothers to run the tours for him, and Christopher Lord's first impressions of the country were good. 'The Bulgarians asked Bloom how many hotels he wanted and offered to build them,' he says. 'He offered to send 50,000 customers in the first year, but the only person he knew in the travel industry was me. I had already been to check out the resorts and I thought it was a lovely country. Customers loved it although the hotels were simple three-star places, cheap and cheerful. Sunny Beach and Golden Sands were artificial resorts with very good beaches, built for the Eastern Europeans who didn't come because they were broke. They gave us heavily subsidised prices.'

The holiday programme was short-lived as Bloom's empire went bust, but other tour operators took up Bulgaria and in 1966 the authorities set up Balkan Holidays in Britain, which celebrates its fiftieth anniversary in 2016 as a major package holiday company with charter flights from all over the country. Bulgaria is still one of the cheapest places in Europe to have a family holiday, and the quality of hotels has improved greatly over the last twenty-five years.

Romania, with a much shorter coastline, was less successful attracting British holidaymakers, although it soon started to exploit its Count Dracula associations by attracting tour groups to the Transylvanian mountains. Both countries also offer good value skiing.

Another rather curious British tour operator that started in the 1960s was Glasgow-based Black Sea Holidays, but the company's main business was called Sovscot Tours and it was owned by the Soviet-Scottish Friendship Society, which fostered links with the Soviet Union for ideological as well as recreational purposes. An air of intrigue has always hung around some companies that operated tours behind the Iron Curtain, and especially Intourist which controlled all tourism in the Soviet Union although it made partnerships with many British firms.

Intourist was, almost certainly, the world's largest tourism company – but to call it an enterprise would be misleading, as it was more like a monolith. It was the main or only tour operator to Russia and the other Soviet republics from many countries, setting up in the UK in 1938 and continuing into the present century, although the UK operation is now known as IntoRussia. But Intourist was far more than a tour operator. It operated all the hotels and other tourist services during the Soviet era, a vast, state-owned organisation whose cold fingers were in every tourism pie and which was widely believed to shelter many spies among its overseas personnel. To quote its Wikipedia page, Intourist was to tourists what indigestion is to digestion!

As Intourist had no competition, standards were of course poor. Hotels were mainly dreary concrete blocks and (especially in Moscow, where many hotels were built for the 1980 Olympic Games) included immense, sprawling places like the Hotel Rossiya which was at one time the largest hotel in the world. In Moscow, Leningrad (now St Petersburg) and some other most visited cities, each floor in the hotel would be guarded by a stern older woman who gave you your key. She also dispensed handy little booklets in English for a bedtime read, with titles such as *Trotskyism Today – Whose Interests Does it Serve?* and *Cudgels of Democracy versus Fighters for Peace*, extolling the British women who demonstrated at Greenham Common against the deployment of American cruise missiles in the 1980s. Meals were dull (the borscht soup an exception) and would be served at the given time whether you turned up or not. Intourist hotel bars only took hard currency, and sometimes served only brandy and champagne at sky-high prices. The only Russians you were likely to meet here were state snoopers or prostitutes, and if you made a phone call there were strange noises on the line.

Although you were free to walk around on your own, it was difficult to travel except as a group and many parts of Russia and the other republics were off-limits for tourists. But Intourist did encourage groups to travel around, not just Russia but other republics such as Ukraine and Georgia, as long as Moscow and Leningrad were included on itineraries. You did (and still do, for Russia and some other countries) require a costly visa, and airport and currency formalities were a chore. But despite all these problems, the people who wanted to go loved it, and to stand in Moscow's Red Square, in the heart of what American President Ronald Reagan described as the 'Evil Empire', was a thrill.

It was against this background that Thomson Holidays, synonymous with package holidays to the Mediterranean, launched weekend breaks in Moscow for only £29, in winter 1972/73. The weekends were a sensation and gained tremendous media coverage. Thomson used its own Britannia Airways charters from Luton, with Soviet navigators on the flight deck and Russian fighter jets as escorts.

A lot went on behind the scenes to get permission, as this was one of many times when relations with Russia were tense with suspected spies having recently been deported from London. Former Thomson managing director Bryan Llewelyn recalls: 'Two weeks before the first departure, which was fully booked, I got a call from Moscow saying we want you to make representations to the Foreign Office to get the people expelled from the UK let back in, or the flight won't operate. I rang the Foreign Office and they already knew about this demand – probably because the lines were tapped. They said not to worry, and in the end the Russians made no attempt to stop us. Operating to Russia was like opening Pandora's Box, as it was regarded with hostility. It was a coup. We got all kinds of customers, from dukes to dustmen.'

Doug Goodman, who handled Thomson's press relations from 1971–1988, says: 'We took 5,500 people to Moscow that first winter, and when those holidays sold out quickly we sold another 2,500. Because Intourist wanted British visitors it made some amazing offers, and the following winter we added two-centre holidays by overnight train to Leningrad. Over the next ten years our people spread out to Kiev (Ukraine), the Arctic, Central Asia, Siberia and also Mongolia, a satellite of the Soviet Union which printed postcards just for us. It was minus forty degrees Centigrade when we first went to Siberia, in 1979. The BBC filmed us on the ice of Lake Baikal.'

Thomson's holidays to the Soviet Union continued to grow until the mid-1980s, when around 10,000 were travelling each winter, but then a series of problems cropped up which saw Thomson pull out before the break-up of the Soviet Union in 1991. People fell ill because of bacteria in the water at Leningrad, with Intourist being angry when the story got into the British press, and then came the Chernobyl nuclear disaster of 1986 which affected travel to the whole region. 'The Soviet authorities denied there was a problem, but we decided to bring people home and this was another reason our Soviet Union programme ended,' says Goodman. 'Radioactive screening was set up for when our people got back to Gatwick, and we spent an hour rehearsing what the press were going to ask us. But all our people were bothered about was why they had been brought home early!'

Virgin's Richard Branson also dabbled in the Soviet Union, but with less success, hatching an unlikely plan to operate holidays to the Crimean seaside resort of Yalta, then in Ukraine but controversially annexed by Russia in 2014. He was pictured in a pullover beside unsmiling tourism officials, but plans such as this were ahead of the times.

Although there were many challenges operating behind the Iron Curtain, there were some amusing incidents too. Coach tours had started operating all the way from Britain in the 1950s, and people would put their trust in well-known companies such as Wallace Arnold or Excelsior to take them to Russia. Former WA operations director Stephen Barber says: 'We did our first tour around 1959 and it was an endurance test, with the KGB watching us all the time. Our biggest fear was being hijacked in the middle of nowhere, and officials at the borders were often corrupt. People would offer to guard the coach overnight in Leningrad, and when we agreed – it cost only about 50p – someone turned up with a Kalashnikov and watched it all night.'

Tony John first visited the Soviet Union in the late 1960s while managing director of a coach tour operator called Southbound. 'There were some very long days, such as the 700 km from Moscow to Minsk with nothing much in between,' he recalls. 'Crossing borders could be a problem, as in some countries they would put a large mirror under the vehicle looking for hidden Bibles. They would also inspect passengers' luggage and this wasn't a cursory glance, as they would remove English newspapers even if used to wrap shoes.

'The girls employed by Intourist were very good, and people fell in love with them. Ordinary Russians were lovely and very eager to communicate, but officialdom was different. I was once told off for taking a photo of someone eating ice-cream as I was told it wasn't "typically Russian". I was about to take a picture of a tram driven by a rather beautiful woman, but a People's Militiaman said no. We thought we weren't being watched, but our Intourist guide later told me I'd been a naughty boy.

'People expected that hotels standards wouldn't be brilliant, but it was a thrill just to be in Russia,' adds John. 'When it was no longer a thrill to be behind the Iron Curtain, it became a harder sell.'

Most of the countries in Eastern Europe had their own version of Intourist, a state-owned organisation that controlled many or all hotels and tourist services, and a tour operation-cum-tourist office in the UK and many other countries. Poland had Orbis (operating as Polorbis in London) while Czechoslovakia had Cedok, Hungary had Danube Travel, and the so-called German Democratic Republic (East Germany) had Berolina Travel. These operators concentrated

Let's Go!

on cultural and historic tours, and but some couldn't resist politics. Berolina's last brochure, published for the 1990 season, was overtaken by the fall of the Berlin Wall. It is a real museum piece, promoting a May Day tour to East Berlin with an invitation to 'hear the rousing music of working class struggle, thrill to the sight of thousands marching in celebration of International Labour Day, marvel at the colour and pageantry of flags held high by the delegates of countless thousands of Berlin workers'. Berolina didn't realise it would soon all be over.

Some countries were more liberal than others, but East Germany was extreme in its repression and surveillance. The Solidarity pro-democracy movement gathered momentum in Poland during the 1980s, while the popularity of Polish Pope John Paul II, who served from 1978 to 2005, meant even religious tourism was tolerated. Hungary was one of the most liberal countries, allowing Western hotel chains to manage hotels in Budapest before the Berlin Wall came down, and with generally more to buy in the shops. When Hungary hosted the 1990 ABTA convention in Budapest, bringing in thousands of people in the British travel industry who had never been to Eastern Europe before, it was a proud moment for Danube Travel boss Gabor Tarr.

Czechoslovakia, which split amicably into the Czech Republic and Slovakia in 1993, was however one of the harshest regimes, as a result of the failed 'Prague Spring' movement in 1968 which was brutally suppressed by Soviet troops. You could wander the streets of Prague in the evening and see no one about, an extreme contrast to the hugely popular city break destination it became in the 1990s.

Of all the countries in Eastern Europe during the Cold War era, the strangest without doubt was Albania, a small Balkan country sandwiched between what was Yugoslavia and Greece. Under the iron grip of dictator Enver Hoxha from 1944 to his death in 1985, it was an almost totally closed, paranoid Communist country which had broken ties with both the Soviet Union and China, but was full of curiosities including a museum of atheism. It also has the ruins of ancient civilisations, an Adriatic coastline and a mountainous interior, but what attracted the very few tourists who visited in the Cold War era was its extreme political system. They had to be hardy: in the total absence of flights, the most usual route in was by a short bus ride from Titograd (now Podgorica, capital of independent Montenegro) and then a walk across the border, where anyone sporting facial hair had an enforced encounter with a barber.

Although Lord Brothers had looked at Albania in the 1960s, the first company to establish regular tours there was Regent Holidays which was, and is, a leading tour operator to Eastern Europe plus China, North Korea and other oddball destinations. Former Regent director Neil Taylor, who started his travel career with Progressive Tours (a company then linked to the Communist Party) led many tours to Hoxha's reclusive state.

'Our tours were the only way a British subject could get into Albania, so we had people reporting back to the UK in one way or another and sometimes an undercover journalist,' he says. 'Some articles were then published but the Albanians wouldn't have seen them, as there were no communications with the UK or diplomatic relations. We weren't harming the UK by taking people there. We wouldn't have been much help to the British Secret Services.'

Running holidays to Eastern Europe was in some ways straight-forward, as there was no choice in who to deal with – operators had to take it or leave it. 'In the old days, organisations such as Intourist set the prices and the tour itineraries, and little negotiation was possible,' explains Taylor. 'I wanted to develop the Baltic republics, but you weren't allowed to operate tours outside the capital cities of Riga, Tallinn and Vilnius. Large swathes of the Soviet Union were forbidden to foreigners, but gradually things started to change. With perestroika (a reform movement under President Gorbachev) more places opened up, and you could travel beyond the capitals. Throughout the region there were changes. In Poland, dissent was being expressed openly with the encouragement of the Catholic Church.

'Our customers often weren't particularly interested in the political systems of these countries, but they wanted to see somewhere different and there were a lot of contrasts,' continues Taylor. 'East Germany really hit you when you crossed over from West to East Berlin, with its lower standard of living, portraits of the leaders, and general bleakness.

'I never foresaw all the changes after the Berlin Wall came down, when so many people left the state-owned tourism companies to set up their own enterprises. But they were usually naïve, business-wise, and lots of complications came in with fifteen countries in the former Soviet Union and lots of visas needed, except in the Baltics which abolished visas as soon as they became independent.'

Regent became a major specialist to the newly independent Baltic countries of Estonia, Latvia and Lithuania, which later joined the EU, and now they are popular for city breaks as well as touring. Russia, however, is one of the few countries where the tourism flow from the UK has gone backwards. Not only is it expensive, but it is one of the few major tourism countries in the world still requiring visas from British or EU citizens. The UK and Russia have always played a tit-for-tat game with diplomacy, which is reflected in visa regulations. The chilling of relations following Russia's intervention in Ukraine and annexing of Crimea means it is now more difficult than ever to get a tourist visa, with would-be visitors having to go to a Russian consulate in London or Edinburgh in person, to have their fingerprints taken. St Petersburg still attracts plenty of cultural visitors, and can be visited visa-free on cruises. But few British tourists now go to other parts of Russia or other countries of the former Soviet Union, apart from the Baltics – a far cry from the 1980s when Thomson alone took 10,000 a year.

The wars in Yugoslavia were catastrophic for tourism with the six newly independent countries taking varying amounts of time to recover. Most of the Adriatic coastline is now in Croatia, which fought a vicious war with Serbia and Montenegro from 1991–95.This resulted in the shelling of Dubrovnik, the first time a mainstream European holiday destination had been caught up in hostilities since Cyprus in 1974. Fortunately the shelling happened in winter, but tourists had already deserted Dubrovnik and there was no major lasting damage to the Old Town. Only in recent years has Croatia started to get back to the UK tourism figures it enjoyed when part of Yugoslavia, whereas Slovenia – which was not torn apart by war – continued to do well. The loss of Yugoslavia was a major blow for the UK travel industry, but Turkey was developing at the same time to give tour operators another option.

When visiting the former Iron Curtain countries today, it is often almost impossible – the Soviet-era architecture aside – to see any trace of the political system that ruled them. Belatedly, some countries put their monolithic statues in parks or opened museums to the Communist era, one of the most impressive being the House of Terror in Budapest, once headquarters of the Hungarian secret police. Even today many Hungarians won't visit as painful memories are too strong. But if you go to many places – especially Prague, with its vibrant culture and less vibrant stag and hen parties – you would never know what happened here less than fifty years ago. That's the problem with Eastern Europe today – it just isn't different any more, now that McDonalds, Starbucks et al have moved in.

7

1982–1991: They Never Had It So Good

The 1980s-era of Margaret Thatcher, the failed miners' strike and outright commercialism – was a decade of immense growth for package holidays. Growth was made possible by increasing disposable income and computerised reservations systems that allowed tour operators to pile on flight and hotel capacity and cut prices, with travel agents switching from telephone bookings to an automated system called viewdata. Many small travel agents were set up in the 1980s, but they faced massive competition from large chains. Although some package holidays were sold direct to the public, travel agents controlled around 90 per cent of the market.

Until the mid-1980s travel agents were not allowed to discount holiday prices. Only tour operators could make that decision, but when the floodgates opened it led to a price war that meant many more people could afford to go abroad – encouraged, at the same time, by an all-out war between Thomson and Harry Goodman's International Leisure Group (ILG), with Intasun as its main brand. This was the heyday of the package holiday, with many small tour operators also joining in. The number of tour operators belonging to ABTA increased from 440 to 699 during the 1980s, while the number of travel agents increased from nearly 2,000 to almost 3,000, with travel agency branches nearly doubling from 2,448 to 4,548.

ABTA was taken to the Restrictive Practices Court in 1982, with the Office of Fair Trading objecting to its Stabiliser closed shop rule (tour operator members could only sell through travel agency members, and vice versa), its ban on retail discounting and other restrictions. The closed shop was allowed to continue as it was considered in the public interest, with ABTA vetting financial standards and consigning fly-by-night operations to the margins. But ABTA could no longer ban discounting, and tour operators came under pressure to let travel agents cut prices.

The pressure had started a few years earlier and there were two main protagonists. In the unremarkable East Midlands town of Ilkeston, the local Co-op started offering people who booked holidays through its travel agency £10 discount vouchers to be used in the store for each £100 spent on holidays. Ilkeston Co-op's Ken Scott was a canny man who gained nationwide publicity, boasting that he was soon sending more people on package holidays than the entire population of Ilkeston.

Big tour operators including Thomson, Intasun and Horizon confronted him, a time recalled by Horizon's Michael Knowles: 'Ken Scott was a tricky character and quite aggressive. He found us rather arrogant, but we wanted to keep a level playing field. Tour operators agreed that discounting wouldn't be helpful, but Scott got his way. When discounting became endemic, package holidays became heavily price-driven and this was anathema to us. We came under attack in our Midlands heartland, at Manchester and at Gatwick. Thomson, Intasun and Airtours all became very aggressive.'

Tour operators could still make contracts with travel agents forbidding discounting, but attempts to ban discounting were ended by a Monopolies and Mergers Commission ruling in 1986. The second travel agent to challenge the ban, Page & Moy, was one of those giving evidence to the MMC.

David Short, Page & Moy's sales and marketing director, recalls the outright hostility shown by ABTA when it started offering discounts to readers of TV Times, followed by its setting-up of the Barclaycard Holiday Club: 'We were still prevented from discounting by tour operators, so we came up with a scheme whereby people paid the full price but then got a cheque back from us. We then started a discount scheme with Walkers crisps, and the president of ABTA was shown on the TV news shaking a packet of crisps, which just gave us more publicity.

'Travel agents went ballistic over the Barclaycard discount scheme, and one of ABTA's leaders was shown in the press about to cut up his Barclaycard. What he didn't know was that we had just sent someone to his agency to book a holiday using a Barclaycard! People were used to getting discounts on everything else, so why not holidays? It was amazing that the ban on discounting lasted so long, but people have saved probably billions of pounds as a result of what we fought to do.'

Discounting coincided with a massive battle for market share between Thomson and the would-be market leader. Thomson was keeping a wary eye on ILG as it went on the acquisition trail. Matters came to a head for the 1986 summer season when Intasun ramped up holiday capacity, but the times were starting to take a toll on the flamboyant Harry Goodman. Stories about his excessive lifestyle would soon start to appear in the tabloid press.

'Outwardly I was self-assured, but inwardly I was scared as I was self-taught, I left school at sixteen and I'd had no training in business,' he recalls. 'I had a lack of self-esteem, and didn't recognise my own strengths. I was friendly with a very famous pop star as we used to take drugs together, and I used to think that running ILG was rather like a pop concert. Like my friend, I could rabble-rouse and judge an audience very well. But after the show, when he went back to his hotel, he would feel deflated – and so would I.

'Running a company that grows so fast can be a very lonely job, and very often those ventures end in failure. We took risks. There were two sides to me – the businessman, and a bit of a playboy and a villain, which was 20 per cent true. But people who attacked me ignored my charity work. I was "chief barker" for the Variety Club children's charity, and once I raised £100,000 in twenty minutes. I probably gave over £5 million to the Variety Club and I also supported charities in the East End.

'But I was into every excess, and I deserved the tabloid exposes. When you have such a high profile you can't have any kind of foible, but when I went through a personal crisis it was very tough. I'm a people person, but I was surrounded by secretaries and no one could get to see me. I went into rehab for a while, and that's when I bought Club 18–30. I remember a board meeting one day when I just walked out, and vanished for a week. When I came back, my jacket was still hanging on the back of the boardroom chair.

'Thomson hated me,' continues Goodman. 'They allocated millions of pounds to put me out of business, but I'd been tipped off. They were arrogant, complacent and slow-moving, while we had a reputation for shooting from the hip. I did my homework and when I pressed the button, we moved fast. We became a public company in 1981 but I never got on with the City, and the feeling was mutual. I was a kid from the East End who suddenly became chairman of a public company. I was both chairman and chief executive as there was no corporate governance in those days, and I used to spend money like water.'

Eyewitness: Marian White
She worked for Thomson Holidays from 1982 to 2009, spending eleven years overseas as a rep and resort manager in many countries before returning to head office as overseas purchasing

manager and in human resources, where part of her role was recruiting and training.

When I started, the rep's role was very traditional, and people coming into it saw the job as glamorous and exciting. But it's always been a lifestyle choice rather than a job paying lots of money, and you always had to work very hard. There were no mobiles or emails then, so you were fairly independent, and you had to put up with not having the best accommodation, or things like washing machines. In the early days, people on holiday turned to the rep for everything and we were much appreciated, especially by older customers on programmes like Thomson's Young at Heart.

In general it was the more mature reps who provided the best service, and Thomson was good because it always offered excellent training and career progression – but you had to attract the right people in the first place. You needed to have real empathy with customers and not get flustered, and you had to speak the language in the country you were based in. Sometimes you needed to deal with emergencies, even deaths, helping people who had to go to hospital and going to the local police station when they got into trouble.

Over the years things started to change as people became more familiar with destinations, and if they really knew the ropes, they didn't need the old-style rep service anymore because they knew the resort better than many of the reps. Thomson made every effort to make the rep service relevant to customers' needs but began to withdraw it from some hotels, and holidaymakers were given a 24-hour helpline instead. Reps sold excursions and generated revenue, so although the company didn't have the costs of providing a rep, it didn't have the revenue it had before. There was still help and advice on hand when needed.

There was still a rep service in most hotels after the merger between Thomson and First Choice in 2007, but some big destinations such as Mallorca now have far fewer reps than when I started. Reps today have hand-held computer terminals and demand a lot more from their companies, and in general they are getting younger.

Thomson and Intasun were at each other's throats for the 1986 season, and the winner was the customer as holiday prices tumbled. Thomson reacted by piling on capacity itself and bringing back the

Skytours name for its cheapest holidays, as former chairman Roger Davies would later recall: 'The crunch year was 1985 as our prices were rather high, and ILG was determined to become number one,' he said. 'We really had to grow volume substantially and planned a major increase for 1986, wrong-footing Harry Goodman and re-introducing Skytours as our fighting brand. We added one million holidays for 1986 because we were absolutely determined that Intasun would not become too big, and we were fighting each other for aircraft. We proved that if you put a value proposition to consumers, they will dump other purchases and buy holidays.'

All-out competition continued to rage between the big two, but Goodman says efforts were made to agree to a truce – a claim denied by the Thomson side. 'At one of the ABTA conventions, I got a call from Thomson saying we needed to talk,' he says. 'They had hired a private villa where our two teams could meet, but the meeting was a disaster. Thomson was totally arrogant and said it would wipe us out. I wouldn't have it, so I walked away.'

There were casualties in the price war and the biggest was Horizon – the former Horizon Midlands, which rose from the ashes of the original Horizon Holidays to become the third biggest tour operator. It was sitting pretty with a great reputation for quality, its own charter airline (Orion) and some of its own resort hotels, and had acquired a brand called Holiday Club International. That company, formerly Pontinental, was originally the package holiday arm of UK holiday camps operator Pontin's, but was now owned by the giant brewer, Bass.

Horizon's refusal to cut prices came under severe pressure, as former managing director Ken Franklin relates. 'Until the mid-1980s, the industry hadn't developed into really nasty competition, but then Intasun declared war on Thomson and the Horizon board got nervous,' he says. 'Our chairman Bruce Tanner took the view that we needed some backing, and started talking to Bass which he regarded as a white knight. Bass took over our entire shareholding but I wasn't at all happy with that course of action. It was very evident to me that Bass wasn't bringing anything to the table, and that Horizon wasn't doing anything for Bass.'

Michael Knowles, Horizon's former marketing director, takes up the story: 'We were being squeezed by Thomson and Intasun, and Airtours was now snapping away at our heels out of Manchester. We were taken over by Bass to get a cash injection and some stability, and we thought we would be left to get on with it. But Bruce Tanner left as part of the deal and Ken Franklin retired, and Horizon went on a drive to increase volume. As Horizon wasn't as profitable as expected, Bass decided to get out. It approached Thomson and asked if it wanted to buy.'

Bass was also talking to ILG, but Thomson had the cash reserves and took over Horizon in 1988 – what Thomson's Roger Davies called 'the knock-out blow' in its battle with ILG. Suddenly, Thomson was not just big but enormous, foreshadowing the takeovers of ten years later. But the Horizon name was retained for only a couple of years, while the Monopolies and Mergers Commission looked at the deal. By 1990, a very proud name with a forty-year heritage had gone.

'Thomson more or less turned up one day and said, "We own you",' says Franklin. 'I was still on the Horizon board and gave Thomson lots of information on areas of the company it needed to retain, but I was devastated when it emerged that Thomson took us over to close us down. It paid an enormous amount (£75 million) to take Horizon off Bass but then Thomson destroyed it.'

The final word on Horizon goes to Knowles, who later tried unsuccessfully to buy the Horizon brand from Thomson. 'I never understood why Thomson wanted to lose a quality brand that had been around for so long, but even today it is fondly remembered and we had 167 people at our fiftieth anniversary reunion in 2015. The feeling for that company is tremendous, and everyone says that working for Horizon was the best time of their lives.'

Many of the hotels used by Horizon were brought into the Thomson brochures, and as both operators had an emphasis on quality, they were a natural fit. Thomson had gradually increased the quality of what it offered, and a highly amusing advertising campaign (viewable on Youtube) showed a suited, bowler-hatted gent with umbrella inspecting hotels and awarding 'T' ratings, jumping into a pool and limbo-dancing while fully dressed. The message was 'you don't have to hope for the best', and that message hit home.

Doug Goodman, Thomson's press officer from 1971–88, says: 'This advertisement made people realise that real people went out to inspect hotels, and it put us ahead of our competitors. To start with you could get away with a bit of exaggeration in brochures, but by then everything had to be accurate and a team of writers visited every hotel to check things like how far it really was from the beach. But people also wanted low prices. I remember when we relaunched Skytours as a budget brand, and I sat up all night concocting a story about holidays costing only £25 that made front page news. A whole new group of people could now afford to go abroad.'

Whether or not Thomson did deliver 'the knock-out blow' to ILG, competition continued to be fierce and not just between the big two. Tour operators including Global had been swallowed up but Cosmos carried on, as did names such as Falcon (by now part of Owners Abroad) and destination specialists such as Olympic Holidays (Greece and Cyprus).

Owners Abroad, which would rebrand as First Choice in 1994, started in the 1970s by arranging flights for overseas property owners. It acquired companies including Falcon, Martyn Holidays, Twentys and, in 1990, Redwing, which itself took in former British Airways-owned Enterprise and Sovereign, plus Greece and Turkey specialist Sunmed. Owners Abroad also set up its own airline, Air 2000.

The huge increase in package holiday availability was also made possible by bigger aircraft, especially the Boeing 757. In charter configuration tour operators could pack 228 seats into this model, about one hundred more than the original version of the Boeing 737 which remained the workhorse of the charter airline business. British Airways' 757s seated only 195. Another step forward was the twin-aisle (wide-bodied) Boeing 767, introduced by Britannia in 1984, seating up to 273. These new aircraft delivered further economies of scale, and could cross the Atlantic when restrictions on flying two-engined aircraft so far over water were relaxed. The Boeing 757 could not reach Florida or the Caribbean non-stop, so refuelling was usually done in Bangor, Maine. Later versions of the 767 could achieve this, but 767s were just as useful on the busiest routes to the Mediterranean. Both types remain in service today.

The mid-1980s were a time when tour operators faced major challenges to their bottom line, according to John MacNeill, who was with Thomson from 1971 to 1989 and managing director of Thomson Holidays from 1982 to 1985. 'Not only were travel agents starting to offer holiday discounts, but they were also offering free travel insurance which took away another income stream from tour operators,' he says. 'There were four sources of income for a tour operator – the holiday price itself, room supplements such as sea view, profits on insurance, and getting people's money up-front and earning interest on it. But interest rates started to drop, and people started to book later. It was important for customers not to pay a lot less for the same holiday as someone sitting next to them on the plane, because they had booked just two weeks before departure. So Thomson introduced Square Deals, discounted holidays where you didn't know which hotel you'd be going to until you arrived. The discount on holidays booked late could be substantial, but by selling the last few seats on the plane we could make big profits. That was necessary as we lost the other income streams.'

Thomson also developed winter holidays successfully, and one way it did this was to offer long-stay holidays in resorts such as Benidorm to the over-60s. Its brand name for these holidays was Young at Heart, and most big tour operators had similar programmes such as Golden Times or Golden Days. These holidays were something of a time warp as they featured sequence dancing, bingo and other old-fashioned entertainment, and eventually disappeared as older people became more demanding in their tastes. Long-stay holidays were so cheap that tour operators claimed it cost less to spend two or three months in Benidorm than to heat your own home throughout the winter.

Holidays for the eighteen to thirty age group were also changing. Club 18–30 had been joined by competitors such as Twentys, while the big tour operators also got involved with youth brands such as Thomson's Freestyle. But at the same time, this type of holiday became infamous for lashings of booze and illegal substances.

David Heard, who was at Horizon Holidays when it started Club 18–30 in 1965 and bought it from Horizon in 1972, left in 1983 to set up a different operation called Buddies. 'The problem was that it takes a lot of energy to set up an excursion programme for young people like we used to do, and some reps thought it was easier to just get people pissed and get kick-backs from the bars they took them to,' he explains. 'Loutish behaviour became a problem in the 1980s and I started getting calls from the tabloids. There was a huge fight in Magalluf and although it didn't involve our clients, the mud stuck. Only a tiny minority got into trouble but of course the tabloids loved it.

'The culture had changed by the 1980s, and as more people were travelling independently because of cheap charter flights, our USP disappeared. People who weren't our clients latched on. When Harry Goodman bought Club 18–30, he asked me what he should do with it. I said he should take it up-market, to new destinations, and give people who had grown up with Club 18–30 something to move on to. These people were buying their own houses, and were more independently minded.'

But while Club 18–30 stayed much as it was, Heard's new operation Buddies was aimed at the slightly older, more experienced customer. Hotels were of better quality, meals were taken in top restaurants and casinos, and some people even dressed up. Heard sold on Buddies in 1985 and moved out of the travel business, and has watched with some horror as the youth market, travelling mainly independently, turned increasingly nasty.

'Drugs have now taken over, and the adventure aspect of the early days has all gone,' he laments. 'It's now all about drink, drugs and hedonism, but people don't remember getting pissed or stoned. What they do remember are things like horse-riding on the beach or scuba-diving, which we used to offer.'

Another defining feature of the 1980s was the growth in travel agencies, especially Thomson-owned Lunn Poly and Thomas Cook, which set the scene for the main battleground of the 1990s. Lunn Poly more than doubled in size in only five years to about 500 'holiday shops' by the end of the decade, but didn't only sell Thomson holidays. Intasun didn't have its own retail shops, but had very close relationships with many independent agencies which it entertained at lavish parties. Horizon had only a few of its own shops, but with its own airline and its own travel agencies, Thomson was ready for the next stage of battle.

MacNeill, who moved on from Thomson Holidays to become Lunn Poly's managing director from 1985–89, says: 'The next stage became controlling the distribution of your holidays, but although Lunn Poly incentivised staff to sell approved tour operators, we didn't differentiate between Thomson and others, such as Horizon. It wasn't until much later that Lunn Poly became almost exclusively an outlet for Thomson.

'Our strategy was to open mainstream holiday shops, and we didn't offer things like foreign exchange or rail tickets. Part of the reason we grew so quickly is that the opposition looked down their noses at us and didn't regard us as "real" travel agents.'

While all these developments were ongoing, another horse was coming up on the rails – and galloping very quickly. Seen in retrospect, there are some similarities in the rapid growth of Intasun in the 1970s and 1980s, and Airtours in the late 1980s and 1990s. Both were run by self-made men who left school in their mid-teens, Harry Goodman and David Crossland. In a little more than a decade, David Crossland's Airtours grew from nothing to become the second biggest package holiday company.

Airtours might be an obvious name to give a tour operator, but the letters A, I and R referred not to a means of transport but to Albert and Ivy Roberts, a couple who sold their travel agency to Crossland and used the name Airtours. Crossland had started working in Althams Travel in his home town of Burnley, Lancashire at the age of sixteen in 1963 – a company which started as a grocer in 1874 and still exists today as an independent travel agent. But he soon moved on, acquiring Pendle Travel Services in 1972 and starting a tour operation in 1980 as Pendle Airtours, selling 900 holidays to Malta. The following year he sold 23,000 holidays, and by 1987 that total had grown to 365,000 – mainly low-cost package holidays to the usual destinations. That was the year Airtours was floated on the London Stock Exchange – coincidentally, the same year that ILG was taken back into private ownership.

Crossland – who sold off his travel agencies in 1986 to concentrate on Airtours – was renowned as an entrepreneur who notched up some notable firsts, including charter flights to Barbados, which started in 1987 with holidays costing from £299 for two weeks. Like Goodman before him, he brought in expertise including some from outside the travel industry, from organisations including Granada and Marks & Spencer. But he stayed close to his roots, establishing his headquarters at an old mill in Helmshore, Lancashire just a few miles from home.

Rapid growth was not without pain, however – especially for some of Airtours' long-haul customers. By 1989 it was chartering Boeing 747 jumbo jets to fly people to Florida and Hawaii, but one proved to be so unreliable it was dubbed 'the flying pig' by the press which had reporters camped at Manchester airport to report on customers' woes. Andy Cooper, who joined Airtours as a lawyer that year, had a baptism of fire as he became a regular in the courts trying to fight off litigation.

'It was a horrible time, and at one point we had five hundred people stranded in Vancouver on their way back from Hawaii,' he recalls. 'We ruined 20,000 holidays that summer, but the Airtours name became well-known and people forgot why they first heard of us. Our lead-in price was £299 for Jamaica based on four sharing a room, but the reality was there might have been only one room in a hotel that could fit four adults in. We aimed to add a new and interesting destination each year, such as Kenya, Thailand, even Australia.'

Eyewitness: Diana Hanks
She handled complaints by holidaymakers for ABTA and Thomson Holidays between 1973 and 1987, before moving on a business with a poorer public image – timeshare.

ABTA did a lot of work with the Office of Fair Trading to improve things for the package holiday customer, and legislation such as the Trade Descriptions Act of 1968 and Unfair Contract Terms Act 1977 made tour operators improve their booking conditions and how they described resorts and hotels. The ABTA arbitration scheme, introduced in the 1970s, is independently run and very helpful if a complaint reaches deadlock.

As package holidays expanded there could be lots of problems, as with Tenerife where there were many half-built hotels. Customers became more savvy over the years and the Small Claims Court was a threat that tour operators had to take seriously, but fraudulent claims also started to increase.

Here are some of my favourite extracts from complaint letters, and they are all genuine:

- *The brochure advertised Spanish flamingo, but there wasn't any.*
- *We had no electrics for three days. The rep didn't show up to explain anything, which left us completely in the dark.*
- *We were put in room 208 with lots of foreign chambermaids that started at 7 a.m.*
- *The beds were hard, the pillows lumpy. The large gap under the door allowed the lizards to enter and repose on the ceiling. I suppose they would as the beds were so awful.*
- *My wife had the sole. I was presented with the heel.*
- *The rep said it was a vegetarian rat in our room and so did not count as vermin.*
- *I took a party of fifteen women to Benidorm and have quite a lot of complaints.*
- *If my seats are not sold I would like them sent to me as proof.*

[And tour operators reply:]

- *There is only one complaint that holds water and unfortunately it didn't – the swimming pool.*
- *The rep who you say was dressed very untidily was in fact one of your fellow passengers.*
- *I am sure you will accept that power failures, prostitutes and beetles are items over which we have no control.*

Despite this rapid growth, Airtours' glory days still lay ahead. Harry Goodman's attention, meanwhile, had turned beyond what he knew best, package holidays. It was to prove his undoing, but when the end came for ILG it was due to events beyond anyone's control. Many claim that Goodman was a visionary as well as an opportunist, and there was no doubting that his vision for a pan-European, low-cost scheduled airline was a decade ahead of its time.

In the 1980s airlines, like most of commerce, were still regulated in the European Union, with 'single market' legislation not taking effect until 1993. But Goodman diversified Air Europe by applying for scheduled as well as charter routes, and setting up joint ventures in several other countries. Air Europe's first scheduled routes were to Spanish resorts – a move also made by Monarch, Britannia and Orion. But when Air Europe started flying to cities such as Paris, Munich and Rome despite the objections of British Airways and other national carriers, it was venturing into unknown territory.

'Europe had just voted to liberalise aviation, so I knew an open market was coming,' says Goodman. 'I put in a bid for British Caledonian, which was the second biggest scheduled airline, but when that was about to be taken over by British Airways in 1988, its European routes were put up for grabs as part of the deal. We applied for every route and got them, plus the departure slots at Gatwick. Air Europe was the first airline to do what EasyJet and Ryanair are doing now – the first low-cost airline, ahead of its time. But I was still told I couldn't offer low fares to Paris. So on the first flight, I gave every passenger £25.'

With its European partners, Air Europe set up bases in Spain, Italy, Germany and Norway. Goodman himself became even more of a celebrity, being entertained to lunch by Margaret Thatcher and mixing with more elevated company when Air Europe started flying to Rome: 'As a joke, I asked if the Pope could attend – and I later found out that a large sum was paid into a cardinal's account to make that possible,' he claims. 'There was an event in the Sistine Chapel and I was asked to give a speech, but as I'm Jewish I asked someone else to do it. The Pope agreed to shake hands and have his photograph taken with everyone present. I met lots of other celebrities – even Prince Charles and Lady Diana. I was living a dream.'

Stuart Hulse, in charge of Air Europe's PR, preferred the airline's boss Errol Cossey to act as the front man. 'I could see what a bright bloke Harry was, but he was not the right man to put in front of the media when promoting an airline,' he says. 'He couldn't raise money in the City, but he got it from Japanese banks.'

It takes massive resources to set up a scheduled airline to compete against the big boys, as Laker had found. Air Europe did this in preparation for the liberalisation of European aviation, but then came events outside anyone's control which hit all airlines hard. In August 1990 Iraqi dictator Saddam Hussein invaded neighbouring Kuwait, leading to the first Gulf War when a US-led coalition succeeding in ousting Saddam from Kuwait at the end of February 1991. Fuel prices rocketed, and for possibly the first time in a major conflict, there was a direct threat to use missiles to bring down civilian aircraft. The effect on most airlines was devastating with business people ceasing to travel. Air Europe was flying virtually empty aircraft and leeching cash at a terrible rate.

Within a few days of the first Gulf War ending, on 8 March 1991, ILG and all its airlines and tour operations went bust, with 4,000 job losses. As with previous tour operator collapses, the 30,000 or so package holiday customers abroad at the time were brought home in an orderly way and people holding bookings reimbursed – but not so the people who had bought tickets on Air Europe scheduled services, some of whom lost their money.

'The airline was not a drain on us but no one could have foreseen what happened,' says Goodman. 'Overnight, the load factor on our Paris flights [the proportion of seats sold] dropped from 80 per cent to 15 per cent. We broke some rules, but we never missed an interest or capital payment, and we were put into liquidation by the banks. We went bust with £5 million in our account but I'm not bitter about it. If you play to win, don't be surprised if you lose. I came from the slums of the East End of London to meeting royalty and the Pope and I'm grateful, not bitter.'

There followed what Goodman describes as his 'wilderness years', but when he did start going again to trade events, he was well received. In 1998 he became directly involved again, this time with a new venture called TV Travel Shop which grew very quickly with the cable TV boom, broadcasting programmes about holidays while inviting viewers to book through a call centre. TV Travel Shop was a retailer rather than a tour operator, and sold the packages of all big companies – even Thomson. 'I never went to Thomson's Greater London House headquarters in my Intasun days because it was beneath them to talk to me,' he says. 'When I went there to do a deal for TV Travel Shop, I thought there must be some people turning in their graves.'

He also got a good commission deal from Airtours, and recalls meeting its boss, David Crossland, who was by then number two behind Thomson. 'He asked if I didn't resent how Airtours had grown in my place, but I told him I would have done the same thing. Airtours had the same entrepreneurial spirit.'

The success of TV Travel Shop restored Goodman's reputation, and it had achieved annual turnover of £200 million before being sold off by venture capitalists in 2002. Goodman left, but in 2005 bought an online cruise agency which proved to be a loss maker and later went bust. Apart from a little consultancy work, Goodman – aged seventy-seven – is now retired but defiant, an admirer of EasyJet and budget supermarkets. He is reflective and aware of his place in history.

A few days after ILG collapsed in 1991, a leading newspaper ran a profile comparing him to Icarus – 'the man who flew too close to the sun'. The entrepreneur who had loomed large in the package holiday then airline worlds for a quarter of a century can now look back with pride at what he achieved.

Hugh Morgan, who worked for Goodman from 1966 to 1990, says many people who became future industry leaders started by working for Intasun or ILG – including Peter Long, who went on to head what's claimed to be the world's biggest tourism company, TUI.

'Harry surrounded himself with a good bunch of people, and he was living the life of Riley rather than sitting in the office looking at balance sheets all day,' recalls Morgan. 'He made and spent fortunes and could be ruthless, but he should have no regrets.'

8

Far Away

Even in the earliest days of package holidays, it wasn't unusual for people to travel far beyond the Mediterranean in search of sun or new experiences. While most people who travelled beyond Europe went on an escorted tour (see Part 2), a few went mainly to relax or were sure to add time on the beach after a tour, safari or other activity. But the style was usually different to a package holiday in Europe. People usually travelled as individuals, on regular scheduled airlines rather than on charter flights, so had greater flexibility. Almost without exception, they were wealthy.

It's partly because of the British Empire that people have been used to faraway travel (what the travel industry calls long-haul) for so long. If they were accustomed to spending weeks or months travelling by sea to Africa, India or even further afield, it was easy by comparison to fly there even if journeys were arduous by today's standards. Most countries retained strong links with Britain after independence, meaning plenty of flights. Countries where English was widely spoken were especially attractive.

The Caribbean quickly became the top destination for faraway sunshine holidays, especially Barbados, Jamaica, St Lucia, the Bahamas plus, further north, Bermuda. Mauritius and the Seychelles also became popular, all these countries being once part of the empire. It took a lot longer for countries including Thailand and the Maldives to become favourite places for the British, but now they are much in demand.

The faraway country always regarded as most attractive is of course the US, but until Intasun's audacious introduction of Miami Beach in 1980 few people went there in search of sun, and fewer still stayed in one place. People went to America on tour, to see the cities or stay with friends or relatives, until Florida began grabbing the attention.

As with package holidays to the Med, the biggest single factor making faraway holidays affordable was the jet aircraft. By the late 1950s you could fly across the Atlantic in speed and comfort on board a Boeing 707, which more than any other aircraft shrank continents and the distances between them. This was celebrated, or lamented, in popular songs such as 'Leaving on a Jet Plane' by John Denver and recorded by American folk trio Peter, Paul and Mary, or 'Early Morning Rain' by Canadian singer Gordon Lightfoot. But although the first intercontinental jets such as the Boeing 707 and McDonnell Douglas DC-8 were game changers, they had limited range.

The history of one of the world's longest air routes, from London to Sydney, is enlightening. Qantas, which began life as Queensland and Northern Territory Aerial Services, started a Flying Boat service from Sydney to London in 1938, taking nine days although only seventy hours were actually spent airborne, with thirty-six stops! The cost (one-way) was £200, or £12,150 in today's money. By 1947, using a Lockheed Constellation, the journey was down to four days with only six stops, fifty-five hours being spent in the air. When the Boeing 707 started on the 'Kangaroo Route' in 1959 the journey time was cut to thirty-four hours, but the limited range of the 707 (and commercial considerations) meant stops still had to be made in Perth, Jakarta, Singapore, Calcutta, Karachi, Beirut and Zurich.

The next and even bigger game changer was the twin-aisle, wide-bodied Boeing 747 'jumbo jet', which first flew to Britain in 1970. When Qantas introduced it in 1971 the journey time from Sydney to London was cut from thirty-four to twenty-five hours with only two stops, in Perth and Bombay (now Mumbai). There has been only one significant cut in journey time since then, with the longer-range Boeing 747-400 making one-stop journeys possible in twenty-one hours. Although a lightly loaded Boeing 787 can travel between London and Australia non-stop, airlines do not see this as desirable for economic reasons and no reduction in journey times is likely in the foreseeable future. The world's longest non-stop commercial flight, in 2015, was by Emirates from Dubai to Panama City, a distance of 13,821 km covered in seventeen hours and thirty-five minutes.

The Boeing 747 changed faraway holidays not just because of its range, but because of its enormous size seating 430 passengers compared to 110 in the 707 introduced by Qantas in 1959. The same challenge was experienced by airlines all over the world as they introduced Boeing 747s and smaller wide-bodied aircraft such as the DC-10, as suddenly they had many more seats to sell. Inevitably, fares dropped dramatically and discounts below the published fare became widespread as the age of the 'bucket shop' cheap fares agency arrived. Airlines not only cut fares but often set up their own tour operations (such as Speedbird, later renamed British Airways Holidays), or started working more closely with established holiday companies wanting to expand.

The age of the jumbo jet was still a few years away when Kuoni first arrived in the UK, buying a company called Challis and Benson and starting its first tours in 1966. The company that would soon become synonymous with faraway travel, achieving a dominance that Thomson never had in European package holidays, was founded by Alfred Kuoni in Switzerland in 1906, and already operated tours from several other European countries before starting in the UK. While Kuoni was a mainstream package holiday company in some countries, its young London-based manager Peter Diethelm thought the UK was already too competitive to risk that.

Instead he pulled off the first of many coups, chartering a Vickers Viscount VC-10 (not to be confused with the McDonnell Douglas DC-10) to run holiday flights to Mombasa, Kenya, at a cost of £199 for one week at a beachfront hotel – half the price of the scheduled return air fare. Kuoni grew rapidly, but not by operating charters which incurred substantial risk. As demand increased and bigger aircraft arrived, scheduled airlines began to offer attractive fares linked to tours, especially to the Far East. In 1973 Kuoni took over its main rival, Houlders, becoming top company for faraway holidays. It has held that position ever since and remained market leader in 2015, a change of ownership during that year meaning German company Rewe now runs it.

Kuoni continued to operate charters from time to time, as it pioneered flights to Rio de Janeiro in 1976, Luxor (Egypt) in 1986, the Maldives in 1987 and Acapulco (Mexico) in 1989, while in 1984 it started chartering Concorde to the Caribbean. The big package holiday companies started faraway holidays when they had the right aircraft available, such as Thomson using Britannia Boeing 707s to the Caribbean around 1970, and Clarksons with its ill-fated Court Line TriStars to St Lucia in 1973. Airtours would become a charter operator to the Caribbean and Thailand in the 1980s and 1990s, while Thomson operates its Boeing 787 Dreamliners today to the same places. But in general most tour operators use scheduled airlines for faraway travel, and the choice of airlines and routes has increased enormously.

Kuoni has sailed happily through all these changes, and was one of the first to computerise, in 1979. In 1980 came a master stroke, a programme called Kuoni 3 to three-star rather than luxurious hotels, aimed at attracting Mediterranean package holiday customers to make the big leap forward. 'These people represent our future,' said Diethelm. 'We consider ourselves to be the BMW of the travel industry and regardless of whether you drive a three series or seven series, you will always buy class and quality.'

Another director of Kuoni, the late Brian Whitham, wrote at the time: 'The profile of the traditional long-haul traveller has changed, and radically. Clients used to be almost exclusively the company director type taking a second holiday in the winter. Now they come from all social strata. They are garage owners, restaurant managers – anyone, in fact, with disposable income. This turnabout has occurred because there has been a fifteen-year history of people doing the rounds of popular European holiday resorts, and now they want to do more with their holiday than just spend it on the beach. They want to see things and do things, and sit on the beach as well.'

It was far-sighted when introducing Kuoni 3 in 1980, but could not have foreseen what started to happen in the late 1980s, especially with the growth of all-inclusive hotels. Nowadays people think nothing of flying across the world to do no more than lie on a beach and maybe indulge in water sports, and as Intasun and Airtours were the first to realise, they were happy to do that during the British summer and not just to escape the winter blues.

Kuoni also noted the 'massive over-capacity' available on scheduled airlines by 1980, with some Third World countries starting their own airlines for reasons of prestige rather than sound economics. The increasing cost of European packages, why Intasun started holidays to Florida in 1980, was another factor in the growth of faraway. Kuoni's Whitham added: 'While a holiday to Greece can now easily cost £400 plus, the price of a Far East trip has been held down to much the same kind of figure and sometimes even less. As the popularity of long-haul holidays has grown, so has the number of holiday companies specialising in this type of package, with eighty-plus operators in 1982 when there were only about twenty a few years back. Research suggests that all the companies put together have only scratched the surface of the potential demand for exotic long-haul holidays, which at the moment manage to attract only 2 per cent of the UK market.'

Kuoni has plotted the rise of faraway travel very accurately, publishing its Long-Haul Report every year since the early 1980s. By the middle of that decade, as he watched Thomson and Intasun tearing each other apart in a vicious price war for mainstream packages, Kuoni boss Peter Diethelm was able to boast: 'The greatest satisfaction for us is that we have given the lead for long-haul to grow profitably at a rate of 20–25 per cent a year without throwing the industry into a price war. We have done this by continuously improving real value for money, and by narrowing the gap between the price of an ordinary two weeks in the Med and a more exotic faraway holiday.'

Kuoni's brochures have reflected people's dreams and aspirations over the years, as the emphasis has gradually broadened out from simple beach holidays and a few tours. Now it offers an ever more sophisticated range of faraway experiences with a growing emphasis on spa treatments, weddings and honeymoons, more all-inclusive, and more luxury options. Tastes have changed, usually for the better, and Wendy Kenneally, who started working for Kuoni in 1989, looks back on some of the holidays it used to offer with a shiver of horror. In 1980 it was selling a 'Night Life Special' holiday in Bangkok which was unashamedly aimed at men going for sex, while hotels with a similar focus were also available in the Thai resort of Pattaya.

'We were always a reputable company, but this sort of holiday was acceptable in those days,' says Kenneally, Kuoni vice-president of purchasing and customer experience. 'Over time, this type of holiday became less acceptable and we had to ask, do we want to cater for that? In terms of reputational damage, it would be impossible to offer that kind of holiday today.'

Even photography of bikini-clad women is frowned on in many brochures nowadays, and the imagery used is far more aspirational in an age where anyone can take a great photograph with the average digital camera or phone. Hotel standards have improved enormously, first in Asia and the Caribbean but now throughout the world, but Kuoni doesn't have such a strong focus on all-inclusive as some tour operators. Pick up a charter-based holiday brochure for Mexico, for example, and there is nothing but all-inclusive.

Managing people's expectations of a faraway holiday used to be more of a challenge, as Kenneally explains: 'People always expected luxury when they went long-haul, or at least similar standards to in Europe when there was a massive difference especially in Africa and Asia. People don't talk about culture shock any more, but twenty or thirty years ago, the foreignness of these places really hit them. As we were selling dreams, brochures were not as truthful as they are now. People would look at guidebooks and TV programmes, but the research they did was very limited. They trusted the travel agent, but some agents who mainly sold Europe weren't very knowledgeable.'

Thailand became Kuoni's top destination in the 1980s, but was later overtaken by the Maldives which remains number one today. The availability of direct flights is often crucial to a country's success, and when visitors to the Maldives no longer had to travel via Sri Lanka, it started to take off. The rapid growth of wealthy Middle East-based airlines, especially Emirates but also Abu Dhabi's Etihad and Qatar Airways, has opened up one-stop flying to many previously inaccessible places. They fly direct from the UK regions as well as from London, and Dubai and Abu Dhabi have become holiday destinations in their own right and not just for stop-overs.

'Airlines such as these have really upped their game, and the standard of on-board comfort, food and entertainment is now much better,' says Kenneally. 'It's the same with hotels, when you look at spa options for example. Spas were always important in Thailand, where it was more about culture than treatment, whereas twenty years ago you might only see a hairdressing salon in many hotels as people were more concerned with how they looked than how they felt. Many customers now want a spa wherever they go, and the male aspect has come in as it used to be regarded as seedy for a man to have a massage.

'Starting in the Caribbean, weddings are also a very important part of our business. It used to be very difficult to get a licence and other paperwork, but it quickly became a conveyor belt with lots of brides wandering around Caribbean hotels. Then hotels started limiting weddings to one a day or even one a week, and nowadays wedding parties are much more demanding and want to know every detail in advance. Honeymoons, wedding anniversaries and other special occasions are also very important to us.'

Kuoni has always been dominant in faraway holidays, but of course it has hundreds of competitors. British Airways Holidays and Virgin Holidays were set up to feed traffic onto their parent airlines, and a few other general faraway specialists have stayed the course such as Hayes & Jarvis, an independent company run by Melba and Tom Correia, who sold it to First Choice before it became part of TUI. Thomas Cook concentrated more on tours than faraway beach holidays, but now has a major resort programme called Signature. But most faraway tour operators are much smaller, often specialising in a particular country or part of the world, although that can be risky when natural disasters, political or economic problems come into play.

Cox & Kings can rightly claim to be oldest travel company in the world, but only started operating tours to India in 1970 and is now a leading up-market tour operator to the Indian sub-continent, Latin America, Africa, the Middle East, the Far East, Europe and Australasia. The company's history goes back to 1758 when Richard Cox was appointed regimental agent to the Foot Guards, and soon Cox & Co became the agent for many British regiments. Rival banking and shipping agency Henry S. King & Co. merged with Cox after the First World War, being sold to Lloyds Bank in 1923 after which the shipping agency became separate, running tours and organising travel around the empire, especially to Egypt, India and South Asia.

In 1970 it was bought by Grindlays Bank as part of a deal with Indian Prime Minister Indira Gandhi to develop tourism into the country, as Cox & Kings chairman Tony Good explains. 'We are the world's oldest travel company, while Thomas Cook is the oldest tour operator. When we started our first tours to India (£191 for a week at the Taj Hotel, Bombay) it coincided with India and Pakistan going to war, so we had to introduce other destinations and not replicate what companies such as Thomas Cook were doing. We now operate out of other countries too, and growth out of India has been enormous.

'Faraway holidays will continue to grow as more people realise the world is available at a very reasonable price, whereas forty years ago only a small percentage could afford it. But there have always been crises, especially the price of fuel, and also political problems. Visas can also be an issue, whereas for Australia, you can get a visa electronically within minutes.'

The US and Canada have always been approached differently to other faraway destinations, with more visitors wishing to explore independently. A significant number (especially for Canada) are regarded by the travel industry as VFR (Visiting Friends and Relatives) – also a major factor in travel to Australia, New Zealand and South Africa. Demand for North America was frustrated by high air fares up to the 1960s, when 'affinity group' charters were allowed but only for members of clubs or associations. In 1972, the rules were changed to allow Advance Booking Charters (ABCs), and some companies who started running these charters developed into fully fledged tour operators in the 1970s.

Malcolm James started in 1960 with Pan American, moving on to Canadian airline Wardair and then Dan-Air, and was still working in 2015 running his own niche tour operation to the South Pacific, Transpacific Holidays. In 1975 he joined Jetsave, a company set up by entrepreneur Reg Pycroft, which still exists today as part of TUI.

'Affinity group charters had turned into a circus, as we were issuing membership cards with air tickets for organisations such as the Bromley Rose Growers Association,' he remembers [another was called the Left Hand Club]. 'These clubs were dreamed up to get access to cheap flights, and there was good availability of second-hand Boeing 707s and Britannias to operate charters. The cost of fuel was not an issue before 1973.

'Jetsave was effectively running an airline with other people's aircraft, and we developed our first holiday programme in 1977 to sell more than just tickets. Jetsave was a new kind of animal, doing publicly what had been done surreptitiously. We were selling 100,000 seats a year by the time I left in 1981, to destinations all over America and Canada.'

Stuart Hulse, who was Jetsave's PR man, adds: 'Advance Booking Charters were a huge success, and I remember making a media splash with return flights to New York for £45. Price controls didn't work, as when they were abolished for package holidays in 1971, and the media had pages of publicity on all the new offers.'

The Boeing 747 really changed things as it allowed scheduled airlines to offer fares competing with charters, spelling the gradual decline of transatlantic charters except to Florida and seasonal flights to Canada. The entrepreneurial spirit of Freddie Laker was taken up by Richard Branson's Virgin Atlantic, which launched in 1984, first to America but later to the Caribbean and other faraway destinations including Hong Kong and South Africa. Like Laker, it later became embroiled in legal action against some competitors.

Nigel Jenkins, who helped set up Unijet in 1981 and sold it to First Choice in 1998, had also worked for Jetsave and remembers how scheduled airlines on both sides of the Atlantic tried to protect their privileged, high fare position: 'The 1970s were a really exciting time, bringing low-cost transatlantic travel to the masses,' he says. 'But the reaction of scheduled airlines was scary, and all kinds of dirty tricks were going on. But it was a very profitable time for Jetsave, as people used to put down deposits nine months in advance of travel and pay the full amount two or three months before. Jetsave never had less than £15 million in the bank.'

Malcolm James adds: 'Transatlantic charters had peaked by the mid-1980s as there was a huge increase in cheap fares by scheduled airlines. Deregulation came early to America, and all the restrictions on fares were swept away. There were a lot of mavericks around in the 1970s – people like Harry Goodman, Freddie Laker and Reg Pycroft. The travel industry has now matured into something which is sounder and more respectable, but the fun has gone.

'Look how things have changed. When I started putting people on flights fifty-five years ago, people would board in their Sunday best. Now they go on board in shell suits, and the expect air travel to "just be there". They are now over-protected, and the latest EU rules on compensation for delayed flights will lead to increased fares. But there is still a place for the small, specialist tour operator to destinations like the South Pacific, where we can add value.'

The rise of discounted air fares from the mid-1970s created a new kind of tour operation, packaging up air fares, hotels, car rental and tours with total flexibility, something charter flights with their rigid operating patterns could not offer. Companies such as Jetset, Travel 2, Gold Medal, Travelbag and Trailfinders could sell anything from a simple discounted air fare to a totally flexible, tailor-made, round-the-world tour, without the risk of running charter flights.

John Bond, who bought the UK operation of Jetset in 1992 from its Australian owners, says technological developments have also helped in making faraway places affordable. It introduced a reservations system called Worldlink to confirm hotel, car rental and tour bookings instantly before the internet age.

'Now the public can buy everything online, but there are still so many anomalies that people turn to a specialist,' he says. 'For example, you can buy a club-class outward flight on some airlines and return in economy class, for less than the economy return fare. Airlines are not only our partners but our biggest competitors, but in general they don't want to undermine their brands by offering very low fares when they can offer low fares linked to a tour. People booking direct on the internet still don't have access to the lowest fares, and if something goes wrong and they haven't used a tour operator, who are they going to turn to?'

The benefits of booking through a tour operator have been proved in crisis after crisis, especially when travelling to faraway countries where extreme weather and political upheaval are regular occurrences. The Boxing Day tsunami that devastated countries around the Indian Ocean in 2004 is just one example – but tour operators of any kind still face a daily battle to prove their relevance.

Eyewitness: Graham Lancaster
He acted as a spokesman for ABTA and later the Federation of Tour Operators (FTO) for over twenty-five years.

It was on a Bank Holiday when the worst and most distressing crisis in my many years' serving the industry hit the headlines, and desperately transformed so many lives and communities. It was Boxing Day 2004, and it showed how the media played an important role alongside so many others in responding.

An earthquake off the coast of Indonesia, measuring over nine on the Richter scale, caused the huge tsunami which would hit the coasts of thirteen countries and lead to the deaths of over a quarter of a million people. The most badly affected coastlines included some popular holiday centres in Thailand, especially around the west coast of Phuket island, in the Maldives and parts of Sri Lanka. Overall there were some 10,000 British tourists enjoying a Christmas break in these areas – around 6,000 on inclusive tours booked with tour operators, and some 4,000 travelling independently.

Everyone played vital roles as the industry's crisis management plans went into action, including tour operators' staff in head offices and resorts, charter and scheduled airlines, travel agents, accommodation providers, local partners, tourist boards and the industry's trade bodies. Other key partners immersed in responding to the crisis were the Foreign and Commonwealth Office, with its Consular teams in London, relevant embassies and also its rapid deployment teams, the Metropolitan Police Service, including its call handling teams, and aid agencies.

The media's role was also pivotal, and the FTO and ABTA worked closely throughout to co-ordinate press briefings. The media issued the FCO's helpline number and passed on tour operators' advice to their customers with future bookings. Journalists also reported on the flights rapidly laid on by tour operators and their airlines to bring back customers, and how distraught clients still in resort awaiting repatriation were being heroically looked after by tour operators' reps and hoteliers.

With virtual real time reporting that comes with 24/7 rolling news, all this was immensely helpful to the smooth operation of FTO members' emergency plans, and also helpful to families and friends at home desperate for updates on their loved ones. The UK and world media continues to this day to monitor progress in the areas and communities so devastated by the tsunami, helping ensure that the world never forgets. The travel industry and the media are a partnership working for the traveller.

9

1991–2001: The Big Get Bigger

History repeated itself in 1991, as the collapse of one big tour operator created the opportunity for another to challenge Thomson's cherished number one spot. While Harry Goodman's Intasun filled the gap left by Clarksons in 1974, it was David Crossland's Airtours that came up strongly after 1991 when Goodman's International Leisure Group (ILG) collapsed. But the parallels only go so far. While Intasun was a small player in an undeveloped business in 1974, Airtours was already a significant publicly owned company in 1991. After a decade of uninterrupted growth, package holidays were now big business and poised to grow even more.

The first Gulf War, with Saddam Hussein's threats to bring down civilian aircraft within range of his missiles, was a nasty blip from which package holidays soon recovered. Saddam was ousted from Kuwait, but not toppled, in February 1991 – too late to save ILG, whose Air Europe offshoot didn't have the resources of state-owned airlines. Thomson had swallowed up Horizon three years earlier, and wasn't targeting further expansion. But Airtours, which had already announced plans to set up its own Airtours International charter airline for 1991, was hungry.

Andy Cooper, a senior lawyer who had joined Airtours in 1989, recalls: 'Our strategy was to be number one. Thomson had been consistently the largest tour operator for many years, and 8 March 1991 when ILG collapsed made a huge difference to our business plan. Suddenly, it was game on. Until then we had been mainly Manchester-based with a small presence at Stansted, but now Gatwick was available too. On the day ILG failed, David Crossland had two private jets waiting to secure as many hotel beds as we could from ILG. Thomson was rather off the ball, and allowed us to grow faster than we anticipated.

'David Crossland did much more to change the market than Thomson during the years up to about 2000, when he was most active. He was a visionary, incredibly smart, but realised he needed the right people around him.'

Another factor in Airtours setting up its own airline was the troubles encountered by Dan-Air, a leading charter airline since the 1960s, which also operated many scheduled routes. When the bankrupt airline was sold to British Airways for a nominal £1 in 1992, a lot of charter capacity disappeared and the options for independent tour operators started to shrink. Airtours set up its own airline but it lacked a vital ingredient to take on Thomson – it needed its own network of travel agencies. The Pickfords chain was acquired in 1992 and Hogg Robinson's retail agencies (Hogg Robinson retained and developed its business travel interests) in 1993. Ironically, Crossland had sold his own Pendle Travel agencies to Hogg Robinson in 1986 and now had them back again. This set the tone for the battle between the big tour operators in the 1990s. While Thomson had built up its Lunn Poly chain to over five hundred shops and Airtours was assembling its own chain, other tour operators felt exposed.

'Airtours bought travel agencies partly so it could expand, but also to put itself in a safer position as Thomson-owned Lunn Poly sold about 20 per cent of its holidays, and that relationship could go wrong,' explains Cooper. 'David Crossland took the concept of vertical integration – with a tour operator owning both an airline and a retail network – to a new level. Thomson had had that model for a long time, but the three parts weren't really integrated. Crossland brought it all together.'

Pickfords and Hogg Robinson were united under a new high street name, Going Places, and further travel agencies were acquired including the Travelworld chain. While Intasun had fought Thomson a decade earlier without its own retail chain, but the backing of many independent agencies, Airtours could now control its own destiny. A discount battle between Lunn Poly and Going Places erupted in 1995, and as both chains continued to sell other tour operators, they were drawn into it too.

Like Intasun in the 1980s, Airtours attacked Thomson with lower prices and, in general, lower quality hotels. 'Our hotels were three-star, not as good as Thomson's, and 40 per cent were sold as "lates" within a few weeks of departure,' says Cooper. 'If you sell that many late holidays it's very profitable in a year of high demand, but when demand is lower you can get your trousers very muddy. But by around 1994, there was a lot of soul searching about the quality of our holidays. Customers were demanding better quality and more honesty in tour operators' brochures.'

Steve Endacott, who joined in 1991 as commercial director, takes up the story: 'When I started it was a very reactive business based on price – we would wait for competitors to launch, then undercut them by £10 to see if we could make money. Thomson was market leader in quality, as well as numbers, by a mile – but it was very complacent, and slow, and there for the taking. The key to Airtours' success was David Crossland's down-to-earth approach, deciding what the customer was prepared to pay and then making the costs fit. Caribbean holidays for £299 were one example.

'Crossland was an entrepreneur, but the most corporate entrepreneur I ever knew. He brought in the right people, including some from Thomson, but we still had a "stack it high, sell it cheap" approach. We got away with it for a few years, but then the complaints ratio had reached 4 or 5 per cent which was way higher than our competitors. One year we had a purge and dropped over one hundred hotels. If we hadn't done that, we couldn't have continued to grow. But every year in the 1990s, we had double digit growth. We had load factors (the proportion of seats sold on a flight) of 98 per cent or more, and we were always cheapest in the lates market.'

Richard Carrick, who joined Airtours as marketing director in 1993, also recalls a time when Airtours appeared to be flying by the seat of its pants. 'The majority of our customers got a great holiday at a fantastic price, but the quality of a lot of hotels left much to be desired and we were often on the BBC's *Watchdog* programme,' he says. 'Sometimes our customers would be on the plane while our reps were running around resorts trying to find them somewhere to stay. We opened up destinations like the Dominican Republic where the quality of hotels and other services was lacking, and I had to pick up the pieces when it came to the PR fall-out. A lot of customers recognised that they could not have afforded to go to these places except at prices like ours, but at times we were paying out in compensation almost as much as we were making.

'We got rid of a lot of hotels to avoid our brand being completely trashed. We went through a kind of Damascene conversion, and our image improved substantially as journalists and travel agents came to recognise. As with Intasun in the 1980s, we had gone for growth at almost any cost. But now Airtours was growing up.'

Chris Mottershead, who became UK boss of Thomas Cook in 2015 and was boss of Airtours in the late 1990s, agrees that Crossland's personal role was crucial. 'The UK was a cash cow for Airtours and the profits made allowed it to make acquisitions across the world,' he says. 'It was very commercially driven, growth-focused and willing to challenge the norm, looking for new destinations and creating mass-market cruising. Thomson looked stale by comparison. But when Crossland took a back seat, things started to go wrong. It started to drift, people left, and Thomson took full advantage. The spirit had disappeared long before the merger with Thomas Cook.'

Thomson and Airtours certainly didn't have it all their own way, however, as other forces were at work which would create the 'Big Four' by the late 1990s. With breathtaking speed, a new mass market tour operation had grown up from the ashes of ILG run by some of its former bosses, taking over many of the hotels used by Intasun and other parts of the ILG empire. But the people who put together Sunworld didn't have the resources to do it themselves. Fortunately they found a wealthy and needy partner, Spanish-based Iberotravel, which had contracted many of Intasun's hotels and found itself badly exposed by ILG's collapse. The partners moved very quickly, as ILG collapsed in March 1991 but Sunworld was up and running within weeks, in time to take plenty of bookings for that summer as consumer confidence returned.

The man who headed up Sunworld, Peter Long, had joined Intasun as an accountant in 1984 and would go on to become the most important figure in tour operating in the twenty-first century, as head of the giant TUI empire. Regarded by his peers as a very sober businessman, he was the diametrical opposite of Intasun's Harry Goodman, who brought him into travel. But in March 1991, he showed his entrepreneurial streak.

'What came out of the ILG collapse was a realisation that tour operators had to be properly financed,' says Long. 'What tends to happen when a big company collapses is that the capacity that was lost is replaced, plus about 30 per cent. It wasn't possible to save ILG, but there was a lot of goodwill around and the backing of a very strong partner to supply us with the hotel beds. Sunworld had real success, and grew very quickly to become number four. But it grew without having its own travel agencies, and that was a weak model. We became reliant on competitors for many of our own holiday sales.

'Thomson and Airtours built up huge retail networks. David Crossland at Airtours was an entrepreneur but very prudent, and he built a hugely strong position. But as it got bigger he became more distant from running the business, like Harry Goodman. Success is often down to instinct and intuition, and avoiding the mistakes of over-expansion.'

Sunworld's growth was indeed rapid, but in number three position behind Thomson and Airtours was a group of disparate tour operations under the banner of Owners Abroad. Key parts of its empire were Falcon Holidays, the Sovereign and Enterprise brands previously owned by British Airways, Martyn Holidays, Greece and Turkey specialist Sunmed, and youth brand Twentys. In the absence of its own retail network Owners Abroad made an alliance with Thomas Cook, but after rebranding as First Choice in 1994, thoughts turned to setting up its own retail network.

Roger Allard, who had joined the then small company selling flights to villa owners in 1973, says: 'I have always been an aviation man, and I acquired tour operators by default, sometimes for no money when they got into trouble. We set up our own airline Air 2000 in 1987 because we were Dan-Air's biggest customer, and if Dan-Air got into trouble (as it did) we would have gone down too.

'The trade re-arranged itself very quickly after the ILG collapse, but Owners Abroad was a collection of tour operations with no strategic plan and it needed to be rebranded. But I left in 1993, as I'd been there for twenty years and needed a change. Every day was a mini-crisis and although my business was my hobby, it was very stressful.'

Owners Abroad was one of the first companies, ahead of Airtours, to start acquiring tour operators and airlines in other countries. In 1988, just a year after starting Air 2000, it helped set up Canada 3000 based in Toronto, a charter airline flying Canadians to Florida, Mexico and the Caribbean during the long months of winter. The reason for this venture was simple, but the solution far-seeing – Air 2000 had aircraft to spare during the British winter, whereas winter is peak season in Canada when more aircraft were needed.

It was primarily Airtours, however, that looked abroad for further expansion. It continued to grow in the UK, making an unsuccessful hostile bid for Owners Abroad in 1992 but acquiring Aspro Holidays and its charter airline Inter European in 1993. It also bought long-haul tour operator Tradewinds and acquired a fleet of four cruise ships to make cheap fly-cruises available from ports such as Palma, Mallorca. But further expansion in the UK was made less attractive when a Monopolies and Mergers Commission enquiry into the travel business started in 1996.

In 1994 Airtours acquired the largest tour operator in Scandinavia, Scandinavia Leisure Group, including an airline called Premiair and ownership of a group of hotels known as Sunwing. One of Canada's biggest tour operators, Sunquest, followed in 1995 – and by 2000, Airtours controlled tour operations, retail shops and airlines in the

UK, Scandinavia, other parts of Western Europe and North America serving three million customers a year. Airtours had been a publicly quoted company since 1987, and in 1996 a stake of nearly 30 per cent was acquired by Carnival Corporation, a giant US cruise company.

Like Airtours, Thomson had taken advantage of the European Single Market, which took effect in 1993, to launch tour operations in six European countries. Package holidays were no longer organised country-by-country, but on an international basis achieving great economies of scale. UK companies were exporting their expertise in a big way, but it wasn't a one-way process. A key development came in 1992 when Thomas Cook (see chapter fourteen) was acquired from Midland Bank by a partnership of Germany's third biggest tour operator, LTU, and German bank WestLB, which took full control in 1995.

Foreign ownership in the package holidays business was established in the 1960s as Cosmos – one of the longest established operators of package holidays and escorted tours – had been Swiss-owned since it started in 1961. Kuoni, also Swiss-owned, arrived in 1965. This was also the year when the Canada-based Thomson Organisation moved in, but the Thomas Cook deal was different. Suddenly it was off the hands of its cautious British owners and part of a multi-national. By the mid-1990s, Thomas Cook remained one of the biggest UK travel agency chains despite the growth of Lunn Poly and Airtours-owned Going Places. It had its own escorted tour operation with some 150 years of history behind it, but not its own mass market package holidays.

The new German owners were acquisitive, and in 1996 they moved to take over Sunworld which had grown to be the UK's fourth largest package holiday operator in only five years. This marked Thomas Cook's first serious entry into mass market packages, although it had dabbled in them since the 1960s. In just over a decade, Thomas Cook would grow to be the number two.

Manny Fontenla-Novoa, a former Thomas Cook executive and one of Sunworld's founders, says: 'Sunworld didn't have a retail business but Thomas Cook had supported us from the beginning, and as vertical integration began to take hold Thomas Cook felt exposed. Sunworld wanted to buy Thomas Cook but as it still had financial operations, it was more like a bank. It made sense to sell Sunworld to Thomas Cook, so I found myself back there and ended up staying until 2011.'

Steve Endacott, who was with Airtours at the time, adds: 'Thomas Cook needed its own package holiday operation, as competitors were cutting off the supply of holidays to its retail chain. It was getting like the Cold War, with big tour operators threatening to cut Thomas Cook adrift. It had been left out in the cold.'

Peter Long joined First Choice – the former Owners Abroad – on the sale of Sunworld, and comments: 'First Choice was a plc with access to finance, but 60 per cent of our holidays were sold through our competitors' travel agencies and that had to change. We set out to create the First Choice retail chain by buying regional chains including Bakers Dolphin in the South West, and a joint venture with a Co-operative Society to set up Holiday Hypermarkets, giant retail stores with equivalent space to fifteen average sized shops. Over the next ten years we built this up to the point that 60 per cent of our holidays were sold through our own network.'

First Choice was the first big tour operator to apply its own brand to travel agencies – something that Thomson didn't do until the next decade, and Airtours never did. Independent travel agencies often felt shut out when this happened, while independent tour operators questioned whether customers would come looking for them in travel agencies bearing one of the big names. But the tide was turning, and big travel agency chains were increasingly selling their own brands rather than third parties. This – and a reduction in consumer choice – was one of the key points when the Monopolies and Mergers Commission started its investigation in 1996.

Its report came out in December 1997, and by ruling that there was still plenty of competition and no need to start breaking up the big companies, it opened the floodgates to a rash of takeovers that was likened to a feeding frenzy. The acquisition of medium and small tour operators by Thomson, Airtours, First Choice and Thomas Cook – who became the Big Four – speeded up dramatically in 1998, making some entrepreneurs who decided to sell out seriously rich. Within a couple of years, nearly every company worth buying had been snapped up and power in the travel industry was concentrated in just four pairs of hands.

Despite the many takeovers that followed, many small tour operators not only survived but thrived – but not in the mainstream package holidays business. Some made a good living by concentrating on particular countries, such as Greece or Turkey, while others concentrated on faraway countries or niches such as sports or other activities, or particular types of accommodation. Many belonged to the Association of Independent Tour Operators (AITO), which is still going strong in 2016 with over 120 members.

Christopher Kirker, who was chairman of AITO in the 1990s, says: 'The MMC's decision was not in the best interests of the customer or the concept of choice, but at that time small tour operators were beginning to recognise the potential of the internet, and many destinations were becoming much more accessible. AITO succeeded in getting a lot of publicity that opened people's eyes to an alternative kind of travel company, and they began to realise that there were tour operators catering for their individual needs.'

The biggest prize in the feeding frenzy was Unijet. Formed in 1981 with the original intention of selling cheap holidays to American university accommodation (hence the name), it had grown rapidly by selling charter flight seats. It became part of aviation broker Viking International, starting selling more holidays to America, and grew so fast that it set up its own airline, Leisure International, in 1989. By introducing the latest version of the Boeing 767 it could fly non-stop to Florida and the Caribbean, and started the first non-stop flights from the UK to Las Vegas. It also started package holidays to the Mediterranean, concentrating on self-catering. By the late 1990s it had grown to become the fifth biggest tour operator with over one million customers a year.

Nigel Jenkins, one of Unijet's founders, remembers how difficult it was to get established in places like Barbados, where Airtours had moved in. 'Airtours was like an Intasun Mark 2 – aggressive, and pushing the boundaries,' he says. 'We were trying to contract hotels only to be told that these hotels would never see an Airtours customer again if they gave space to us. But we were so successful that we were approached by both Airtours and First Choice asking if we wanted to sell. It became a Dutch auction. If Airtours had bought us, it would have leapt ahead of Thomson to become number one. If First Choice had succeeded, it would have become the second biggest ahead of Airtours. Either of these deals would have created enormous synergies by taking out layers of costs. The Dutch auction went on for six months, and in the end we sold to First Choice for £110 million. We were very fortunate. We had a very profitable business with £31 million on the balance sheet, but I cared about our brand and I was the last director to agree to sell.'

What do you get, when you buy another tour operator? Thomson had acquired its big rival Horizon a decade earlier, and closed it down. First Choice, which acquired Unijet's airline, market share and a substantial amount of cash, was to keep the Unijet name for several years and took on some of its people, including Jenkins, who went to work for Peter Long. 'Peter was a frustrated entrepreneur, an accountant who had the trader instinct,' says Jenkins. 'He wanted me to stay to bring more entrepreneurship into the business.'

Long adds: 'The two big moves we made, simultaneously, were to buy Unijet and long-haul tour operator Hayes & Jarvis. We then thought that we didn't want just a mainstream business, and started buying specialist tour operators such as Citalia (Italy) and Sunsail (yachting), and we started to expand in Europe, especially in Spain with Barcelo. We then bought adventure tour operators including Exodus, and the adventure sector was more profitable than the mass market because it was more value-added. We created product diversity, and geographical diversity, while developing the core First Choice brand with quality hotels available only through us.

'When you buy a tour operation, you are buying a client base, a position in the market and a management team. If you don't keep the management you will lose a lot of business, as when Thomson bought Horizon.'

First Choice became so attractive that Airtours even tried to buy it, but Airtours was more successful in swallowing up several smaller tour operators in the late 1990s including Panorama, Greece specialist Manos, city break operators Bridge Travel Group and Cresta, long-haul operator Jetset, coach tour operator Leger and Direct Holidays, its first venture into direct sales as opposed to selling through travel agents. Some of the sums paid were breathtaking, with Direct Holidays – run by ex-Owners Abroad man John Boyle – changing hands for £86 million.

Richard Carrick's job at Airtours was to bring together the purchases, and he says: 'It was a challenge to manage so many brands, but the vast majority of acquisitions did make sense. Bridge Travel and Cresta were well down the list of priorities as city break operators don't use charter airlines, and didn't fit the vertically integrated model. There was an element of buying companies to keep them out of the hands of our rivals, and with our own big retail network, we needed different kinds of holidays to sell.'

Andy Cooper, also with Airtours, adds: 'Some acquisitions were opportunistic, including Bridge and Cresta which were controlled by the same Belgian company, and Jetset. Leger never fitted in, but some acquisitions were all about driving business for our 700 travel agencies, or for our airline. The rush for acquisitions was partly driven by our shareholders.'

Some very famous names were hoovered up in the process, including Panorama, started by Sussex fishmonger Adrian Hayes in 1954 as he wanted somewhere warm for his own holidays. Panorama opened its own hotel in Es Cana, Ibiza, in 1966 – and until then the village had no electricity. It later became a specialist in Tunisia and by the mid-1990s, when owned by Justin Fleming and Nick Munday, it was one of the biggest tour operators out of the Irish Republic.

'It was clear that the big tour operators wanted to get bigger to utilise their aircraft fleets, and another thing we gave Airtours was entry into the Irish market,' says Fleming. 'It costs more for tour operators to build up a business than to buy it, but some of these acquisitions didn't turn out as they hoped. Accountants did their due diligence procedures, but can only look at the figures they are given.

'The value in a brand only remains while it is a brand. Once Panorama was fully absorbed into Airtours and later Thomas Cook, it had no reason to exist any longer and duly disappeared. There is an argument that separate brands should be allowed to grow, but as time goes on a brand loses its identity.'

Jetset was one of the last to be sold in the feeding frenzy as John Bond, who owned the specialist in North America, the Far East and Australasia, feared that the so-called Millennium Bug would devastate computer systems and make him unable to operate. He sold in 1999 but bought back Jetset in 2003, a highly unusual move. While Jetset has survived back in private ownership, many of the brands bought by the Big Four didn't last long.

'The Big Four were growing so fast that they didn't have a grip on their accounts, as their booking systems were inefficient,' says Bond. 'During the period Airtours owned Jetset, it faced various crises including 9/11 and SARS (Severe Acute Respiratory Syndrome), which hit travel to the Far East. Turnover went right down and I heard Airtours was going to close it, but it would have cost them more in redundancies than to sell to me. It's been a great pleasure to build it back up again.'

The Canada-based Thomson Organisation's long involvement in the UK travel industry came to a successful end in 1998 when the Thomson Travel Group was floated on the London Stock Exchange with a valuation of £1.7 billion. Nothing much changed at first, but as a publicly owned company (as were Airtours and First Choice) it had to behave differently. Its share price collapsed when it threatened another price war with Airtours. There were management casualties as a result, as it became clear that the days of risk taking and all-out battle were coming to an end.

Another factor in the 1990s, that influenced some company owners to sell up, was the increasing legal liability faced by tour operators. The Package Travel Regulations came out of the EU and were law in the UK by 1993, when people on package holidays or tours could take legal action against tour operators even if the fault lay with an overseas hotel. John de Vial, who worked at Thomson in the 1990s and is now head of financial protection at ABTA, says: 'The Consumer

Protection Act of 1987 also had an effect, and ABTA anticipated the changes in its code of conduct in 1990. The industry matured and became more sophisticated, and some hotels had to do a lot of work to continue selling through tour operators. But there were also a lot of tour operator failures.'

Thomson's expansion continued, with purchases including ski operator Crystal, North America specialist Jetsave, and Australia and New Zealand specialist Austravel, all of which survive as it didn't make sense to apply the Thomson brand to these sectors. Magic Travel Group, including Magic of Italy and Magic of Spain, was eventually dropped.

Thomas Cook's purchase of Sunworld made it a serious player in mass-market package holidays for the first time, but it didn't stop there as it also acquired Flying Colours, a short-lived airline- and tour-operating group including Sunset Holidays and Club 18–30 (also see chapter fourteen). It also bought Inspirations, cities specialist Time Off and Neilson Holidays, and in 1999 Thomas Cook merged with Carlson Leisure and rebranded Sunworld, Sunset and Flying Colours as JMC Holidays and JMC Airlines.

This was an era when many people felt the fun had gone out of working for mass-market tour operators, and it was also an era when brands became all-important and huge amounts of money were spent on consultants, brand strategies and launches. JMC is a case in point, as the well-known Sunworld and Sunset brands were swept aside and no one knew, or cared, that J, M and C were the initials of John Mason Cook, son of the founder Thomas.

Hugh Morgan, whose long career working for Harry Goodman ended in 1990, had headed up Flying Colours and became a director of Thomas Cook after the buy-out. 'Thomas Cook was a retailer that didn't understand tour operating at all,' he comments. 'When it bought Sunworld, Sunset and Inspirations, its own travel agencies didn't want to sell them as they made more money selling other tour operators. We had to rebrand them and decided to come up with a name other than Thomas Cook, because independent travel agents would feel we were cutting them out. JMC's slogan was "unwrapping the package" and it even wrapped up a real Boeing 757 in brown paper for the launch. JMC was a complete and total nonsense, and we spent millions on the rebranding. It lasted for only a few years and was a debacle of the first order.'

An ironic twist in the branding debate was to follow. Thomas Cook had been German-owned since 1992, but in 2001, having sold off its global and financial services divisions, it was acquired by another

German company, C&N Touristic. Would JMC become C&N, another set of initials that were meaningless to the British holidaymaker? No, as within months C&N had rebranded its whole operation as Thomas Cook to make the most of 160 years of tradition.

Things now moved very quickly, as C&N had targeted a Thomson takeover before switching its attention to Thomas Cook. But instead Thomson was bought by Preussag, a giant German company part-owned by Lufthansa which was seeking to diversify away from its industrial base, for £1.8 billion. Preussag actually owned part of Thomas Cook at the time, but sold off this stake. In 2002 Preussag would be renamed TUI (Touristik Union International), laying the foundations for becoming the world's largest tourism group with listings on stock exchanges in Frankfurt and London.

Package holidays had been big business for a long time, but now they could be ranked alongside the top businesses in the world. With two of the Big Four in Teutonic hands, German towels were well and truly on British sunbeds.

10

City Slickers

According to research by ABTA in 2015, city breaks are the most popular type of holiday with 54 per cent of people in a survey having visited a city in the previous twelve months – more than the 50 per cent who go on beach holidays. But tour operators are hardly involved at all now, with the vast majority of people going online to book low-cost flights and accommodation to put together their own break. With the rise of peer-to-peer booking portals such as Airbnb, using private accommodation, hotels are now under threat as well as the few remaining city-break tour firms.

Partly because Great Britain is an island – and long before the Channel Tunnel opened in 1994 – people who wanted to go to Paris, Amsterdam or another Continental city had little idea how to go about it, so went to a travel agent or tour operator. The 'naughty' image of Paris has attracted British people for centuries, and by the 1950s people had started going again as France recovered from the war. Tour operators were slow to consider alternatives, but in 1967 two companies, Time Off and Travelscene, were set up to sell city breaks including alternatives to Paris.

Time Off is one of the most fondly remembered tour operators of any kind, because of the customer care, attention to detail and sheer 'style' of its boss, Roland Castro. It was never big in numbers terms, but its reputation was far greater than its size. While it is easy enough for any tour operator to offer luxury hotels at sky-high prices, the genius of Roland Castro was to find hotels in every category from one- to five-star with a personal guarantee that they would offer excellent service. They were presented not in a standard brochure with photographs of the Eiffel Tower or Colosseum, but in pocket-sized pamphlets adorned with water colour paintings of city scenes. When you had booked your break you would be sent another pamphlet by an independent travel writer describing the city in often quirky terms – examples included *The Romance of the Metro*, for Paris, and *The Discreet Charm of the Luxembourgeoisie*, for Luxembourg. Another series of pamphlets was entitled *How to Spend Less and have More Fun in ...* , with tips about eating, drinking and sightseeing. With your travel documents you would also be sent a city map, with hand-written stickers and colour-coded arrows indicating the location of your hotel, the nearest public transport, and restaurants where you could pre-book meals. Time Off breaks included a voucher for a drink and snack at a café typical of the city, and all this added up to a package like no other.

Roland Castro (1923–2006) was a rarity in the travel business, an Oxford-educated intellectual who stood apart from his mainly tradesman peers, but who nevertheless played a full role in travel industry politics. Born to a wealthy Jewish family in Egypt, he worked in publishing before setting up Time Off to provide the kind of immersive city experience he himself enjoyed. He could be difficult to work for as his attention to detail was legendary, one example being that when he inspected a hotel, he would check how easy it was to reach the bath taps in case you were elderly. Unlike some of his competitors, he did not provide airport-to-hotel transfers as he wanted his customers to start thinking for themselves the moment they arrived. The Time Off map was all they needed. Castro had close personal relationships with many of the hotels he used, meaning it was never too much trouble to cater for a special guest or special occasion.

Like other companies, Time Off expanded in the 1970s beyond the starting points of Paris and Amsterdam to include Brussels, Bruges, Swiss and Italian cities, and further afield. He remained distrustful of Eastern Europe where Time Off standards were harder to achieve, but by the 1990s he was facing intense competition, fewer discerning customers, and a harsh regulatory regime with the Civil Aviation Authority making strict demands on all tour operators. Despite being voted Best Travel Company in *The Observer* awards in 1995, he sold Time Off the following year to Thomas Cook, which closed it down in 2003.

Castro harboured thoughts of a comeback which he would call City Lights, but times had moved on, low-cost airlines and online booking had arrived, and he was over seventy. When he sold Time Off, a customer wrote: 'Can it be possible that your wonderful, unique Time Off has been sold to the giants? Your company was the last vestige of a civilised time when personal, intelligent service was important. One felt valued and known by you, although we never met.' Even at its height, when Time Off was handling 50,000 customers a year, Castro himself would sometimes answer the phone-in reservations. 'Reference Roland,' he would say, 'as in Roland Rat ... [a TV cartoon character].'

Travelscene was a very different animal, which grew to become the largest city break operator with over one hundred cities not only throughout Europe, but extending to New York, Boston and some other faraway countries. Started in 1967, Travelscene also operated the Dutch bulbfields programme it took over from Clarksons, and tried unsuccessfully to run charter flights to Paris at a time before the Channel Tunnel when air fares were high. It also offered city breaks by ferry, especially on routes from Hull.

John Harding joined Travelscene in 1981 and worked there until it went bust in 2004, during a time of tremendous growth followed by catastrophic decline. By 1981 it was second biggest behind the Bridge Travel Group, whose brands included Paris Travel Service and Amsterdam Travel Service.

'People would go to Paris one year, and the next year Amsterdam, and then ask where next?' he says. 'They would take their main holiday by the beach and a city break in spring or autumn, and we also started doing Christmas markets. We were able to expand in the 1980s when airlines such as Air Europe started operating, as before then air fares were rigidly controlled by IATA (International Air Transport Association). Whether we sold 5,000 or 100,000 seats a year, the fare was the same. The high-water mark of city breaks came in the early to mid-1990s, when we were so successful that companies such as Thomas Cook were selling our holidays under their own names. But then the low-cost airlines came in, and they dissolved the glue that held city break packages together. We had to respond by selling city hotels without flights, but our average selling price was down 60 per cent on the package price. When Travelscene went down in 2004, it was a sad end for a great business, but one that just wasn't sustainable anymore.'

Low-cost airlines started to target European cities several years before Mediterranean resorts, and at first they didn't want to work with tour operators. Ryanair soon dominated air travel to Dublin, but EasyJet was a more important player to European cities, starting flights from Luton to Amsterdam, Barcelona and Nice in 1996 a few months after its making its debut, to Glasgow and Edinburgh. With internet booking starting at about the same time – EasyJet had sold one million seats online by 1999 – city-break packages were dealt a mortal blow. Companies including Thomson scaled back, while Cresta – which, like Bridge Travel Group, would be sold to Airtours – diversified into short breaks to holiday resorts. The Cresta brand passed to Thomas Cook which finally abolished it in 2015.

But it wasn't all doom and gloom, and Travelscene was to be the learning curve for a luxury city break operator, Kirker Holidays, to get off the ground. Now a highly successful company offering short breaks or longer holidays to cities and leisure destinations around the world, Kirker also takes some of its inspiration from Time Off with its attention to detail and water-colour illustrations, although its brochures are full-size.

Christopher Kirker joined Travelscene in 1982, at a time when city break customers usually booked a grade of accommodation rather than a particular hotel. He wanted to offer a more up-market experience, and when he started Kirker Holidays in 1986 he had a piece of luck: 'The US had just started bombing Libya, and as Americans were worried about travel, I was able to walk into the grandest hotels in Europe and do great deals, because they were empty,' he says. 'It was the same with airlines, and I was welcomed with open arms. I had a very clear idea of what I wanted to do and have never wavered. I wanted to offer private limousine transfers, and good quality hotels for any duration you wanted. Kirker Holidays would also provide lots of information on museums, restaurants, nightlife and shopping, with our local agent providing the tickets.

'When the low-cost airlines started, I knew that companies which just offered flights and accommodation would find it very tough, but a company that could offer a one-stop shop could still flourish. If you don't add value then no business can survive, as you have to prove to customers that you're offering a service that is difficult to arrange on your own. But if you book hotels and flights online yourself, you're just a number. If you turn up and find you're in the wrong type of room, who's going to help you?'

Kirker would sell the company that still bears his name in 2002, first to venture capitalists who later sold it on to Kuoni. Former Thomson executive John MacNeill then became managing director, continuing with its founding principles while adapting to the new reality of low-cost airlines and online booking.

'Low-cost airlines made a big impact very quickly, so we began to diversify to countries including Russia, and leisure breaks to non-city destinations such as Andalucia and the Greek islands where you go to relax,' says MacNeill. 'We also started making more use of Eurostar trains, with its leisure premium class being our quoted price. Kirker Holidays still has a mix of luxury and the best available hotels for a discerning traveller, but other city-break operators fell away because low-cost airlines trampled all over them. Kirker's Concierge restaurant-booking service is highly prized, and it can put you in the best rooms such as overlooking the Grand Canal in Venice.'

A few other companies still sell city breaks – examples are Thomas Cook and Osprey Holidays – but it is ironic that while many brands disappeared, the number of cities and places you can fly from increased enormously due to low-cost airlines. Tour operators will now make up a package on EasyJet or Ryanair, and while some people might still miss frills such as club class, the convenience of local departures overcomes that.

You can now fly to many European capitals from airports all over the UK, and not just the capitals but many provincial cities too. Some routes might exist mainly for migrant workers, but also appeal to people who want somewhere really different. Sometimes people will head off for a weekend just because fares are low, with no idea about what to do when they get there. You can fly from Bristol to Vienna, for example, or from Liverpool to Kaunas (Lithuania), booking a hotel through a link from the airline's website or on any number of third party sites. But you're probably not buying a package, and if anything goes wrong, you're on your own – with no one like Time Off's Roland Castro to look after you.

'We are very privileged to have all of Europe on our doorstep, with most cities reachable in two to 2½ hours,' says Kirker. 'The quality of hotels, restaurants and museums is improving all the time, and nowadays visiting a city is a completely different cultural experience. I have been to Venice every year since 1967, and I am still finding new things to do.'

11

2001–2007: End of the World as They Knew It

The Big Four tour operating groups came into the twenty-first century lords of all they surveyed – bloated and self-satisfied after gobbling up many independent companies in the feeding frenzy of the late 1990s. Hundreds of small niche tour operators remained, but the middle ground had all but disappeared. Figures from the Civil Aviation Authority show that in June 2000, the Big Four accounted for 56 per cent of all holidays covered by its Air Travel Organisers Licence (ATOL) scheme, while the top ten had a massive 68 per cent share of the cake. Thomson was licensed to carry over 4 million; Airtours 3.3 million; JMC Holidays (Thomas Cook) 2.8 million; and First Choice 1.9 million. Airtours was in fact even bigger as it owned Direct Holidays (516,000), which still had its own licence. First Choice also owned fifth placed Unijet (820,000). In the following years Airtours was to briefly overtake Thomson as the biggest.

But then, at the peak of their powers, these vast empires began to show signs of stress. The cracks in the hull were hardly visible at first, but soon the ships were starting to list and Airtours, in particular, was taking in vast amounts of water. Steve Endacott, who first worked for Airtours in 1991 and returned briefly in 2003, describes it thus: 'It was like piloting an oil tanker. The rocks ahead of us were the low-cost airlines, and the lighthouse illuminating the rocks was the internet. But we just couldn't change course.'

Low-cost airlines and the internet are inextricably linked. The two airlines which, indirectly, took over much of the package holiday business would soon become some of the biggest online names in any sector, but at first they were modest call centre-based operations. Ryanair had started as a small Irish regional airline in 1985, when it carried only 5,000 passengers (it now carries over 80 million a year). But it soon started to challenge Aer Lingus and British Airways on Anglo-Irish routes, and by the mid-1990s it was responding to deregulation of airlines in the EU to fly to and between other countries. EasyJet first flew in 1995, with the telephone number of its Luton reservations centre emblazoned across its aircraft. From those humble beginnings of flying people to Scotland for £29 – as cheap as a pair of jeans, it proclaimed – it has grown to carry nearly 70 million passengers a year across Europe.

Low-cost airlines had a radically different approach not only to scheduled airlines, but also to the charter airlines owned by tour operators. Scheduled airlines used to charge such high fares that they could afford to run their flights half-empty before low-cost airlines came along, and never reduced their fares close to departure. Tour operators, in contrast, were keen to sell the last few seats at a knock-down price because they had covered all their costs, and whatever price they got was pure profit. Low-cost or no-frills airlines turned this approach on its head, in a business model based on that of Southwest Airlines in the US. They start by selling seats very cheaply, months before departure, making up revenue by charging for 'frills' such as luggage, seat allocation (more recently), and on-board meals, plus changes to reservations. But if you book just before departure, their fares might well be higher than mainstream airlines charge.

The big tour operators could afford to ignore low-cost airlines simply because they didn't fly on package holiday routes at first, although by the turn of the century these airlines were hitting sales of city-break packages. In any case the Big Four were pre-occupied digesting the enormous meal they had made of their smaller brethren, and grappling with this new phenomenon called the internet. They certainly realised that online sales would grow, but their first crack at designing websites soon came to look clumsy. Faraway market leader Kuoni was one of the first to go online, in 1999.

But if low-cost airlines were not seen as a problem and the potential of the internet was not understood, a new threat to tour operators suddenly appeared, literally, out of the blue. When two of the four hijacked aircraft slammed into New York's World Trade Centre on 11 September 2001 – with the four crashes claiming nearly 3,000 lives – the whole world stopped to look on in horror. There was an immediate impact on sales of all foreign travel as people felt afraid to go away, and trade newspaper TTG ran a lurid headline, 'Tourism on Terror Alert'. Many tour operators were soon blaming all their problems on 9/11, when the issues they faced ran much deeper.

Endacott set up a call centre in 1999 called Holidays by Phone, plus a company called Holiday Taxis so people could book airport transfers – another vital part of the traditional holiday package – online. He agrees that in the early 2000s, there was little understanding of how low-cost airlines would develop. 'Holidays were still booked by either walk or talk – you walked into a travel agent, or you rang a call centre, and the age of click was yet to come,' he says. 'Low-cost airlines had no impact on my thoughts at all in 1999, but by the time I rejoined Airtours in 2003, they were beginning to push us out of the closer destinations in the Mediterranean, especially Spain. To start with they kept to the cities, but by 2002–03 EasyJet in particular had started flying to the resorts and tour operators were starting to get worried. We could see that the low-cost airlines had huge aircraft orders and very low leasing costs.'

Hugh Morgan joined Cosmos, then the tenth biggest tour operator, in 2001, after a long career including Intasun and Thomas Cook. He recalls how quickly low-cost airlines took over some resort areas – especially the Costa Brava, after Ryanair opened a base at Gerona airport.

'I remember seeing EasyJet's 01582 phone number on the sides of its planes, and I was extremely dismissive of them as I felt they didn't have a hope,' he says. 'No one in package holidays perceived low-cost airlines as a threat, but they crept up on us and bit us on the backside. Ryanair came into Gerona, calling it Barcelona when that was fifty miles away. Tour operators pulled out of Costa Brava resorts such as Lloret de Mar in 2002–2003 because Ryanair was getting massive subsidies, and we couldn't compete. I remember a meeting at Luton airport attended by all the big tour operators, when people from the Catalonia regional government flew in – on Ryanair, of course – to talk to us. They told us they weren't going to give us any money, and after all tour operators had done for the Costa Brava, that was disgraceful. They just didn't listen, and the subsidies given to low-cost airlines helped them buy more efficient aircraft, which was a game-changer. By now, many people were so used to going to places like Benidorm, the Costa Brava and Mallorca that they didn't need tour operators anymore.'

EasyJet and Ryanair were not interested in running their own package holidays, but they soon forged alliances with a new breed of travel company created by the internet to offer 'click-throughs' from airline websites to book accommodation, resort transfers and car hire. Known variously as bedbanks or Online Travel Agencies (OTAs), companies including Lowcostholidays and Expedia were soon to become major competitors to traditional tour operators (see chapter thirteen). The whole package holiday business would become realigned and fragmented, while the Big Four decided how to react.

The Cosmos group – a great survivor in mass market packages since it started in 1962 – was better placed than some of its bigger rivals, as it sold lots of charter seats to property owners and independent tourists through a brand called Avro, and set up its own bedbank called somewhere2stay.com. Its airline, Monarch, had to adopt the low-cost model.

Should the Big Four have become more aware of the threat posed by low-cost airlines? Peter Long, the pre-eminent figure in package holidays in the twenty-first century, thinks not as he regarded them as totally different businesses. As chief executive of First Choice and later joint head of TUI, he identified early the need to be different from the new upstarts.

'Their model is based entirely on price, and they were really starting to grow by the early 2000s,' he says. 'For First Choice it was all about providing packages and creating experiences which were different such as our holiday villages, with a choice of restaurants, entertainment and crèches for children – we set the standard for the club holiday concept. We stood aside from destinations like the Costa del Sol where people owned a lot of property and were not buying packages, but expanded in the Greek Islands and Turkey. We introduced more all-inclusive hotels, whereas in the mad dash for growth in the 1980s and 1990s, it was more about self-catering.

'Thomson, in the early 2000s, was rather confused. It started to look like Expedia by offering hotel-only bookings and flight-only. But the danger in doing this is that you undermine your own tour operation. The low-cost airlines grew, but mainly for short breaks which were not our market.'

First Choice stood aside from battle to concentrate on what became called, in marketing speak, 'differentiated product' – packages to hotels that can't be bought through anyone else. Long's decision proved to be a master-stroke. Nigel Jenkins, who stayed on with First Choice after Unijet was sold in 1998, says: 'The good thing about selling holidays that no one else sells is that you can't be beaten on price. If the appeal is strong and it's the only show in town, you can charge what you like and stay out of price wars.'

While Thomson may have been confused, the situation at Airtours was much more troubling and 2002 was its annus horribilis. By this time it was a huge international group with fifteen million customers worldwide and had been rebranded as MyTravel, representing phenomenal growth in a little over twenty years since a minor tour operation was started by a travel agency in east Lancashire. Its UK/ Ireland division was led by Airtours but also included Direct Holidays, Panorama, Manos, Bridge Travel, Cresta, Tradewinds and other brands, plus the Going Places retail chain and MyTravel Airways, formerly Airtours International.

When MyTravel was launched as the new brand in 2002 it produced a brochure called Our Future saying, 'It is time to transform ourselves again'. But all wasn't well, behind the scenes, and it didn't have even a medium-term future as an independent company. In the autumn of that year a 'black hole' of nearly £1 billion was discovered in its accounts, with TTG running the headline 'MyTravel Meltdown' as it issued its second profits warning in four months. Its share price dived to a ten-year low amid warnings of a second Iraq war, as MyTravel struggled for survival and sold off brands including Eurosites. The crisis came much to the alarm of founder David Crossland, who had been planning to retire. He would later tell the Manchester Evening News that those events were 'very sad' and that he himself lost a lot of money. In December TTG reported that MyTravel was back from the brink, but that the many banks owed money had ordered a major restructure. By the time Crossland did move on the following year, a new management team was in place.

Airtours legal chief Andy Cooper also left in 2003 and suspects that the group would have gone under if behind-the-scenes activity at government level hadn't stopped that happening. 'David Crossland was a details man, but by then he had moved away from the day-to-day running of the company,' he says. 'We seemed to be sailing along but there was a knee-jerk panic after 9/11, when bookings were flat and the horror was still being felt. The auditors objected to our accounting practices, so MyTravel had to issue a profits warning. The rebranding went a long way towards saving the company, as people didn't know what MyTravel was.

'The share price collapsed and we stopped paying our bills – winding-up petitions were arriving every week. The Civil Aviation Authority bottled the decision to revoke our licence as it thought the situation was too complex to pull the plug. When ILG went bust in 1991, it was simply a tour operation and an airline. But MyTravel also had a huge travel agency chain and international businesses. Deals were done to save it but from then on it was treading water. But Airtours' legacy is more about people than the brand. It was an incredible learning curve for many senior people in travel, and a lot of them have ILG and Airtours on their CVs.'

Richard Carrick remained with Airtours from 1993 to 2002 except for a short career break in 1999, and when he returned he helped set up a low-cost airline called MyTravelLite, which never became big. 'MyTravel was a change of image aimed at the City as much as consumers, and looking back it makes more sense now than it did at the time,' he says. 'When the company went through its tricky patch, the Airtours name was sheltered because it was MyTravel getting the flak. 9/11 caused a huge dip in the market, and MyTravel had to resubmit its accounts. That combination of events was a perfect storm, and the heyday of package holidays would soon be over.'

Dermot Blastland, who headed First Choice's UK business from 1996–2007, says: 'MyTravel wasn't a well-run company and wasn't making money from its core business, with its Going Places retail shops even giving away free winter holidays if you bought a summer one,' he says. 'It was offering discounts on bank holidays and if you can't make money then, you never will. Holidays had become commoditised, which is why First Choice went down a different route with holiday villages. Online sales were becoming important, but some tour operators went online too quickly and their systems kept crashing.'

Peter Long adds: 'By about 2001-02, we believed that online was the perfect medium to showcase our product. But there were few online transactions back then, in contrast to 2015 when 55 per cent of TUI's holidays are sold online. It was First Choice and Thomson that led the way.'

The wounded MyTravel ploughed on, but John de Vial, who joined in 2005 to handle customer relations, says it recovered strongly over the next couple of years. 'It was a fantastic challenge to join MyTravel but also a risk for me, as the jury was still out on whether it would survive,' he recalls. 'Its reputation had been tarnished, but a new team came in led by corporate turn-around specialists. They nursed it back to profitability, but consolidation had to happen in the industry and it was simply a question of how.'

There is no doubt that 9/11 was a severe blow to the travel industry, but it had a deeper impact on airlines than tour operators with big names such as Swissair and Sabena (of Belgium) going out of business, and low-cost airlines getting stronger as a result. There were no collapses among major tour operators as a direct result of 9/11, but profits slumped. The Civil Aviation Authority reported that the number of holidays sold during summer 2002 was down by 6 per cent – the worst fall since after the first Gulf War in 1990. MyTravel and Thomas Cook performed worse than Thomson, which remained steady, and

First Choice, which actually grew. But it could have been much worse. Reaction to 9/11 meant that many people wanted to take holidays closer to home in familiar countries such as Spain, but a more severe impact was felt in faraway holidays.

Kuoni's business slumped by 16 per cent in the year to September 2002 to under 300,000 holidays, but its then managing director, Sue Biggs, had to consider other problems. 'The traumatic events of 11 September 2001 had a severe and immediate impact on 2002 bookings,' she wrote. 'But despite promising signs in 2002 that the worst was behind us and the world was doing its best to return to normal, this optimism was shattered within months by the tragic bomb in Bali in October, followed by the Mombasa attack in November.

'Ever since 11 September the world has become a much more volatile place with traditional travel patterns disrupted, perhaps forever. Whole countries have had their tourism industry decimated, and during 2004 – courtesy of the [second] Gulf War, followed by the outbreak of SARS (Severe Acute Respiratory Syndrome) and the threatened attacks in Kenya – nine major destinations were declared out of bounds.' Most of these were in the Far East, while the Indian Ocean benefited from increased visitors only to be devastated, along with Thailand and some other Far East countries, by the Boxing Day tsunami that year.

While package holiday operators were busy worrying about the impact of 9/11 – in some cases blaming this for cancelling charter flights – the low-cost airlines continued to grow, with online providers of accommodation and other tourist services growing alongside them. Ryanair, despite dominating areas such as the Costa Brava, was mainly focused on European cities and routes popular with migrant workers. EasyJet was much more of a threat to tour operators, taking over British Airways' low-cost offshoot Go in 2002 (and later GB Airways in 2008) and growing exponentially at regional airports all over the country, on resort as well as city routes.

Nigel Jenkins, of Unijet and later First Choice, recalls: 'When they started flying to Faro (Portugal) and Malaga, we saw them as competition. But they struggled to compete with the number of seats we offered on charter flights, on the key days of the week when hotels and apartments changed over. In Faro, this was on Thursdays and on the Costa Blanca it was Fridays, while Greek resorts always changed over on Tuesdays and Fridays when one lot of customers flew out, and the next lot flew in. But over time this changed, and those patterns have now gone.'

Low-cost airlines were seriously troubling the big tour operators by the mid-2000s, but for many small tour operators they were an absolute godsend. Small companies selling sunshine destinations used to have plenty of charter flights at their disposal, but this had changed by the 1990s with the disappearance of independent airlines such as Dan-Air. Charter airlines controlled by the Big Four had taken over, often pricing smaller companies out of the market. The Big Four were increasingly selling mainly through their own travel agencies rather than competitors or independents, while smaller tour operators found it harder to get their brochures on display. Thomson rebranded Britannia Airways as Thomsonfly in 2003, while the historic Lunn Poly name was ditched on its retail shops in favour of simply Thomson in 2005.

Monarch Airlines became the only charter airline of any size available to smaller tour operators at a decent price, and there were limited scheduled flights to resort destinations until the low-cost airlines came along. Then the choice expanded rapidly, not only from major airports such as Gatwick, Manchester and Glasgow, but from regional airports all over the country. Low-cost airlines proved to be the making of some companies, including Classic Collection, and the making of airports that had never had many charter flights, such as Liverpool.

An up-market company specialising in top hotels around the Mediterranean, Classic Collection is old-fashioned in many respects with most sales through travel agents, bookings by phone rather than online, and a heavy investment in brochures. Its boss Nick Munday had been part of a team that sold Panorama Holidays to Airtours, with whom he stayed on for a couple of years. 'By 2001 Airtours was out of control for fifty different reasons, including buying a German tour operator that made a massive loss, so it was no surprise to me when it was revealed it had lost nearly £1 billion,' he says. 'I moved on and bought Classic Collection, and set about building it up.

'Big tour operators were very good at filling charter flights to capacity and operating them seven days a week, with hotels all geared up to either seven- or fourteen-night holidays. I couldn't see how EasyJet or another low-cost airline could operate more efficiently, as there was no demand for odd-duration holidays like three or ten nights. But when the low-cost airlines arrived people could fly on any day they wanted, from a wide choice of airports.'

The customers of smaller, up-market tour operators such as Classic Collection and Prestige Holidays didn't at first want to travel on this new type of airline, put off by the scramble for unallocated seats and the reputation of airlines which were, undoubtedly, attracting a type of customer who couldn't afford to fly before. Ryanair's controversial boss Michael O'Leary promised to 'bombard you with as many in-flight announcements and trolleys as we can' in a bid to boost on-board revenue. People who enjoyed club class on resort routes operated by GB Airways were disturbed when it was taken over by EasyJet, and all flights became egalitarian. Soon there was no choice but low-cost airlines and a diminishing number of charters, but the convenience of flying from local airports made passengers who disliked low-cost airlines think again.

Eyewitness: Ron Hughes
Few 'new' package holiday destinations have emerged in the twenty-first century but an exception is Cape Verde, an island nation off West Africa. He started Cape Verde Travel in 1995, long before the big tour operators went in, and offers holidays to all ten islands.

I ran a travel agency in East Yorkshire called Eastgate Travel, and I set this up at the age of forty-two after a career in social services. I was looking for a niche, but it wasn't easy to find something no one else was doing I first heard about Cape Verde through a junior football tournament when our local team was playing one from there. I couldn't find it in any of the guides, but I found out Cape Verde Airlines was flying from Amsterdam, and they were very co-operative. It needed tourism because it didn't have much else, and many of the people worked abroad.

I wanted to run a tour programme somewhere small, where I could know every property. My customers love islands, research where they are going in-depth, and bring the words "culture" and "somewhere different" into a conversation. All the islands are different, being a mix of mountainous volcanic islands like Santiago and Fogo, and the flat sandy islands with the best beaches, including Sal and Boa Vista.

It was inevitable that TUI and Thomas Cook would go in, but they stick to all-inclusive hotels in Sal and Boa Vista, and people who want something different come to me. All-inclusive can be damaging, but when hotel groups are given the land to build, they construct roads and other services. I'm 50-50 about whether all-inclusive is beneficial, but tourism brings in plenty of money and local housing has certainly improved. Development is continuing, especially in Sal, with investment schemes so that people can own part of a hotel themselves.

Cape Verde has kept its character, apart from parts of Sal and Boa Vista. I've spent a lot of time there and got to know the local

*people, and I'm trying to make a positive contribution. I saw a
lot of deprivation when I was a social worker in England, but
tourism is the other side of social welfare, providing enjoyment
rather than dealing with misery.*

By the mid-2000s, the pressures on the Big Four caused by low-cost
airlines, new ways of booking holidays online, and the lingering effects
of 9/11 and other atrocities, were beginning to tell. Their world really
had changed out of all recognition, and their solution was not to buy
smaller companies this time, but to buy or merge with each other.

First Choice made the first move, as Peter Long explains: 'By the
mid-2000s, the market was over-crowded with new competitors and
there were too many holidays on sale, putting pressure on margins.
Consolidation was always going to happen, and in 2006 First Choice
decided to either be the biggest, or to sell our mainstream package
holiday business. Airtours and Thomas Cook then decided to merge,
and this gave us an opportunity as First Choice was the logical partner
to come together with Thomson.'

Manny Fontenla-Novoa, who had become Thomas Cook's chief
executive in 2003 (also see chapter fourteen), says both his company
and MyTravel joined the bidding when First Choice put its package
holiday business and airline (formerly known as Air 2000) up for sale.
'I had the backing of my board, and we were progressing discussions
with First Choice. Alongside these discussions I was approached by a
major shareholder in Airtours [then called MyTravel] stating that they
would support the idea of a merger between the two companies,' he
recalls. 'The attraction of Airtours was that it had fantastic businesses
in Scandinavia and North America that Thomas Cook didn't have,
and there was no overlap at all in Europe, except in the UK.'

Following this merger, TUI bought First Choice to put alongside
Thomson. 'The majority of the brand decisions were easy to make,
with Thomas Cook becoming the lead brand,' says Fontenla-
Novoa. 'However specialist brands such as Cresta, Club 18–30 and
Neilson continued to co-exist. Decisions about people, locations and
management were much more difficult.'

The Airtours brand was kept on as the budget end of Thomas
Cook's package holiday range, and after several years in the doldrums
it was revived in 2016 under new Thomas Cook UK boss Chris
Mottershead, himself a former boss of Airtours in the 1990s. Steve
Endacott makes a brutal assessment of what happened to MyTravel
after merger: 'Thomas Cook destroyed MyTravel, including its people,
its knowledge and its systems. All the talent was lost, and 98 per cent

of My Travel's people took redundancy when its headquarters in Rochdale was closed and everything moved to Thomas Cook in Peterborough.'

John de Vial, one of the few MyTravel people who did move to Peterborough, adds: 'MyTravel was courting both Thomas Cook and First Choice as a lot of dancing around was going on, and we had to be doing the matchmaking. It wasn't sustainable to carry on with four large groups, and First Choice felt it was about to close the deal when it happened with Thomas Cook. The key thing with Thomas Cook is that the deal involved no debt, with 48 per cent of the shares in the new group going to MyTravel's investors.

'There was a positive feeling in the new company, and we didn't feel we were the poor relation. But in reality, it was very difficult and very political. Very few people at any level in MyTravel stayed on, as it was quite a clash of cultures. I have no complaints about what happened personally, but I was very pleased to leave Thomas Cook after eighteen months.'

The merger between Thomson and First Choice went smoothly, with First Choice top management put in charge. Long, who headed the new company TUI Travel, says: 'Our number one priority was to create a single business with one culture in a proper merger, not a takeover. Our second priority was to drive synergy and continue on our journey of offering holidays that you couldn't buy anywhere else. The scale of the new company allowed us to sell most of our holidays through our own channels rather than through third parties, and that reached 90 per cent.'

The mergers created two huge publicly listed companies, but their hold on the package holiday business was slipping. Competitors to TUI and Thomas Cook were not just each other and smaller tour operators, but the new breed of bedbanks and Online Travel Agents who were mushrooming on the back of continuing expansion by low-cost airlines. But as the Big Two rather than the Big Four, at least they were better prepared for the challenges ahead.

12

Mountains High

The lure of the Alps was more powerful than the lure of the Mediterranean sun, until package holidays became big in the 1960s. People went not just to admire the scenery but to gulp the pure mountain air, and in the nineteenth century the wealthy would head for the lakeside spa resorts of Europe in search of a cure or at least a re-invigorating holiday. Although the British gradually lost interest or faith in healing waters – shunning mineral spas both at home and abroad – the tradition of a healthy holiday in the mountains was revived strongly after the Second World War.

Strong though this appeal was, winter sports holidays rather than summer activity breaks became big business by the 1970s. Our interest in winter sports goes back much further, as the Ski Club of Great Britain was founded in 1903. Dr Henry Lunn, whose name lived on in the Lunn Poly travel agency chain for over a century, took his first ski party abroad in 1898, to Chamonix in the French Alps. Within a few years Lunn had a substantial business taking skiers to Switzerland by train and ferry, but as a Methodist minister he frowned on frivolity and would have been appalled by the booze-fuelled après-ski activities of a few decades later. Lunn also operated summer tours with an educational purpose, but only the wealthy could afford them. Skiing was certainly well established by 1920, when D. H. Lawrence's novel *Women in Love* (filmed by Ken Russell in 1969) featured a dramatic scene where the four protagonists go skiing in the Alps, and the character Gerald wanders off into a blizzard to die.

Happier times were promised by tour operators, and in 1934 a very famous name made its debut which remains one of the most important companies today. Inghams was founded by Walter Ingham (1914–2000), who had gone to school in Austria where his father was working, and developed a passion for winter sports which continued after he returned to Britain and started work himself. 'Very soon I found that selling typewriters gave little job satisfaction and no skiing, and I also discovered that with a party of fifteen, the leader got a free railway ticket and free place at a hotel,' he wrote. 'So, in the autumn of 1934 with £25 in the bank, I left Remington and put into *The Times* agony column and similar papers invitations to join a private skiing party to Austria. The first party was formed for Christmas 1934, staying at the Hotel Jagerhof at Schoenberg in the Tyrol.

'That winter I was able to organise four or five more such parties, and finished the season with £80 in the bank. Within about two years our main activities were ski holidays and ski mountaineering in the winter, and mountain walking in summer. We extended our activities into the French Alps and French seaside resorts, as well as organising leisurely coach tours. This was a particularly fortunate move as by March 1938, when Hitler annexed Austria, we already had good connections in France.'

It took until Christmas 1948 to resume skiing holidays after the war, when an Inghams party went to the Tyrol. The 1952–53 programme was presented as 'Inexpensive Ski Parties for Young People, designed for students, ex-students and near-students'. The choice of sixteen-day holidays included Bretaye in Switzerland, Obergurgl and Grafenhast in Austria, and Courchevel in France. All cost 28½ or 29½ guineas (around £30, or £840 at today's prices), including travel, chalet accommodation, meals, ski hire and instruction. 'There are no baths but, in normal circumstances, hot showers may be taken daily,' advised the brochure. 'In the evenings the local Hotel des Bouquetins provides a warm welcome with no obligation to spend much money. This has been the scene of many very enjoyable dances and parties – with no "closing time".'

Growth was rapid in the 1950s, and one of Inghams' innovations was to charter trains from French Channel ports with a bar carriage for dancing. The Snow Sport Specials had a very bohemian atmosphere as passengers drank and danced the night away across Europe, despite frequent interruptions as the gramophone needle bounced about. Air travel was still not firmly established by the time Walter Ingham sold it to Swiss holiday organisation Hotelplan (which is still the parent company) in 1962. Under Hotelplan Inghams would grow to become a much bigger company, but Walter Ingham was not the only ski pioneer to have a lasting legacy. The other big name, which again continues today, was Erna Low – who was also Inghams' main rival.

Erna Low herself (1909–2002) actually started before Ingham, putting an advertisement in the *Morning Post* in 1932 promising a fortnight in Austria over Christmas for £15, 'arranged by young

1902 brochure by Thomas Cook (Thomas Cook).

The way we were ... a Butlins chalet in 1936, when the first holiday camp opened in Skegness (Butlins).

Thomas Cook customers were flying by 1939 (Thomas Cook).

A family skiing in Switzerland, 1938 (Erna Low/ *Aiming High*).

Erna Low, known as 'the mad woman of Old Brompton Road' (Erna Low/*Aiming High*).

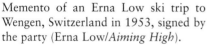

Memento of an Erna Low ski trip to Wengen, Switzerland in 1953, signed by the party (Erna Low/*Aiming High*).

Smith's coach tour brochure from 1938 (Neil McMurdy Collection).

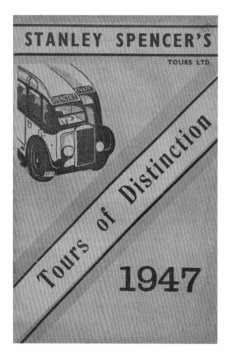

Spencer's Tours of Distinction in 1947 (Neil McMurdy Collection).

Salopia coach tour in Somerset, 1938 (Neil McMurdy Collection).

The Bon Sol Hotel, Mallorca in the 1950s (*above*) and (*right*) today.

Fishermen in Benidorm, 1955 (Benidorm Tourism).

Hotel construction in Benidorm, 1965 (Benidorm Tourism).

Promoting honeymoons in Mallorca, 1956 (Mallorca Tourist Board).

Benidorm today (Benidorm Tourism).

Palma Nova, Mallorca, 1961 (Mallorca Tourist Board).

Palma Nova, Mallorca, 1969 (Mallorca Tourist Board).

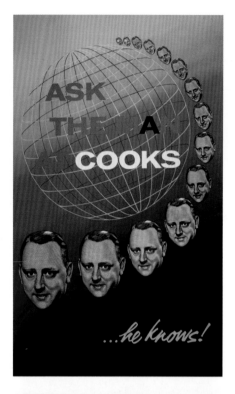

Asking the Man, 1962 (Thomas Cook).

Rail and coach travel were very important to Thomas Cook in the early 1960s (Thomas Cook).

A Cosmos brochure from 1964 (Cosmos).

A Panorama brochure from 1953 (Justin Fleming Collection).

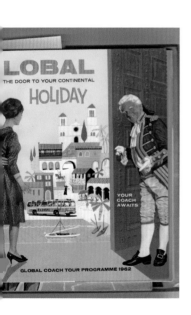

Global took an elegant approach to coach tours in 1962, (Tony John Collection)

All the staff of Riviera Holidays are thought to be in this photo, taken at Southend airport in 1965. They include (front row, from right) Roger Lambert, Aubrey Morris and Sid Silver, who later became the boss of Cosmos (Roger Lambert Collection).

Erna Low's brochure reflected overseas currency restrictions in 1966 (Erna Low/*Aiming High*).

TV celebrity Hughie Green on Universal Sky Tours' brochure in 1959 (Thomson).

A Swans Tours brochure from 1962 (Hugh Walton Collection).

A football team for Harry Goodman's Sunair prepares to give Mallorcan hoteliers a beating in 1967. Harry is standing, second left, while fifth and sixth left are directors Mike Prior and Joe Hyman, with Doug Weston kneeling second from right (Doug Weston Collection).

Smith's Happiway Spencer customers in Spain (Neil McMurdy Collection).

Salopia was a large coach tour operator by the 1960s (Neil McMurdy Collection).

Thomson customers in a Spanish
nightclub in 1969 (Thomson).

On the beach with Thomson in 1969
(Thomson).

It's muddy for Exodus
in the African jungle
(Exodus).

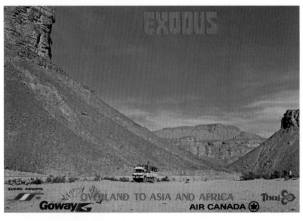

An Exodus brochure
from 1977 (Exodus).

A quartet of *TTG* front pages across over forty years. In 1958 it reflected the growth of air travel, and in 1971 celebrated the end of price control on package holidays. The author wrote the story announcing cheap holidays to Florida in 1979, while in 2001 *TTG* warned about the consequences of 9/11 (*TTG*).

Intasun's brochures instantly stood out because of 'that girl'.

The one that got away. Clarksons went bust soon after its winter 1974–75 brochure appeared (Doug Weston Collection).

The glamour of package holidays was boosted by pretty girls, and Olympic Holidays boss Basil Mantzos looks in his element at the ABTA convention, in Athens in 1976.

Olympic Holidays brochure from 1969 (Colin Brain Collection).

Time Off brochure for Paris, and 'How to Spend Less' in Barcelona.

Time Off founder Roland Castro.

The Thomson seagull logo was prominent for many years, as in this presentation to Manchester travel agents by Northern sales manager Gordon Clark (centre), with Thomson's Roger Lambert far left. Cliff Jones (second right) reflects on the hospitality offered to agents in the Eyewitness [on page 62] (Doug Goodman Collection).

Being Thomson's press officer had its perks. Here is Doug Goodman in Mallorca with Mary Stavin, who won the Miss World title for Sweden in 1977; and in Moscow's Red Square, with an unknown Santa Claus (Doug Goodman Collection).

Club 18–30 brochures from 1967 (David Heard Collection) and 2004. Was it really more innocent back then?

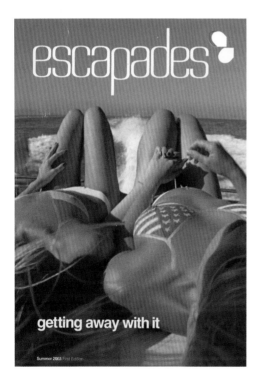

Youth brand Escapades pushed out the boundaries in its 2003 brochure, with girls holding hands as waves crash on the beach.

The start of something big … a Pendle Airtours brochure from 1981 (Thomas Cook).

Thomson reps in 1988 (Thomson).

Intasun's Harry Goodman pictured with
Pope John Paul II at the Sistine Chapel
in Rome, as Air Europe is launched in
Italy.

Intasun's Harry Goodman rubbed
shoulders with the finest, including
PM Margaret Thatcher, the Queen
and Diana, Princess of Wales (Harry
Goodman Collection).

Viennese Graduette for young people'. Only four young people travelled, plus a middle-aged female chaperone for the young Erna. 'We stayed at the Hotel Post [in Solden] and spent a hilarious Christmas,' she recalled. 'My party did not like caraway seeds, salami sausage and plumeau beds, and when I rose in defence of my home country, they used to put a little notice on the table, "Joke in Progress". There were no lifts, not even a bus to Obergurgl. We just walked uphill on seal skins and enjoyed our gluhwein the more for all the exercise we took.'

Low was born and educated in Austria, and started leading ski parties to supplement her income as a London language tutor, visit her sick mother, and indulge her love of the sport. After a colourful career during the war, she formed Erna Low Travel Service in 1947 when Switzerland, which had kept out of the war, was a particularly desirable place to visit. Her first brochure 'To Sun and Snow with Erna Low' appeared in 1948, also including Austria where tourists were allowed 'special food allocations'. Extended house parties in the UK were another of Erna Low's specialities, with an advertisement in *The Times* in 1952 inviting readers to 'enjoy a gay holiday in interesting company with a small party to Paris, Mallorca, spring skiing in Austria or an Easter party in Hampshire by the sea'.

The sense of danger surrounding winter sports was sometimes part of their appeal, with bad weather and accidents (sometimes fatal) being regular occurrences. Eight Erna Low customers were among eighteen who died when a bus carrying a party of skiers was blown into a ravine in Arlberg, Austria in 1952. Fortunately the company's name did not appear in newspapers whereas, if such an accident were to happen today, the consequences for a tour operator could be much more severe. But accidents did not damage the appeal of skiing, which young people saw as exciting and liberating. Erna Low used to share Inghams' Snow Sport Special trains, which continued into the 1960s. She wrote in her brochure: 'There is no holiday like a ski holiday. You start enjoying yourself the moment you enter the bar/dancing car, shaking and twisting your way across the Continent to the tunes of the latest pop music.'

The first ski charter flights, operated by Inghams and Poly Travel (which would soon join Lunn Tours to form Lunn Poly) operated for the 1960/61 season. Skiing holidays would soon benefit from the same economies of scale and mass market dynamics as package holidays to sunshine destinations, but for skiers air travel brought problems too. Most skiers wanted to take their own equipment, which airlines either couldn't accommodate or wanted to charge a lot for. Some resorted to wearing heavy clothing and boots on flights to avoid excess baggage charges, but the jet age brought much faster transit to the slopes and lower prices than rail travel. Ski operators were poised for rapid expansion, and by the early 1960s Erna Low had teamed up with Ski Club of Great Britain to take 10,000 on holiday each winter, with a choice of 150 resorts.

Another pioneer of skiing holidays was Colin Murison Small, who briefly worked for Erna Low and set up a specialist tour operator called Small World which offered a sometimes quirky take on countries including Greece. He had started skiing as a schoolboy in 1949, and by 1956 was driving a minibus to Spain's Costa Brava for summer holidays with a group of friends. In 1958 he was taken on as a courier by Erna Low despite his lack of experience, and as with so many holiday pioneers, he soon learned from the company he was working for and set up on his own. The following winter Murison Small ran his first ski chalet party holiday, to Grindelwald in Switzerland, costing thirty guineas for two weeks, with the journey by rail and cross-Channel ferry taking about twenty-four hours. He too found his customers through a small advertisement, in *The Times*. Small ads sometimes worked in reverse with single travellers announcing they wanted to join a holiday party.

Two girls were dispatched earlier that day to act as chalet hostesses, arriving only eight hours before the party to find and equip the chalet, and buy enough food and drink to get started. 'That done, they needed to digest the layout of the town, find where the ski school met and ski passes were bought, and generally acquire enough knowledge to be one-up on the guests,' writes Murison Small. 'It was an impossible task but, of course, they effected it. Chalet parties had started.'

The girls earned only a pound or two a week, but had free board and lodging and of course free skiing. 'Most of the parties were rated a success by both sides – the girls enjoyed looking after them and the guests appreciated their labours,' he adds. 'But one Air Force group got off to rather a bad start when it transpired that they had misunderstood the meaning of the brochure expression, "the girls will do everything they can to keep you happy", but otherwise all was fairly amicable. What the girls didn't enjoy was waiting for the housekeeping money to arrive from London. This was often because it hadn't been sent, for the very good reason that there wasn't any. Luckily we were working in an honest country in an era of mutual trust, so they were able to smile nicely and be extended credit by the local shopkeepers.'

He then introduced villa parties in summer destinations including Greece, while ski chalet parties continue to be popular today although on a larger and much more organised basis. Inghams has over sixty chalets each sleeping up to thirty people, equipped with log fires, saunas or hot tubs, and of course free wifi, with gourmet food, fine wines and highly trained staff.

Chalet parties are an almost exclusively British idea, as Murison Small points out. 'We made it possible to ski in a top resort without breaking the bank,' he writes. 'There are several possible reasons why the idea never caught on with other nationalities, but the British are more cliquey than most others and enjoy making up groups of like-minded friends.'

Austria and Switzerland were the original skiing destinations, and as they had been welcoming tourists since the nineteenth century many resorts had developed in a charming and personal way with skiers usually staying in traditional inns or small hotels. They were often able to retain that appeal, although many Austrian and Swiss resorts grew in the 1960s. Austria benefited from the European Recovery Programme or Marshall Plan, an American initiative to help rebuild countries affected by war. Austrian resorts such as Arlberg, Ischgl, Obergurgl and Kitzbuhel benefited greatly from investment in hotels, ski lifts, cable cars, transport and general infrastructure

France, however, only came on the scene in a big way in the 1960s, by developing purpose-built resorts with mainly large hotels and self-catering complexes. The French developed resorts to take maximum advantage of the slopes, some being at very high altitude, whereas resorts in some other countries had developed in a more haphazard way. Erna Low responded to the new popularity of France, which in time overtook Austria and the more expensive Switzerland to become top destination for winter sports. It was particularly attractive to the growing number of experienced skiers.

Many other factors contributed to the growth of skiing in the 1960s, including higher standards of tuition and new designs of skis, boots and other equipment which made the whole experience less of a chore. Another important development was increased interest from school parties, with Erna Low winning a contract to provide ski holidays for thousands of children from Wales by the mid-1960s, including a financial subsidy by the Glamorgan education authorities. The improving standard of roads meant coach holidays to the ski slopes were also developed, for both schoolchildren and adults.

Yet more countries wanted a slice of this growing business, including Italy, Yugoslavia, Bulgaria and Romania, with the Eastern European countries also investing in purpose-built resorts. The British left some countries behind, however. Switzerland and Norway both lost out to lower-priced competitors, although Switzerland still appears in mainstream brochures. Year after year, the numbers heading for the Alps and other European mountain ranges increased with nothing seeming to threaten the continual growth curve. It was not until many years later, as global warming began to take its toll, that a lack of snow became more than an occasional problem, especially in lower altitude resorts.

By 1967, around 250,000 British people were taking winter sports holidays each year, and proof that skiing had really become mass market came with the arrival of Clarksons, then the biggest package holiday operator to the Mediterranean. Winter sports had been the preserve of tour operators with specialist knowledge, but skiing was particularly attractive to big companies with their own airlines or long-term flying contracts, because they needed better productivity from their aircraft fleets in the winter. Clarksons started a programme called Snowjet in 1966, and by 1969 it was handling 15,000 skiers a season. As with sunshine packages, mass-market tour operators brought prices crashing down and attracted people who had never considered skiing before – sometimes with painful consequences!

Despite charter flights, mass market tour operators and major resort development, skiing was still a minority interest into the 1980s. Swans, better-known as a package holiday operator, also tried to broaden the appeal of skiing as Hugh Walton, who joined in 1970, recalls.

'Swans was ahead of its time in creating a new market for skiing, using pensions where people paid extra for using a shared bathroom,' he says. 'This was a time when holiday surcharges were common because of currency fluctuations, and I remember having to collect the extra money at the airport using the simple rule that if you didn't pay up, you didn't travel.'

Inghams took over Swans in 1976, but in 1981 came the launch of a tour operator that would change skiing more radically – Crystal Holidays. It grew to become the largest ski operator, a position it still holds today under the ownership of TUI. Thomson already had its own ski programme when it bought Crystal in 1997, keeping it out of the hands of rival Airtours and operating Crystal and Ski Thomson side-by-side for many years after TUI's acquisition of Thomson in 2000. TUI is set to abolish the Thomson brand by 2017, and Crystal is now its sole winter sports operation.

One of Crystal's greatest coups was introducing ski holidays to the US and Canada, as Hugh Walton recalls. He joined Crystal in 1986, moving to Inghams in 1995 and retiring in 2015. 'It was a great thrill for skiers to fly long-haul, and they couldn't believe the quantity of snow,' he says. 'The Americans and Canadians had invested a lot in their resorts, and another advantage was that they spoke English. European resorts started to suffer in the 1990s as prices increased and snow conditions deteriorated.'

Andy Perrin started as a rep in Crystal's first season of 1981–82, staying until after the acquisition by Thomson, but he now heads up

Inghams. 'There wasn't much growth in skiing at first, as Inghams was the top operator but charged premium prices,' he says. 'We saw the opportunity to grow, and Crystal, Thomson and Neilson Holidays picked up former Swans clients who were younger than those of Inghams. We had a desire to innovate, and we introduced charter flights to Denver, Colorado for 1989–90 as Europe had had a couple of bad seasons with poor snow conditions. Resorts such as Vail, Breckenridge and Aspen appealed to experienced skiers and sat alongside elite European resorts such as Zermatt, Verbier or Val d'Isere.

'Back in the 1960s, skiing was perceived as elitist, snobby and for toffs. Swans started changing that in the 1970s, but Crystal was the driver of change in the 1980s when prices came down, volume went up and it became a lifestyle thing. In the 1960s and 1970s going to Spain was adventurous, but by the 1980s people were thinking of a winter holiday too.'

The number of skiers using a tour operator increased from 170,000 in 1980–81 to 730,000 in 1998–99, when France accounted for 29 per cent, Austria for 22 per cent, Italy for 18 per cent and the USA and Canada for 9 per cent. Nothing, it seemed, could stop the growth, but the twenty-first century brought a series of challenges including low-cost airlines, a weak pound and recession. Higher fuel prices and high taxes, especially Air Passenger Duty, led to the scrapping of charter flights to the US and Canada although you can still take a ski package there on scheduled airlines. Reinvestment in European resorts happened at the same time as skiing in North America declined.

'Low-cost airlines had the biggest impact after about 2004–05 when they increased the number of flights,' says Perrin. 'They helped the short break come into skiing as people could try it out for a few days rather than commit to one or two weeks, as with charter flights. A lot of people say low-cost airlines stole our business, but they increased the number of skiers and nine times out of ten, if you're comparing like with like, tour operators can still offer a better deal.

'But after the financial crisis of 2008, we lost a third of the market over the next three winters – not just tour operators but the do-it-yourself skiing market too. People regard skiing as a second holiday, and while keen skiers have stayed with us, the market hasn't yet returned to the high point of a few years ago and will take a considerable time to do so.'

Schoolchildren on skiing trips have also declined badly, and for that Perrin blames successive governments. 'The number of schoolchildren going skiing was almost as big as the number of adults, about 750,000 a season,' he says. 'But then legislation changed in about

1993 so that you couldn't take children away during term time, and the Christmas and Easter holidays are the most expensive times of year. That was an absolute crime, as children never went skiing just before exams. They learned a healthy new sport, a language and they gained self-confidence. A child would get infinitely more out of a week learning to ski than a week at school doing the same things as the week before. Children who were 11–15 in the mid-1990s would have been the core of the skiing market now, but because they never learned to ski as children, they are less interested as adults. We are working very hard to attract new people to skiing, but there is no magic wand.'

But Perrin remains upbeat, adding: 'Unlike most other sectors of the travel business, people have a massive passionate attachment to skiing. They will spend every day of the holiday skiing, and along with higher standards, less queuing for ski lifts and less time needed to learn to ski, this has brought us through troubled times.'

Many more people now put together their own ski holidays using low-cost airlines, accommodation websites and online booking of resort transfers, but as with beach holidays the tour operator offers far more protection when something goes wrong as often happens with skiing. Inghams' Hugh Walton can recall some poor winters in the Alps when snow was in short supply, but the 2013–14 season was the best for twenty years. The following winter, however, brought more problems with a late but massive snowfall on Boxing Day. 'Cars without winter tyres were skidding and blocking the roads, and 29,000 people were stranded around Val d'Isere,' he says. 'It was utter chaos and cost us £250,000 in extra hotel costs and bringing people home, but at least some people appreciate what a tour operator does for them. Another of our strengths is that we fly from over twenty airports, more than the low-cost airlines.'

The tour operator Erna Low made a comeback despite changes of ownership, with Erna Low reinventing herself as a spa holidays specialist before returning to the company she founded in 1995 (aged eighty-five) and helping produce the first Erna Low brochure for sixteen years. She disapproved of the mass market from the start, and the company is now an up-scale, tailor-made specialist. Always an eccentric, she left the office one day in June 1996 saying she was 'just off to watch Wimbledon' and never returned, dying aged ninety-two in 2002.

The company is now run by Joanna Yellowlees-Bound, who joined straight from university in 1982 and says the principles of its founder live on. 'I feel she is still over my shoulder looking at me, and we have retained her focus on customer care which is more important in skiing than sunshine packages,' she says. 'There are still hotels in our programme that we used in the 1960s, and we have clients that first travelled with Erna Low thirty or forty years ago. It is a constant battle to attract new people into skiing, but the low-cost airlines help us. We can offer so many routes without the commitment of charters, and if people can buy a cheap flight, they will spend more on accommodation. The market has fragmented and is no longer dominated by large tour operators, but we can book a full package or just the accommodation and transfer.'

Lakes and Mountains

Well-off British people started visiting the Alps in the nineteenth century to improve their health – a trend recognised by Sir Arthur Conan Doyle, the creator of Sherlock Holmes. When he decided to kill off Holmes in a mutually fatal tussle with his arch-enemy Professor Moriarty (only to bring him back from the dead by popular demand), the venue he chose was a mountain path overlooking the Reichenbach Falls in Switzerland. A plaque now marks the spot of that fictional encounter, and in the resort town of Meiringen below the falls you can visit the Sherlock Holmes Museum, surely one of few in the world devoted to a fictional character. The Parkhotel du Sauvage features in the story 'The Final Problem' as an inn called the Englischer Hof.

Harry Chandler, whose Travel Club of Upminster was a pioneer of package holidays in the 1950s and 1960s, started his career by taking people to the mountains of Bavaria in southern Germany in 1937, before war interrupted his progress. Switzerland was his first destination after the war because it was still a land of plenty, and he wrote: 'My clients had little money to spare, so they were not inclined to purchase excursions when they arrived. They walked everywhere because it was the cheapest thing to do, and I walked with them.'

A pioneer of walking holidays was the Ramblers Association, which operated its first tours in 1947 and grew to become Ramblers Worldwide, offering walking holidays all over the globe. Austria, Italy and Switzerland were its first destinations, with most of its tours described as 'hard walking' of six to eight hours a day in mountainous terrain. But it also arranged holidays to countries such as Algeria, warning: 'A certain amount of dirt and discomfort must be expected as the places where we stay have as yet been little visited'.

Ramblers quickly built up a loyal following, as related in the booklet *Idealism and Realism*. 'A member once said he wouldn't be surprised to find a Ramblers leader emerging with a flask of hot coffee from the snout of a glacier,' it notes. Annual reunions were held in London including a sold-out event for 3,000 people in 1954, and by the 1960s it was also selling cycling, sailing and horse-riding holidays, although a skiing programme was dropped in 1963. The standard of accommodation improved steadily, with the comment in the 1970s: 'It was twenty years after post-war discomforts and shortages. In another twenty years, simple inns were simply out.' The Ramblers Association also owned package holiday operator Wings from its start in 1956 to its sale twenty years later.

In some cases, introducing summer trips to the same places where people went skiing – so-called Lakes and Mountains holidays – was almost an afterthought, but one that made perfect sense. Tour operators could get better prices from hotels and airlines if they could offer year-round business, and could face cash flow problems if they didn't have a summer programme. Some skiers were keen on experiencing the mountains in summer too, although the age range of summer visitors was usually older.

In the 1960s Inghams was one of the first ski companies to start a Lakes and Mountains summer programme, which has grown to be very big today. Some countries and resorts which don't offer skiing are available in summer, including Germany and the Italian lakes, but Austria and Switzerland remain very popular year-round. Inghams chief executive Andy Perrin says: 'The Lakes and Mountains customer is typically fifty-plus, but this age group is totally different to over-fifties thirty years ago. They don't want coach excursions any more but to go walking, biking and boating.'

Hugh Walton adds: 'Skiers are very price-driven, whereas there is great loyalty for Lakes and Mountains holidays. These people might be over fifty but they are fit, in good health, and will even try activities like parascending. But the numbers are shrinking, mainly because of the popularity of cruising and long-haul holidays. They are off to Cambodia or to see relatives in Australia, as the world is getting smaller.'

Must be Santa ...

The annual migration of reindeer is a celebrated event in Lapland, the region of Finland, Sweden and Norway above the Arctic Circle. A far more recent but equally remarkable annual event is the migration of thousands of British families to Lapland in December, to meet Santa Claus.

The trips usually involve some 'easy' winter sports, but usually have nothing to do with skiing although that may be available at the resorts where Santas (there are indeed many, especially in Lapland) live. As in all aspects of the travel business there are great experiences on offer and some mediocre ones, but in general the standard is far higher than it used to be if you're prepared to splash out, as many families are.

Canterbury Travel claims to be the originator of the Santa Claus break, starting in 1970, and for a few years in the 1980s it offered charter flights to Lapland by Concorde. The 1980s were the decade when this type of fantasy break really took off, with Cosmos being the first mass market operator to get involved in 1986. Credit for building up a highly lucrative business, if only for three weeks of the year, must go to Finland. Here the tourism authorities seized the initiative to profit from the tradition that Santa Claus and his reindeer do indeed live north of the Arctic Circle.

Santa breaks operate on charter flights, and provide a welcome bonus for tour operators at what is usually the quietest time of year. At first flights operated only to Rovaniemi, the main town in Finnish Lapland. Here the man in red is resident every day of the year in Santa Claus Village, but at busy times the queue to meet him stretches around the block. To quote from the village's website: 'When Santa Claus declared Rovaniemi as his hometown, he told how his home at Ear Mountain (Korvatunturi) was revealed at the beginning of the last century and how this closely guarded secret spread the world over. In order to retain the privacy of his secret location, the Elf folk decided to build a place where Santa could meet people from near and far at the Northern Arctic Circle.'

It sounds romantic, but isn't. Most tour operators soon decided this was not right for their customers, and started establishing their own mini-villages in the forest in conjunction with hotels. Here they can control every aspect of the experience, from offering every family a private meeting with Santa in a log cabin, to providing a range of activities and seasonal food in a party atmosphere. Activities usually include trips by dog or reindeer sledge and snowmobile, with the possibility of seeing the Northern Lights, and skiing at mountainous resorts including Levi and Saariselka.

At first mainly day trips were offered, but with a four-hour flight in each direction these can be exhausting especially for young children, and complaints soon started about everything being rushed. Although day trips are still available, three- or four-day trips are now the norm with prices from around £700. Some tour operators, such as Transun, do the vast majority of their business in just three weeks of the year. Satisfaction rates for tour operators are generally good, despite problems including flight delays and sometimes a lack of snow in early December. Lapland breaks have proved so popular that feeble imitations are now offered in the UK, but rarely a season passes without some kind of tabloid exposure either about holidays in Lapland or their UK equivalent. More than for any other type of holiday, Lapland operators are selling a dream.

13

2007–2015: Unravelling the Package

It's almost impossible to appreciate the full impact of the internet on how people book their holidays, especially when the situation changes almost weekly as new online tools become available and Google prepares to become more directly involved in travel. Ever since online sales started to take off in the early years of the century, a shrill chorus predicting the demise of traditional tour operators and travel agents has grown louder and louder. But the travel industry is resilient, and adaptable. While many travel agents and tour operators have fallen by the wayside – a trend which predated online sales by at least a decade – those that remain are mostly highly professional and focused on areas where their services are still in demand and they are able to make money.

The internet effectively makes travel agents of all of us, and if we don't want to search multiple websites to put together combinations of flights, accommodation, resort transfers, car hire and excursions, then Online Travel Agents (OTAs) such as Expedia, On the Beach, Lowcostholidays and Travel Republic can do that for us. New technology has made this possible, allowing OTAs and more traditional tour operators to see live availability of flights, hotels and other services, confirming bookings instantly. And then there are what's known as the aggregators, sites such as Travelsupermarket, Skyscanner and Kayak that don't sell you anything, but make their money every time you click through to one of the sites they recommend. The effect of all this is to commoditise everything, reducing booking holidays to the lowest common denominator which is, of course, price.

The online bazaar also invites us to become tour operators ourselves, sourcing all the elements of a package not just from companies with a UK presence, but suppliers based anywhere in the world. Not only can we book all these things, but we can find out all about them in advance down to the smallest detail – taking a virtual tour of a hotel or villa, for example, or choosing exactly what kind of flowers you want for your dream wedding in the Caribbean. We don't need to take suppliers' word that they provide great service – we can consult TripAdvisor, and read any number of apparently unbiased customer reviews about hotels, restaurants, tours and much else. Want to go to Bora Bora? There were 15,900 reviews on TripAdvisor during a quick search in early 2016. Because it registers what you have looked at before, TripAdvisor knows where you might be thinking of going before the home page has fully loaded. And if you want to book right now, you can either through TripAdvisor itself or through links to major online sites such as Booking.com, Hotels.com or Expedia. Simple!

Yet traditional tour operators and travel agents survive, although many of the latter have moved off the street to become homeworkers for organisations such as the giant Travel Counsellors. Why? The reluctance of some people to book online only partly explains this, and if these are mainly older people, then when they die off tour operators and travel agents will die off with them. Another reason why they survive is the growing number of cash-rich, time-poor people who just can't be bothered spending what could be hours online, and would rather leave it to a trusted professional. The independent travel agents that survive have reclaimed their role as honest brokers, while the holiday shops of Thomson and Thomas Cook concentrate on selling their own holidays to the exclusion of almost everything else.

Daniele Broccoli, a long-standing board member of ABTA, runs his own small travel agency in Peterborough, not far from Thomas Cook's headquarters, and also a small tour operation called Typically Italian and Typically Spain. He has ridden the ups and downs of the online revolution, with the availability of so many low-cost flights being a major boon. 'The internet has become too clever and too confusing for many people, and much of the time people don't know who they are actually booking with,' he says. 'When you read customer reviews on TripAdvisor you wonder why people can criticise an authentic but simple hotel in Italy just because it offers only cheese, ham and cakes for breakfast.

'Even younger people are coming back to packages now, and listening to their parents' advice. A group of lads going away together might book online, but if you're taking your girlfriend away for a special occasion, you don't want to get it wrong and you come to a travel agent. People know they have to pay an extra £2.50 for ATOL protection [the Civil Aviation Authority's licensing scheme], but people will pay that so their money and their holiday are safe.'

Since the Big Four became the Big Two in 2007, they have slimmed down considerably. TUI brands Thomson and First Choice have started to grow again, and Thomas Cook is hoping to get back on track after severe cut-backs and flirting with bankruptcy in 2011 (see chapter fourteen). Civil Aviation Authority figures show that the big tour operators have shrunk while online players have grown, but CAA figures no longer tell the whole story because some online companies have decided either to side-step CAA regulations by basing themselves abroad, or act simply as agents claiming they don't need an ATOL. The CAA and ABTA both hope a situation that could put people's money at risk will be rectified when new regulations come in by 2018 (see Part 3).

In 2007, the combined operations of TUI UK (Thomson and First Choice) were licensed to take about 7.3 million people on holiday, while the combined operations of Thomas Cook and MyTravel (Airtours) were licensed for about 5.2 million. Expedia and Travelocity were the only online players in the top ten, with Expedia being the only other company licensed for over a million. By 2010 TUI was down to 5.1 million, and Thomas Cook to 4.1 million. By 2012 they had cut back even further with both licensed to carry just under four million, while Expedia had dropped back as new online players were starting to make their mark. Travel Republic was licensed for 335,000 and On the Beach for 300,000 – the same as Cosmos, once one of the top five.

The top ten companies in 2016 are radically different, although TUI retains top spot being licensed for 4.75 million, with Thomas Cook at number two a long way behind with just over three million. Also in the top ten are First Aviation (Monarch, formerly Cosmos and Avro) with 2.2 million, and up-and-coming Jet2holidays.com with 1.5 million, Expedia with 1.2 million, On the Beach with just over one million and Travel Republic with 659,000. On the Beach has tripled in size, and Travel Republic more than doubled, since 2012, but some big players don't show up in the figures. Lowcostholidays, which sells in the UK and other countries but operates from Spain, is thought to organise up to one million holidays.

The retrenchment of the Big Two is evident in all sorts of ways, especially in resorts and at airports including Gatwick which is now awash with EasyJet's orange after it overtook British Airways as largest airline. Peter Long – joint chief executive of TUI's global operation until he retired in 2015 to become chairman of Royal Mail – has continued to steer it away from territory inhabited by low-cost airlines, with Ryanair operating many more resort routes in 2016 than at the start of the decade. TUI concentrates on exclusive sub-brands such as Sensatori, a range of luxury hotels offering gourmet dining, spas, sports and wellness activities, and all-round pampering, which can't be bought through any other company. It also has a growing range of faraway holidays as Thomson Airways was the first airline in the UK to introduce the Boeing 787 Dreamliner, with seventeen due to be in service by 2016 operating to 'new' destinations such as Costa Rica. The Dreamliner is claimed to offer brighter, airier cabins so that passengers arrive feeling more refreshed after an intercontinental journey.

'We have cut back on selling cheap flights and are now selling more holidays,' says Long. 'When Thomas Cook hit its crisis in 2011 we were able to persuade many more resort hotels to switch and sell exclusively through us, and with our Dreamliners we are building a very strong position in the Caribbean and are number one for holidays to Jamaica. Customer satisfaction is high, and I am not bothered about what low-cost airlines or new online players such as Airbnb do. They are not competitors. That is not our business.'

The role of tour operators and the reputation of the package holiday have been strengthened by various events, including an unprecedented natural phenomenon. When the Icelandic volcano Eyjafjallajokull erupted in April 2010, it released an ash cloud that quickly covered much of Europe and grounded flights throughout the Continent due to a risk that ash would be sucked into engines – a risk that has since been disproven, meaning there would probably be much less disruption if a similar eruption happened again. But in April 2010 the grounding of flights was unprecedented, and for several days no one knew if the ban on flying would last for weeks or months. In the event most flights got back to normal within a week or ten days, but massive disruption was caused with tour operators looking after their customers at huge cost to them. Passengers who had just booked seats on airlines, or had booked their own accommodation, were often left stranded facing extra costs that often took months to reclaim, if they could be reclaimed at all.

'We had 140 aircraft throughout Europe stranded by the ash cloud, but people got the message that tour operators looked after them,' says Long. 'A combination of the warranty that TUI offers to customers with the unique holidays we offer, and plus points such as the Dreamliner, makes us into a power brand. In the early days tour operators didn't care whether people returned to them year after year, but now we have a lot of loyal customers. About 70 per cent of our hotels are on long-term contracts or operated by partners such as Riu, and you can't buy these holidays anywhere else.'

Long was justifiably bullish as he prepared to leave TUI and turn his attentions to the problems of Royal Mail, and the fact that someone who ran package holidays has now taken over an ailing national institution proves how tour operating has come of age. TUI and Thomas Cook are now huge, corporately focused businesses with no room for sentiment. While Thomas Cook is celebrating its 175th anniversary in 2016, and is surely too good a name to ever be replaced, the same is not true of Thomson. TUI announced in 2015 that it is phasing out nearly all its package holiday brands, including Thomson, in favour of the master brand by around 2017, spelling the end of a name that has been market leader for nearly half a century.

Long is unapologetic about the loss of the Thomson name, with the TUI brand due to be applied to high street travel agencies as well as package holidays and the Thomson airline, although First Choice may be retained. 'If you started a new tour operation today you would have a single brand, as that is a stronger proposition,' he says. 'The TUI "smile" logo is widely recognised, but we will not rush the rebranding and we have already tried it out in Holland.

'There is a lot of emotional attachment to the Thomson name, but the same was true of Lunn Poly and Britannia Airways, and who remembers them now?'

The decision has caused outrage in some quarters, however – including Dermot Blastland, who was managing director of TUI Travel from 2007 to 2010. 'Thomson's confidence has come back like it did in the 1970s, and dropping the Thomson brand is utter nonsense,' he says. 'Coca-Cola might be a global brand, but will people in the UK buy a TUI holiday? The TUI smile is already familiar on planes, but it will spend as much on rebranding as it will save by basing the airline in just one country.'

As TUI and Thomas Cook introduce more hotels exclusive to them opportunities open up for others, especially the new online players. Many of the cheaper hotels abandoned by the Big Two have been snapped up by the bedbanks and OTAs.

Steve Endacott has an interesting perspective on how the package holiday business has changed, as he started with ILG, moved on to Airtours but has spent most of the twenty-first century setting up new types of tour operations. He became chairman of Teletext Holidays in 2015, a company that started as a call centre linked to advertising on TV displays, but is now an OTA protecting its customers through the ATOL system.

'The type of holidays that we take hasn't changed, but the way we book them has because of low-cost airlines and the internet,' he says. 'The big tour operators educated customers to book late to get the best deals, but they are now public companies and that's too big a risk, so they have run away from that scenario. There was no sudden moment when online companies started to package up holidays on demand, what we call dynamic packaging, but it was happening by about 2004–05 and really got going a few years later. The internet started showing up lots of OTAs offering the same holidays, exposing the soft underbelly of the big operators and putting them under attack. So they have retreated and now sell holidays exclusive to them.'

Endacott helped set up Jet2holidays.com, which has grown quickly in recent years to become one of the top ten tour operators licensed for 1.5 million customers. Jet2 is a low-cost airline based in Leeds that grew out of a cargo carrier called Channel Express, operating its first flights in 2003 and expanding rapidly from airports in the North, Scotland and Belfast, East Midlands airport being its most southerly base. By 2004 it had already handled one million passengers and in 2007 it started package holidays, opting for a fully-fledged, ATOL-protected tour operation. Jet2holidays.com moved rapidly into Airtours' heartlands after Airtours slashed back in size. In 2007 it was handling only 34,000 passengers but by 2014–15 the number had topped one million – growth of nearly 3,000 per cent in eight years. Jet2holidays.com might be a new online player but it is old-fashioned in some respects, selling resorts such as Benidorm and re-introducing resort reps.

Dermot Blastland moved on from a traditional tour operator to an OTA, as a director of Loveholidays.com. 'You might not be able to book a TUI Sensatori hotel through us, but although TUI may have exclusivity in the UK for many hotels, these hotels could still end up in online bedbanks,' he says. 'Not everyone can afford four- and five-star hotels, and the big tour operators seem to have forgotten Intasun's message in the 1980s that cheap holidays sell. As TUI removes more mid-range hotels from its programme, that releases more stock for the OTAs.

'I see TUI today as positioned somewhere between Waitrose and Sainsbury's in quality terms. OTAs have been allowed to grow because the big operators have been walking away from the middle market, and at Loveholidays.com we look after people. As TUI and Thomas Cook have become smaller, the commodity market in holidays has been taken over by OTAs. You might go to TUI for your main holiday at a Sensatori, but for a quick break you'll probably come to an OTA.'

Soon after merging Thomson with First Choice in 2007, TUI responded to the growing demand by making First Choice a totally all-inclusive brand, while Thomson continued to offer all-inclusive alongside half-board and bed-and-breakfast holidays. All-inclusive holidays started with French-owned Club Med in the 1950s, when beads were used to pay for drinks. Today's style of all-inclusive started in the Caribbean in the 1980s, where Sandals became the leading resort operator and now has twenty-four hotels. The trend started in islands where resorts were often isolated with nowhere close to go out for a meal, while in Jamaica, at that time, there were major concerns about crime and safety.

By the twenty-first century the trend had spread to Europe including Spain, Greece and Turkey, where there were plenty of places to go out and it was safe. In Europe existing hotels were often adapted, which proved to be less successful than purpose-built resorts with acres of space. All-inclusive has been very divisive in some places, with local bars and restaurants feeling that hotels have driven them out of business. Demand for all-inclusive holidays took off during the recession that started in 2008, as families wanted to budget for everything in advance and know they wouldn't have to pay extra for food, drinks or snacks at any time of day. All-inclusive now accounts for over half the holidays sold by the big tour operators, but they have no exclusivity on this. OTAs are also heavily involved, especially with new purpose-built resorts in Turkey.

When low-cost airlines started they kept to destinations that could be reached within about two hours from the UK, to get the best productivity out of their aircraft with three return flights a day. But by the second half of the decade they were spreading their wings further afield to Turkey, Greece, the Canary Islands and even Egypt. Ryanair and EasyJet were geared to continual expansion with extensive orders for new aircraft, including models such as the Airbus A321 which can carry over 200 passengers on flights of over four hours. These developments opened up yet more scope for the OTAs, as by now the public were hooked on low-cost airlines.

Andy Cooper, who left MyTravel in 2003 to head up the Federation of Tour Operators, was increasingly called upon to 'talk up' the benefits of taking a package as many more people went online to book low-cost flights and hotels separately. 'Our message was that tour operators will look after you when things go wrong, but that is not a message that works,' he says. 'In the pre-internet era you more or less had to use a tour operator and travel agent, but we sold only seven- and fourteen-night holidays and people got more flexibility when the low-cost airlines moved in.

'Destinations such as the Canary Islands wanted to encourage low-cost airlines to get a higher number of visitors, but they didn't appreciate the downside as hotels are undermined when people on a budget go to apartments and other types of accommodation. Average spending per head was a lot higher in the Canaries before the low-cost airlines went in, and their passengers often stay for just a few days.'

As with mainland Spain and Portugal a few years earlier, expansion of low-cost airlines proved beneficial to up-market companies such as Classic Collection. There are now literally millions of possible combinations of flights, hotels and different room types, with prices changing by the hour and only 'guide prices' in brochures. Nick Munday, the company's boss, says: 'Tour operators are brilliant at putting together tailor-made holidays if customers know what they want, but if they simply say have you got something cheap in July, it's almost impossible. Prices and availability don't last ten minutes but that's why many people are coming back to package holidays, because they are fed up with all the seats and beds that different websites come up with.

'We are a bit of a dinosaur, hanging on to sales through travel agents, and we still print over one million brochures. Our demise has been predicted by people who never use a tour operator or agent, but in 2014 we had a record year. I concede that 90 per cent of people don't need a tour operator or agent, but we want to grab 50,000 of those who do and we have a choice of 750 hotels.'

The middle ground of tour operating – companies in the mass market but a few rungs down the ladder from the big two – had largely disappeared by the early 2000s, with many companies having been bought by the Big Four. But there were exceptions, including a company called XL which went bust in September 2008 and highlighted the gaps in financial protection that still exist today (see Part Three). XL Airways was a large leisure airline with twenty aircraft, owning various tour operations some of which were quite big, including Travel City Direct which mainly sold the US, and Kosmar which specialised in Greece.

XL's collapse hit 85,000 people who were abroad at that time, and those travelling with its tour operators were brought home or had their money refunded. Passengers who had simply bought tickets on XL Airways lost their money unless they had bought appropriate insurance or were protected by credit cards, and had to pay for new tickets to return home. There was a public outcry when these anomalies came to light. People buying tickets on airlines are still not protected, and as a result of the XL collapse, the ATOL Protection

Charge (a levy to build up a protection fund) was increased from £1 to £2.50 on all packages and charter flights.

The Cosmos group, for so long bankrolled by its wealthy Swiss-based owners the Mantegazzas, began to struggle to the point where in 2014, the family finally sold off the package holiday operator, Cosmos; the airline, Monarch; and other online brands selling flights and hotels, to an investment company called Greybull. Cosmos Tours and Cruises continues under the Mantegazzas' ownership, but the Cosmos name disappeared from package holidays after over fifty years when the new owners adopted the name Monarch for all their operations in 2015. The airline has been scaled back, especially long-haul flights and charters, while the low-cost model continues on flights around the Mediterranean.

Hugh Morgan joined Cosmos in 2002 and is now chairman of Cosmos Tours & Cruises, having retired as chairman of the Monarch Travel Group in 2014. 'Although Monarch Airlines had had some scheduled routes for a long time, the low-cost airlines had a dramatic impact on it,' he says. 'Cosmos was still a successful tour operation, and bankrolled the airline to a large degree. Now Monarch's transformation into a low-cost airline is complete. The changes in tour operating have been driven by players including Lowcostholidays, On the Beach and Travel Republic, and technology has been the enabler because it presents the cheapest price so quickly and bang, there's your package created for you. Some of these guys knew nothing about travel but all about technology.'

Some of the OTAs and bedbanks that now dominate online sales offer literally thousands of hotels across the globe, in city as well as mainstream package holiday destinations, but you have to wonder what level of expertise they offer compared to the traditional tour operator that knows and inspects every property. Some have also caused controversy by insisting they act only as agents of hotels rather than as the principal or organiser of the booking, side-stepping responsibility when things go wrong. Specialist tour operators as well as the bigger names are losing customers to these new players, as more and more people are wooed away by low prices.

Sunvil has steered a steady course since it was set up in 1974 as a specialist in Cyprus and Greece, and in more recent years it has expanded into many areas worldwide ranging from Latin America and Africa to Scandinavia and the Azores. It was a founder member of the Association of Independent Tour Operators (AITO) in 1976 and continues to produce lavish brochures with great attention to detail and customer care. But chairman Noel Josephides – who also became chairman of ABTA in 2013 – says he now fears for the future of companies such as his.

'There are as many small companies as ever, often husband-and-wife businesses that operate on high margins and can take on the increasing costs faced by all tour operators, and who are often offering the kind of holidays that their owners enjoy taking personally,' he says. 'But medium-sized companies such as Sunvil are threatened, as we spend a lot of time coming up with price quotes for tailor-made holidays, which people then hawk around or just go online and book their own flights and hotels. They will look through our brochures and know a hotel is good because we feature it, and then go to Booking.com or a similar site to buy it. That forces us to offer ever more complex holidays, but we need more staff and the volume of bookings is lower. Our difficulty is that we are not getting new customers, who feel they are better off doing it themselves by going online. I don't know if companies like Sunvil will be around by 2020, but if more horror stories come out about the scams of booking online, we might see an upturn.'

The loss of companies with a strong focus on quality and which really care for the countries they feature would be a disaster for anyone who values expertise, but those very small companies who are enabled rather than ground down by the internet may have a brighter future. AITO celebrates its fortieth anniversary in 2016 with about 120 members, and its website reveals that some specialise in particular countries ranging from India to Italy, while others concentrate on activities such as art or adventure, and walking or wildlife.

AITO chairman Derek Moore – one of the founders of adventure operator Explore (see Chapter Sixteen) – says: 'The package holiday market as served by tour operators has two big players who are comfortable with what they are doing, and a large number of small companies who are also in a good position, but the middle range companies are in trouble. Small companies are like speedboats – they can turn around quickly, unlike oil tankers – and because they are owner-managed, they can react to events. They offer niche holidays to a loyal clientele who want their annual fix whether it be horse-riding or wine tours, whereas in tough times people who take sunshine packages might decide to spend on the necessities of life instead.

'One of the benefits of small tour operators is that niche holidays aren't that easy to book online. Their brochures are more like coffee table publications without prices, and although few are online-only, the start-up costs are much lower compared to the pre-internet era. AITO was set up forty years ago to find a cheaper way to offer financial protection to the public and to band together to get seats on charter flights, but today it is also a mentoring service. If you're alone in your office and need someone to talk to, we are a clearing house for ideas and assistance.'

John MacNeill, the former Thomson Holidays and Kirker Holidays boss who advises small tour operators, warns: 'Those specialising in a particular country could be at risk due to world events. They have to realise that the only real asset of the business is them, and that few companies are being bought out these days unless the person running them can be persuaded to stay. The only tour operators likely to be sold in future are those which can grow, not those that are hobbies.'

As the biggest name of all, Thomson, follows Cosmos into history, it is perhaps the small tour operators who are best placed to carry on the tradition of tour operating first established fifty or more years ago. They deserve to be supported and celebrated, even if their holidays cost a little more than the deals you can find online.

PART II

Escorted Tours

14

Asking the Man at Cooks

The teetotal Mr Thomas Cook must surely have been turning in his grave when, soon after the 150th anniversary of the company bearing his name, it acquired a tour operation not exactly known for its sobriety – Club 18–30. The company's journey from global pioneer of the escorted tour to package holiday giant in fifteen countries around the world takes in nearly all the major developments in travel and tourism. As it celebrates its 175th anniversary in 2016, despite the many ups and downs, it could be described as not only a survivor but once again, hopefully, a thriver.

'Ask the Man at Cooks ... he knows!' (there were few female employees in those days) was an advertising slogan which first appeared in 1962, reflecting the absolute trust that the public had in this national institution. Thomas Cook had already been an escorted tour operator for over 100] years but was also the UK's largest retail travel agent – an honest broker which could advise on all manner of travel including rail, sea, air and coach. It booked hotels either independently or as part of a tour, and also provided the all-important foreign currency and travellers cheques which were essential in an era before plastic money. Selling its own tours was an important part of the business but first and foremost, Thomas Cook was a travel agency rather than a tour operator. This, and the changing ownership of the company, explains why Thomas Cook was slow to become a major player in package holidays – something that didn't happen until the mid-1990s.

Although the British nobility had gone in search of art and culture on the so-called Grand Tour of Europe since the seventeenth century, the age of mass tourism only arrived with the coming of the railways. When cabinet maker Thomas Cook organised his first excursion, for a

Temperance Society travelling between Leicester and Loughborough in 1841, the railways were a new phenomenon and a British invention. The world's first steam-powered railway was the Stockton and Darlington, started in 1825, while the Liverpool and Manchester in 1830 was the first to carry passengers on a regular basis. Rapid expansion of railways in the 1840s gave Cook the basis for his business, and when he organised his first long-distance excursion in 1845 (also the first trip organised for profit rather than philanthropy), from the East Midlands to Liverpool, he produced a sixty-page description of the journey and effectively invented the tourist guidebook.

Public demand for rail excursions by those who could afford them was huge, at a time when many had never travelled more than a few miles from home. By 1851 Cook was bringing 150,000 workers from Yorkshire and the Midlands to London for the Great Exhibition and producing a newspaper, *Cook's Exhibition Herald and Excursion Advertiser*. European tours were a natural progression and these followed in 1855, to the International Exhibition in Paris plus 'grand circular tours' to include Brussels, Cologne, the Rhine, Heidelberg, Baden-Baden, Strasbourg and the French capital.

Expansion was so rapid that Thomas Cook became a byword for organised travel not only in Britain, but in many other countries. Cook himself led its first tour of America in 1865, venturing up the Nile in 1869 and organising his first round-the-world tour in 1872, using the newly completed Suez Canal and trans-continental railroads in America. Cook not only opened up the world but took care of all the practicalities, introducing hotel coupons in 1868 and circular notes, forerunners of travellers cheques, in 1874.

Thomas's son John Mason Cook (whose initials JMC would be used for package holidays and a charter airline in the 1990s) was the driving force behind commercial success. Thomas Cook remained in family hands until 1928 when it was sold to Wagons-Lits, a Belgian company providing luxury sleeping train services throughout Europe. When Thomas Cook was sold to a German company in 1992 there was much agonising about a national institution being sold abroad, but this had first happened over sixty years previously. Thomas Cook returned to British control during the Second World War, as Wagons-Lits was based in a country invaded by Germany, and during its centenary year Thomas Cook came close to collapse. It was put under control of the railways, and became a nationalised company in 1948 with the birth of British Railways out of four regional groups.

It remained a state-owned organisation until acquired in 1972 by a consortium including Midland Bank (later HSBC). Like all nationalised companies it was not allowed much entrepreneurial spirit and stood aside while companies such as Horizon, Clarksons, Thomson and Intasun developed mass-market package holidays. As a travel agency chain Thomas Cook sold all these companies and more, while continuing to operate its own escorted tours. But there was a sense that it didn't really approve of mass-market packages, remaining a 'full service' travel agency selling tickets, tours, currency and other types of holidays while high street competitors such as Lunn Poly developed into holiday shops.

Thomas Cook's 'firm hand on the tiller' for nearly three decades, until his retirement as chairman in 1959, was Stanley Adams. He steered the company through the 1930s recession, and in the 1950s looked askance at companies such as Horizon that were promoting the new-fangled package holidays. According to historian Piers Brendon, author of *Thomas Cook – 150 Years of Popular Tourism*, published in 1991,

> ... he was determined that the firm should not stray far from the safe and respectable business of taking commissions from transport companies. He disapproved of advance commitments and risky speculations. He set his face against "fly-by-night adventures" and would not even charter a motor coach. Adams got his way, for he ruled the company with a rod of iron and Cook's managers regarded him as "God with a capital G". State ownership also discouraged the firm from taking bold initiatives. Its nominal overlords simply did not want that kind of bother.

In one of many other books about Thomas Cook, its long-time public relations officer Edmund Swinglehurst adds:

> Over the years, Thomas Cook had become an institution associated in the public mind with Empire and the Establishment, but in the 1950s this was more of a handicap than an asset with consumer society, especially its younger members ...

But as foreign travel took off in the 1960s, Thomas Cook couldn't stand aside completely. It started its own 'Thrift' coach tours in 1960, and 'Topstar' package holidays on charter flights in 1964. It was more comfortable acting as a travel agent and running a wide choice of tours, but in 1968 it tried again to get a foothold in package holidays using British European Airways scheduled services, in a programme called Silver Wing. It couldn't compete on price with companies such as Clarksons, and soon bowed out. By the 1970s, the 'Sleeping Giant' as it was then known was attracting negative publicity, with one writer lamenting the 'strangely monastic atmosphere' of its headquarters in London's Berkeley Street.

As late as 1974, Thomas Cook felt compelled to offer advice to people contemplating going abroad that was only half humorous. Under the heading Deadly Perils, it held forth on the subjects of foreign food, policemen and customs officers, toilets and haggling over prices. It offered ladies this advice: 'Englishmen, from behind their newspapers, glance surreptitiously at the girls but Continentals are more extrovert. It's nice to be friendly but Latin lovers can become a nuisance. If you feel the occasional sly pinch or are pestered by pests, put on your haughtiest and most glacial air like the locals girls do.'

Thomas Cook's moderniser was Midland Bank, which led a buy-out consortium including the AA and hotel group Trusthouse Forte, and soon had sole ownership. Changes did not include a serious move into package holidays, although it continued to chip away at the edges for a few more years. A holiday camp at Prestatyn, North Wales – which it had opened in 1938 – was sold off. Its 100-plus travel agencies were updated and expanded, while more tours were added and the purchase of rival Rankin Kuhn in 1982 added expertise in faraway beach holidays. Thomas Cook remained profitable during the 1970s while the package holiday market was in chaos. After the collapse of the Court Line empire in 1974 it stole a march on other agency chains by promising a money-back guarantee, if the operator of any package holiday bought through its shops went out of business. By moving its headquarters from London to Peterborough it also made a symbolic break with the past, but at the expense of losing management expertise.

By the 1980s there were still plenty of people prepared to ask the man (or now more likely woman) at Cooks, but by now holiday discounting had set in and a new breed of travel agency, epitomised by the fast-growing Lunn Poly, was starting to take over. Thomas Cook dropped some traditional travel agency functions, and when it stopped selling rail tickets customers with an eye for tradition saw this as a betrayal. The Thomas Cook European and Overseas Rail Timetables continued to be published until 2013.

By the 1990s it was being buffeted by great changes in the industry. HSBC acquired Midland Bank in 1992 and the following year Thomas Cook was sold to a German bank. The two biggest tour operators Thomson and Airtours were driving sales through their own travel agencies, leaving Thomas Cook exposed with not enough holidays to sell at a boom time for package sales. WestLB, the new German owner, proved highly acquisitive and took over major tour operators Sunworld and the Flying Colours group (see chapter nine).

Manny Fontenla-Novoa, who moved with Sunworld to Thomas Cook and became its chief executive in 2003, says: 'After buying Sunworld we wanted to continue growing, and first we bought Flying Colours mainly because of its airline, rather than its tour operations. Then we bought the charter airline Caledonian and the tour operator Inspirations from the Carlson Group, and in 1999 we re-branded all package holidays as JMC. That was good as a marketing exercise, as what it was called mattered less. It was about bringing together the disparate operations.'

There seemed a real possibility that the Thomas Cook name might disappear, but when another German giant – C&N Touristic – acquired the company in 2001 it rebranded its global operations as Thomas Cook. People now go on Thomas Cook holidays from countries including Germany, France and Russia.

'We took the decision, probably bravely, to rebrand our package holidays as Thomas Cook and unleash the power of that brand, while keeping specialist brands such as Club 18–30, and Neilson for skiing,' says Fontenla-Novoa. 'That unified us, at a time when Thomas Cook's retail shops were becoming more mass market too. The public did associate Thomas Cook with travel agencies and faraway holidays, but because the name was so well-known, it was easy to extend it into package holidays. But it was a very brave move, and we had to ask Thomson-owned Lunn Poly to sell holidays bearing the name of its biggest competitor on the high street.'

After the merger of Thomas Cook and MyTravel (also see chapter eleven), MyTravel brand Airtours was cut back drastically. Thomas Cook followed First Choice and later TUI with hotel brands and packages available exclusively through its own sales channels.

'By cutting back we were reacting to consumer demand, and a lot of what Airtours had been selling was unprofitable,' says Fontenla-Novoa. It also made acquisitions, including Gold Medal which specialised in air fares and tailor-made holidays to faraway destinations. 'We paid a strategic price for it, because we had a clear strategy to merge it with a similar company called Travel 2, which happened after Thomas Cook sold Gold Medal,' he says. 'We also entered the rapidly growing and profitable bedbank arena with the purchase of Hotels4U, which added to the bottom line from day one.'

The make-up of Thomas Cook's business changed radically in the years that followed, as it became an international travel group with integrated retail, online, airline, hotel and tour operations in over twenty countries. Recognition of the brand was growing and, in the UK, the advertising slogan 'Don't Just Book It – Thomas Cook It', first used in 1984, was brought back. The combination of package holidays, independent travel and travel agency sales (boosted in 2011 by a joint venture with the Co-op's travel agencies) gave Thomas Cook wide coverage of the different ways people were now buying holidays. But some of the acquisitions proved troublesome, and were sold on for a lower price.

By 2011 it had hit severe financial difficulties, which led to a loss of around £400 million in the 2010–11 financial year. Weighed down by debt, this famous old name came perilously close to collapse before a major re-structuring plan pulled it around. It only returned to profitability in 2015, by which time some subsidiaries had been sold off, and its airline fleet and travel agency network had been slimmed down.

Fontenla-Novoa, who left in 2011, cites financial management rather than operational performance for its problems. 'What happened in the run-up to my exit is that whilst we made some very good acquisitions, we were a publicly quoted company. We had to ride out some particularly tough times such as the ash cloud crisis of 2010, the rocketing cost of fuel and a weak pound,' he explains. 'In many markets we were still profitable and doing better than our main competitor on margins, but we had to warn the financial markets that we wouldn't hit our ambitious targets. The City hates profit warnings. I came under pressure and so took the difficult decision to step down.'

Thomas Cook was negotiating credit facilities with its banks and was apparently informed that credit was in place, but then the auditors refused to sign off the business without any qualifications, raising the question whether enough funds had been secured. Thomas Cook had to announce publicly that its annual results would be postponed, and the markets panicked because of all the negative headlines. The company was probably never really at risk of failing, and credit was negotiated very quickly after the crisis.

When MyTravel was merged into Thomas Cook in 2007, the group's transformation into a mass market package holiday operation seemed complete. Although it continued to operate luxury faraway holidays (branded as Thomas Cook Signature) and independent travel with Flexible Trips, its UK operation is package holiday based. The 1,100-strong travel agency chain (the UK's largest), like its big rival Thomson, increasingly sells its own brands rather than third parties. You can still ask the person at Cooks, but in this age of 'directional selling' it can't claim to offer impartial advice.

The company's financial performance was turned around under the brief tenure of Harriet Green, but after the horrors of 2011, another crisis that had been festering in the background gave Thomas Cook very negative headlines. In 2015 during the delayed inquest into the deaths of two children on a Thomas Cook holiday in Corfu in 2006, the coroner ruled that Thomas Cook had breached its duty of care. Bobby and Christi Shepherd died from carbon monoxide poisoning due to a faulty boiler at their hotel, and Thomas Cook was accused in the media of trying to stall the inquest. It was widely criticised for accepting £3.5 million in compensation from the hotel, the Louis Corcyra, its apology to the family being regarded as belated and inadequate. As the crisis rumbled on Thomas Cook's share price suffered, but it then met the family, donated the money it received from the hotel to charity, and appointed a former Sainsbury's boss to look at health and safety. A lasting legacy of the tragedy came when it set up an independent charity called the Safer Tourism Foundation, to fund research and raise awareness of carbon monoxide and other travel risks.

Peter Fankhauser, the group's chief executive officer, described the children's death as 'the darkest hour in the history of Thomas Cook'. The children's mother, Sharon Wood, who is involved with the charity, added: 'The way in which one of the largest and most respected tour operators has treated Christi and Bobby's family is well documented, hard to forgive and impossible to forget. With the Safer Tourism Foundation, Thomas Cook has offered a viable initiative to raise the profile of carbon monoxide and improve carbon monoxide safety both in the UK and abroad. It is all we ever asked for that lessons be learned from our tragedy, so that lives can be saved in future.'

The company certainly faced a torrid time in the years leading up to 2015, but the 'Man at Cooks' appointed in 2015, UK managing director Chris Mottershead, formerly with Airtours and TUI, aims to look forward. The Airtours and Club 18–30 brands were revitalised as it prepared to celebrate its 175th anniversary in 2016, and it is once again offering holidays to Benidorm. Another move, with an eye on the low-cost airlines which have indirectly stolen much of the package holiday business, was to make holiday durations more flexible. It also launched a 24-hour satisfaction promise at over 500 holiday hotels, promising refunds or vouchers worth 25 per cent of the holiday cost if the hotel was not as described.

As with TUI, a high proportion of the hotels sold by Thomas Cook can only be bought through this company, with brands such as Sentido, Sunwing and the new Casa Cook. Mottershead regards

Thomas Cook Airlines as another plus factor, and flights have been introduced to several American cities. 'We are trying to add a level of service that can't be matched by our competitors, and the 24-hour hotel satisfaction promise is part of that,' he adds. 'When hotels are exclusive to us they don't appear on price comparison websites, where everything comes down to the lowest price. That's not where any business wants to be.'

Thomas Cook has a big foot in both the package holiday and independent travel camps, and while it was licensed to sell over three million package holidays in the UK in 2016 (well behind TUI with 4.75 million), it serves over six million customers when sales of airline seats, hotel bookings and other travel arranged by its shops are included. Nearly everything is now branded as Thomas Cook, except for Airtours and Club 18–30. It continues to offer faraway holidays as Thomas Cook Signature, but escorted tours – as first led by Mr Thomas Cook himself more than 150 years ago – are now operated by an American company called Collette under the Thomas Cook brand.

'We see ourselves as a holiday company whether we are selling a complete package, just a flight, or just a hotel,' says Mottershead. 'Every business should be clear about what it offers customers, and that's why we are revitalising Airtours and Club 18-30 rather than shutting them down.' Airtours, Thomas Cook and Signature reflect a 'good', 'better' and 'best' approach, with Airtours aiming to provide the good value it was famous for under David Crossland, and Club 18–30 serving the changing needs of today's clubbers with a fifty-year heritage behind the brand.

The return of Benidorm, in a modest way, is significant. Thomas Cook, like all its major competitors, cut back in North Africa because of the terrorist incidents that blighted Tunisia and Egypt in 2015. Turkey was continuing to sell well for 2016 but 'hundreds of thousands' of package holidays have been added in Spain, Greece, Cyprus, Malta, Portugal and Italy. All these countries were familiar to the package holidaymaker in the 1960s, long before Turkey or Egypt came on the scene.

'Turkey and other "new" countries have very high quality hotels compared to destinations that developed a long time ago, but have forced these more traditional destinations to improve their game,' says Mottershead. 'Places like Mallorca have invested heavily to update what they offer, and the trend is now swinging back to them.

'These days people are looking to travel with brands they can trust, and while it is great to have the heritage of 175 years behind Thomas Cook, you have to be relevant to today when people's expectations are so much higher than they were even twenty years ago. I want to create an organisation that's prosperous, outward looking and moving forward in a growing market. We will continue to offer financial protection through the ATOL system, and having worked in Russia where consumers have absolutely no protection, I have seen how much money people can lose.'

What would Mr Thomas Cook make of the institution he founded in 1841? It's an interesting question to ask on the 175th anniversary, and for sure the teetotaller wouldn't have approved of the limitless booze on offer at all-inclusive hotels. But in many ways, he might look at it with admiration. As former boss Manny Fontenla-Novoa observes, 'It is a great name that has lasted for 175 years, and today still holds dear the founder's values and aims to make travel affordable and accessible to all.'

15

To the Ends of the Earth

SKINS – older people happily Spending the Kids' Inheritance – are often not content to lie on a beach as they want to explore, but explore in comfort. There's nowhere on earth beyond the reach of the escorted tour, although if you want to go to Antarctica it has to be on a cruise, a type of all-inclusive tour. Countries may drop off the tourist map from time to time due to war or natural disaster, and in 2016 it might seem impossible that Syria, Libya or Iraq will ever make a comeback. But all these countries have great historical and cultural appeal, despite the destruction of some monuments by Islamist extremists. You need only consider the resurgence of Iran or Northern Ireland as touring destinations to appreciate that yesterday's closed society or civil war zone could be tomorrow's in-demand places. People who love touring are much less easily put off than the average package holiday customer, and while some have a deep interest in particular countries or cultures, others simply want to tick another country off their list.

Until intercontinental air fares started to tumble in the 1970s, Europe was the main touring destination. But many people didn't want the long trek by coach, so as soon as cheap charter flights became available, tour operators started flying people into Europe for their tour to begin. Clarksons, a name forever associated with cheap package holidays in the early days, also had a major touring programme and in charge of that in the late 1960s and early 1970s was Stewart Wild.

'We started to sell Danube river cruises from Austria using weekly charter flights by Bristol Britannia aircraft,' he recalls. 'These cruises were a good example of Tom Gullick's [the Clarksons MD] risk taking, as to get the best prices, we operated in spring when the river levels might be too high, or in autumn when levels might be too low. The most popular tours were six-day trips using flights to Madrid, Rome, Athens and Bergen in Norway. Nearly every seat was sold, and Thomson followed us into Norway with Boeing 737 charters, but had problems finding enough hotel beds. We were always adding new tours, and were into Eastern Europe long before other tour operators. Customers were happy because we gave them phenomenal value-for-money, by promising to fill a hotel with people outside the main season.'

A company that was never a big name, but continues to offer the oddest places in the world, made its debut in 1971. Regent Holidays could have been an adventure operator as this was how it started with minibus tours to Albania in south-east Europe, then a reclusive and secretive Communist country. Regent was founded by Ulsterman Noel Cairns, who had been to every other country in Europe and decided on Albania after meeting a diplomat from that country in Belgrade. He had also spent a lot of time in Turkey, then regarded as an unknown and very exotic country, which soon became a major part of Regent's business. Another then-unvisited country, Iceland, was introduced in 1975, the same year that Neil Taylor joined the company and it began to diversify. Taylor had a degree in Chinese from Cambridge University and was determined to operate tours to a country which had briefly opened up to tourists in the 1960s, but then closed again due to Mao Tse-tung's so-called Cultural Revolution.

Taylor had first visited in 1971 with the Society for Anglo-Chinese Understanding, and recalls: 'Lights were out for much of the evening with bedtime firmly fixed around ten o'clock. As the day started equally firmly at seven in the morning with quotes from Chairman Mao from a sound system that could not be turned off, perhaps this early bedtime mattered less. Clearly in those days, the Chinese did not do holidays in the normal sense of the word. You either accepted an intensely political tour or you stayed away. Mao died in 1976 and by late 1978 Deng Xiaoping was firmly in control. It is not known whether he had any views on tourism, but certainly one of the earliest signs of an opening to Western ideas was a complete change in the organisation of holidays. It might take a few more years before operators could book specific hotels, but at least we could specify an itinerary and replace a ball-bearings factory with the Summer Palace.'

Regent's first tours to China departed in 1976, using the trans-Siberian railway. It soon gained a reputation for tours to other Communist countries, including Cuba, while continuing to develop Turkey and Iceland. Regent's biggest coup was becoming the first Western tour operator to add North Korea in 1987, which remains the most isolated dictatorship in the world.

'You can now go almost anywhere in the world on an independent tour, except for North Korea,' adds Taylor, who retired from Regent in 2003 but continues to guide visiting groups. 'Previously there were many countries you could only visit on a package tour, but now you can just book a flight and drift. Destinations come and go in popularity, but when people go back three or four times to a country such as China, they do different things. The affluence of many of the older generation is an important factor. A lot of older couples have rock-solid pensions, and many older single people don't have to consider saving for the next generation.'

Regent Holidays has stayed true to its oddball credentials despite two changes of ownership. Many mainstream tour operators have moved into countries including China, Turkey and Iceland, but Regent's Small Group Tours brochure for 2016 includes tours called Kiev and Chernobyl, Classic Belarus, Pioneering Nagorno Karabakh, and Kazakhstan 'Back in the USSR'.

'The core Regent customer is fifty-plus, very curious about countries they are visiting and already very well-travelled, taking four to six holidays a year on average,' says Andrea Godfrey, Regent's general manager. 'We specialise in things that aren't easy to book yourself, like wine tasting in Georgia or visiting a family in Kosovo. A lot of tour operators try out unusual destinations and drop them, but we stay in. We have seen phenomenal changes for the better in many countries, and in some countries people expect there will be challenges such as the standard of hotels, or having the same food for five days. The world situation is our biggest challenge today. Russia is one of our biggest destinations, but we saw a fall in demand after 2015 when you had to apply for a visa in person.'

Eyewitness: Neil Taylor
The former Regent Holidays director now writes guide books and articles, guides tours and lectures on cruise ships.

Recycling is very tempting for writers in the travel business, whether in a blog, for a guidebook, brochure copy or a press release. If the prose is tempting, will anyone notice slight inaccuracies caused by the passing of time? Writing on North Korea fortunately does not pose such a problem. I first visited in 1985 and have returned regularly over the subsequent thirty years. What I would have written then is identical to what I have to say now.

The government has seen the potential for earning foreign currency through tourism, but also the danger of losing even a modicum of control over the visitors who come. Mobiles and laptops are taken on arrival, and only returned on departure. The guides, like their leaders, provide "on the spot guidance" and do not want a second opinion. In fact second opinions on anything simply do not exist in North Korea. There is one department store, one hospital and one library that all visitors see, and none of these actually function. The actors posing as customers in the shop return the goods as soon as the tourists have left. The patients are brought into the hospital for visitors to admire but clearly no treatment takes place there. In the library, there is no access to websites or to books from abroad.

Neither the death of Kim Il-sung in 1994, nor that of his son Kim Jong-il in 2011, has made any difference to tourism. The sense of complete unreality remains in a society ruled by Kim Jong-un, that does not express doubts or admit to any imperfection. Come the evenings this does not matter, when revolutionary opera or terrifyingly brilliant acrobatics take to the stage; there is only one stage that foreigners will see. At the opera, the strength of the music, the actors' intricate costumes and the enthusiasm of the local audience all make up for the lack of any serious plot. Never expect a twist in the tale: communism always wins over capitalism and no mercy is shown to any transgressor.

However the outside world will protrude just before departure, as this is tipping time. Guides are very grateful for whatever they are given and one can picture them, just after the farewells, letting their hair down, literally if they have bought some shampoo, or metaphorically if they buy something else. Their play-acting will not be necessary until the next group arrives.

China was one of the first major success stories for two other escorted tour operators, Bales and Voyages Jules Verne, and Bales' first tours to that country started a decade before Regent, in 1965. Only two years later, the gates to China slammed firmly shut as the Cultural Revolution banned foreign visitors.

Former RAF navigator George Bales started as an air broker in 1947, and with his wife Molly he operated his first tours, to the Holy Land, in 1961. Egypt was introduced in 1962 and India in 1963, these countries becoming its most important destinations. By 1970 Bales was running a round-the-world tour in thirty days for £499 and it returned to China in 1977. Tours were sometimes still priced in guineas in 1970, when an 18-day tour of Ceylon (Sri Lanka), India, Nepal, Afghanistan and Pakistan cost 305 guineas. The sightseeing tour of Kabul included a museum which was partly destroyed by the Taliban in 1996. Bales tours eventually covered most cultural faraway destinations, but in 2009 it was sold to Virgin Holidays which later closed it down.

Voyages Jules Verne was the brainchild of Philip Morrell who spent twelve years with Thomson Holidays, and rail tours were one of its specialities (see chapter eighteen). Thomson Holidays had been the first mass-market operator to breach the Iron Curtain with weekend breaks to Moscow in 1972, and soon after that, while at Thomson, Morrell set his sights on breaching the Bamboo Curtain too. Chinese premier Chou En-lai had invited Lord Thomson to visit even during the Cultural Revolution, which helped prepare the ground.

'I managed to get a letter delivered to the Chinese authorities in 1977 via Tarom Romanian Airlines' weekly flight to Beijing, and within a short time China had agreed to let Thomson in,' says Morrell. 'But Thomson wasn't really interested, so I decided to leave and operate tours there myself. At Voyages Jules Verne I started the Central Kingdom Express rail journey to Beijing and Hong Kong, as an exotic taster for what was to follow, including the first direct flights to Costa Rica and Tashkent.'

Morrell led his first tour to China in 1977, and it soon became the new company's most important destination. By 1980 he was organising a tourism conference in Beijing's Great Hall of the People, but operating tours to China certainly brought challenges in those early days. One of his first customers was an abattoir owner whose main reason for coming was to study the Chinese way of slaughter, but he went home disappointed despite many noisy protests.

Morrell sold Voyages Jules Verne to Kuoni, the long-time market leader to faraway countries, in 1998. Kuoni had always had an interest in group tours, although most of its holidays by that time were either beach-based, or independent tours. Kuoni now has a programme called Journeys which includes escorted tours, rail trips and river cruises in Asia, Africa, the Americas and Europe. This is in response to demand for more immersive or 'experiential' travel, which only works as part of a small group with a maximum size (for Kuoni) of fourteen. Companies such as Explore and Exodus, which started by offering adventure tours, also appeal to travellers who want 'soft adventure' with some creature comforts.

'People nowadays want to control everything about their holiday before they go, but we can still take them on a journey,' says Wendy Kenneally, Kuoni's vice-president of purchasing and customer experience. 'So it's a question of how we can facilitate things for people, while still catering for that spirit of adventure. Everyone knows about the temples and floating market in Bangkok, for example, but how about a cycle ride? People trust us to organise things for them that aren't easy to book online.'

Small group tours are particularly appropriate in offbeat countries such as Rwanda, says Kuoni's Africa specialist Sandra Farmer, with the company for over thirty years. 'All I knew about Rwanda before I went was the genocide and the gorillas, but it is an incredibly diverse and beautiful country which you can visit on a tour and have your expectations changed,' she says. 'In South Africa, we have seen customers meet local people on a tour and then go on to support their children. They form proper relationships with local people who have nothing, but will give you everything.'

A growing number of companies have started targeting escorted tour travellers over the last thirty years, often selling through newspapers and magazines rather than through travel agencies. These include Titan, Travelsphere, Riviera Tours (no connection with Riviera Holidays that became part of Thomson), Collette and Newmarket Holidays, and in some cases the tour experience starts the moment you leave home as a chauffeur-driven limousine is included to take you to the airport.

Customers are almost exclusively fifty-plus, as with Saga which is now part of a huge company offering holidays and financial services to older customers. Saga's origins go back to 1948 when Sidney De Haan opened a seaside hotel at Folkestone, Kent, offering breaks exclusively for retired people off-season. By 1957 he was chartering trains, and the first Saga customers travelled abroad in 1959. By 1970 it was a major operator of escorted tours, starting cruising in 1975 and faraway holidays in 1979. The holiday habits of the over-fifties have, literally, come a long way since the first retired people came on holiday to Folkestone over sixty years ago.

There are now about 25 million people aged over fifty in the UK, and as people live longer and healthier lives, escorted tour operators can look forward to a bright future. Travelsphere is another of the companies targeting globetrotting older travellers, with China, America, Canada, Vietnam and Australia among its top destinations. A growing number of over-fifties are travelling alone, and not always through necessity. A brand called Just You includes single rooms at no extra cost on all its tours, and a high percentage of its customers are women.

Travelsphere and Just You are part of All Leisure Holidays, a company which also specialises in small ship cruises with Voyages of Discovery, Hebridean Princess and Swan Hellenic. All Leisure chairman Roger Allard was once a major player in package holidays with Owners Abroad, later rebranded as First Choice, but he now sees a brighter future in cruising and touring.

'Niche businesses offer greater potential, and cruising gives you the opportunity to travel in comfort to places such as Russia as coach tours used to do in the twentieth century,' he says. 'A lot of our customers live off their pensions and savings, and recent changes to pensions meaning you can take it all as a lump sum will increase people's spending on holidays. The appeal of group tours and cruising comes down to having disposable income, value for money, and meeting like-minded people. Just You is growing because it appeals not just to single people, but to married people who want a different type of holiday to their partners. The age range we appeal to will remain the over-fifties because they are the fastest growing demographic.'

Philip Morrell, who remained with Kuoni for two years after selling Voyages Jules Verne, has also moved into small ship cruising with *Lord of the Glens*, a purpose-built luxury ship in Scotland. He is more downbeat about the future of escorted tours than most of the companies in it. 'A corporate animal like Kuoni couldn't cope with the kind of risks I took as an independent operator, so I steered Voyages Jules Verne away from a more risky type of operation to the mainly structured itineraries it offers today,' he says. 'Group travel is actually diminishing as people become more experienced, and if you look at a company like Noble Caledonia, most of what it does is on ships rather than on tours. There isn't much of a future for tour operators, as in this transparent world of the internet, people seek out the end provider such as the hotel or cruise company. The key to moving forward is to have your own product, such as a ship.'

The Oceans (and Rivers) Wave

Plenty of books have been written about cruising, especially the two long-established companies whose origins lie in Britain, Cunard and P&O. But the briefest of summaries may be helpful here, if only because two of the biggest tour operators became involved and because many tour operators include a short river or ocean cruise as part of an escorted tour.

Until the 1960s, the notion of cruising for pleasure was hardly known. People took sea voyages as a means of getting from A to B, especially across the Atlantic and to the far-flung countries of the British Empire. But even before the Titanic set out on its doomed maiden voyage in 1912, a long journey at sea had acquired a certain glamour that burned even more brightly in the golden era of the great liners, between the two world wars. The word posh is said to originate from the instruction 'Port Out, Starboard Home' scrawled by porters on the luggage of wealthy P&O passengers travelling from Britain to India.

By the 1960s, however, that golden era was over and the companies that operated the great liners were in deep trouble. Air travel had been chipping away at them for a long time, but when the first jets started to fly across the Atlantic and around the world, the age of long-distance sea travel was over. The few companies that continued, such as Cunard between Southampton and New York, moved into the tourism business and marketed themselves as a nostalgic experience.

Many of these companies did not go quietly, however. Cunard, P&O and others reinvented themselves as cruise operators, offering many ports of call during a week or more travelling around the Mediterranean, Baltic or Caribbean. Carnival, the world's biggest cruise line (which owns both Cunard and P&O), was founded in the US in 1972. One of the first ships it bought was the *Empress of Canada* belonging to Canadian Pacific, which was renamed the *Mardi Gras*. But the giant American companies that soon began to dominate cruising didn't make do with second-hand goods for long. When Royal Caribbean's 18,000-ton *Song of Norway* was purpose-built for cruising in 1970, it was considered enormous with a capacity of 724 passengers in 350 cabins. Ever since cruise ships have become bigger, more lavish and more glitzy. The world's biggest are the twin ships *Allure of the Seas* and *Oasis of the Seas*, each weighing in at 225,000 tons with 2,706 cabins accommodating 5,412 passengers. Royal Caribbean brought an even larger ship into service alongside them in 2016, the *Harmony of the Seas*, which can carry 5,479 passengers. Even larger ships are under construction, including one for Costa Cruises able to carry 6,600 passengers.

Thomson was the first big tour operator to spot the potential of cruising in 1973, but pulled out in 1976 as fuel costs escalated. It didn't return to cruising until 1995, when its great rival Airtours had already entered the market, and now owns four ships based around the Mediterranean that are part of the broader TUI Cruises fleet. Airtours moved into cruising when it bought a ship called the *Sunwing* in 1994, followed by three others, acquiring Costa Cruises in 1997 in a joint venture with Carnival. Airtours is widely credited for making fly-cruises affordable for young couples and families, and helping to change the rather stodgy, old-fashioned image of cruising that persisted for much of the twentieth century. Cruise ships also kept

Airtours' charter airline busy, moving passengers to ports including Palma, Mallorca.

Demand for cruising grew rapidly in the twenty-first century, keeping many travel agencies afloat as they moved away from selling package holidays. By 2011 the Passenger Shipping Association (now the UK arm of the Cruise Lines International Association) was claiming that one in eight packages was a cruise, with 1.7 million passengers originating from the UK. The number was similar in 2014, with a major increase in cruises from UK ports as well as fly-cruises. Southampton now handles more passengers than in the glory years of the great liners.

Cruising is a global phenomenon that recession hasn't sunk, as construction takes many years and ships are coming into service now that were ordered before the downturn. Over-capacity means that discounting is rife, while another serious problem is the environmental impact of giant ships. This is felt especially on small islands such as the Caymans, or old port cities such as Venice and Dubrovnik. Small ship cruising is growing almost as an antidote, by companies such as Hebridean Princess and the sail-powered Star Clippers.

River cruising has also grown enormously, especially along the Rhine and Danube, with some coach and rail tour operators advertising 'no fly' holidays including a few nights on a river. It is ironic that air travel, which killed off the big liners but then made cruising accessible in many parts of the world, is now being rejected by some people in search of a more leisurely experience.

16

Looking for Adventure

About fifty years ago, young people started travelling the 'Hippy Trail' across Europe and southern Asia. Their destination was usually the fabled city of Kathmandu in Nepal, but sometimes India or Afghanistan. Their goals were not just fun and adventure but mind expanding drugs and spiritual enlightenment, as popularised when The Beatles met the Maharishi Mahesh Yogi at his ashram in India in 1967. Some were British but many were Australians and New Zealanders, and for them the Hippy Trail was an economic way of travelling to Europe at a time when air fares remained very high.

By the 1980s it was all over, not because flower power faded but because the Iranian Islamic revolution of 1979 closed off the route, while the Soviet invasion of Afghanistan that year made this country dangerous to visit, which it has been ever since. But adventurers found new destinations. Soon they were digging battered trucks out of the mud on long expeditions through Africa, before moving on to South America.

From those pioneering days along the Hippy Trail, or sometimes in North Africa, was born a major adventure travel industry. Adventure travel is alive and well today, although much changed, and a man who has lived through it all is Derek Moore who was one of the founders of Explore. He joined a company called Oasis Safari in 1969, and when that went bust joined Minitrek from 1971–1976. When that too collapsed he worked for Penn Overland, a company with its roots deep along the Hippy Trail, helping set up Explore when Penn closed down in 1981.

'In the early days it was like pirate radio – off the radar,' he comments. 'With Oasis Safari I drove a Ford Transit van on two-week trips to Morocco, which were very primitive and just one stage up from backpacking. I once drove twenty-two hours in one day as there were no driver controls like tachographs at that time. We camped, and if the van broke down I had to fix it. I loved living on my wits.'

Penn Overland proved to be the classroom for many people in adventure travel, and by the early 1970s it had anticipated future trends by introducing shorter tours rather than the long slog to southern Asia, which typically took about ten weeks via Turkey and Iran. 'The first generation of guys running these companies were not businessmen but entrepreneurs, who liked travelling themselves,' explains Moore. 'Penn was the most professional of the overland companies, using proper Bedford coaches. But when they broke down, you might have had to fly thousands of miles to find the nearest dealer. Overland trips appealed only to people who had a lot of time, including Australians. There were all kinds of incidents, but often the press didn't get to hear about them. We used to navigate by compass in the Sahara, but one German group got stuck and died when they ran out of water.'

When Penn closed down in 1981, other companies including Explore soon took its place. Moore says the Iranian revolution was a key factor: 'It killed off the overland business, and although some tour operators started flying over Iran from Turkey, it wasn't the same. I remember being in Isfahan, in Iran, when the first popular uprising happened. I said the Shah would be back in control within three weeks, and that was my last bit of political punditry!

'I was in Rio de Janeiro, still with Penn, when I got a telegram saying it was closing down and I should come home. At the creditors' meeting myself, Travers Cox and Derek Cook said this was a great little business. There were many tour leaders out of work, and we could get a mailing list of customers and had contacts throughout South America, Africa and India. It was an opportunity crying out to us, but because of Iran we couldn't operate overland to Asia any more. But flights were becoming cheaper, so at Explore we chopped the longer trips down into shorter segments, such as northern India and Kashmir. Exodus was our main competitor and clients had no loyalty – it was either Explore or Exodus.'

Young people, like those who had first blazed the Hippy Trail, continued to be Explore's main customers. But as it advertised more widely and travel journalists began to write about it, Explore moved more into the mainstream. 'No one has ever defined what an adventure tour is, but it is for people who don't mind unpredictability,' says Moore. 'It will usually offer local accommodation, meals and tours, and be something of a physical and mental challenge. A group size of twelve is ideal, but overheads are high when you have to pay a tour leader and hire vehicles, so fifteen or sixteen is a better size.

'Long-haul flights were growing in the 1980s, and soon we were operating all over the world still using our own tour leaders. I hit on a formula of using guys straight from university who might previously have joined the Army on short commissions, typically in their early to mid-Twenties. We had them for a few years, before they hit thirty and decided to settle down. To start with there were few women tour leaders, as in some countries in the Middle East and Africa they couldn't do what we needed them to do.

'By 1990 Explore was probably the biggest adventure operator in Europe, but by then a lot of competitors had come along such as Intrepid, Gap Adventures, The Imaginative Traveller and Dragoman. Big tour operators such as Kuoni started to put more active stuff in their programmes, in what became known as "soft adventure".'

In 1993 the Package Travel Regulations, adopted by the European Commission, took effect in the UK. Tour operators became liable for parts of a package they might have washed their hands of before, such as activities or excursions organised by a third party. While package holiday operators were able to adapt fairly easily – taking greater care of health and safety at hotels, for example – the effect on adventure operators was more profound. Suddenly, a tour operator could be sued in a British court if something went wrong abroad.

'The Package Travel Regulations forced adventure operators to be licked into shape and become more professional, while some simply dropped out,' says Moore. 'We saw it as, "Whatever happens, it's our fault". It was easy for package holiday operators to cope, but not if you had a group on a bus or on camels in India. To hold us responsible for everything was totally unrealistic, but the adventure travel industry was fragmented when it came to lobbying politicians.'

Moore recalls one customer writing to *The Sunday Times* complaining about the tyres on their coach in the Swat Valley, in northern Pakistan. But operators were pleased when people wrote to the newspaper to support them, arguing that operators could only use whatever resources were available. 'The problem was that as the adventure travel business expanded, it started attracting people away from mainstream holidays where people expect everything they are promised,' explains Moore. 'But even a yak in Mongolia is subject to the Package Travel Regulations. The regulations didn't limit the destinations we operated to, but what we did when we got there. For example, we could no longer send people on a trip in a fishing boat unless it had ship-to-shore radio.'

The modern adventure travel industry started to take shape by the mid-1990s, with many trips becoming shorter, more European destinations not normally associated with the adventure concept, and an increase in the average age of customers. Soft adventure started to happen in our own back yard – just across the Channel – and leading operators later introduced family adventures.

Moore's direct involvement ended in 2000 when Explore was sold to a company called Holidaybreak, whose brands included short trip operator Superbreak and Eurocamp. It was later sold to faraway operator Cox & Kings, and changed hands for a third time in 2015 when acquired by Hotelplan, the owner of Inghams.

Unlike Explore, several companies were set up in London in the 1960s and 1970s with Antipodean connections. Contiki was formed by New Zealander John Anderson in 1961, the name recalling the Kon-Tiki expedition of 1947 crossing the Pacific by raft between South America and the Polynesian islands. But instead of hitting the Hippy Trail, Contiki operated coach camping trips around Europe, a role it still fulfils today despite diversification into other types of holidays and other parts of the world.

Australian Warren Sandral arrived in London in 1968 and became a driver for Contiki. In 1970 he started operating as North African Tours (NAT) to Morocco, Algeria and Tunisia, but as NAT the company became a mainstream operator of coach holidays to the Mediterranean and the ski slopes in the 1980s. 'I used to put up notices around Earls Court where the Aussies congregated, and in those days North Africa was the Wild West,' he recalls. 'But by the mid-1970s visa restrictions squeezed the Australian market, so we started to target Brits. It was mainly camping tours and skiing.'

Topdeck Travel was set up by 1973 operating double-deckers around Europe, and is still in operation today with more conventional coaches. Transit and Sundowners were among the other companies active during that period.

The history of Exodus goes back to 1974, making it possibly the longest established adventure tour operator still trading. What it called the Trans-Asia Overland had become a well-used route from Calais to Kathmandu using surfaced roads all the way, and it later started an overland London to Johannesburg route – 'a mere sixteen weeks of roadblocks, mud and dysentery'. Arriving in sixteen weeks was regarded as a triumph, with one tour taking twenty-one weeks to reach Johannesburg, including an ambush in Sudan on Christmas Day. By the 1980s, starting in Nepal, trekking had become a major speciality. By 1990 Exodus had taken an overland truck into China, something no other UK company had done for over a decade. 'China is just another destination now, but in 1990 this was more sensational than going to the moon or the South Pole,' says the company.

Philip Normington joined Exodus in 1978, and retains a consultancy role today. 'The London to Kathmandu route was a licence to print money as running costs were so low,' he says. 'There was very little regulation in those days, so anyone could set up an overland company. You could buy a scrap vehicle for £500 and refurbish it, and drivers' wages were very low as I can testify. You could fill up with fuel in Iran for just 1p a litre.

'Kathmandu was the destination as it was the furthest you could drive across Asia without encountering real difficulty. It was a lot less challenging than Africa, which had few surfaced roads and a lot of jungle. When I was a trainee driver, I flew out to Kathmandu and was sitting with other crew when we got a telex saying, "We can't send you any money for the trip – borrow from the passengers"! The passengers had to buy the food and do the cooking.'

Typical customers were English-speaking, sometimes on a gap year from professions such as accountancy or nursing. Bookings for London-Kathmandu dried up after the Iranian revolution, although Australians and New Zealanders still came in smaller numbers the other way. Africa became the main destination for Exodus, but like Explore it had to change because of the Package Travel Regulations.

'We had to start keeping to the advice offered by the Foreign and Commonwealth Office (FCO), whereas in the 1980s, if the FCO said don't go somewhere like Zaire, we went anyway,' says Normington. 'We started doing South America, where the political situation was improving and the roads were better. We stopped doing the old Overland route because of safety regulations and difficulties getting visas.

'We had done shorter trips from the start, including walking holidays in Morocco and Peru. By the late 1980s trekking was the biggest part of our business and as it was relatively expensive, we attracted a different type of customer. In the early days trekking meant camping, but "full service" camping with everything done for you. In Europe, and even in Nepal, we started going for fixed accommodation such as lodges.

'People today want their creature comforts and are more likely to complain when things go wrong, so we have to do risk assessments. Exodus still goes to unusual places, and it is now so much easier to reach them. Countries which were once so emotive are no longer so.'

Exodus' range of adventurous and active holidays now reaches all seven continents, and in 2004 the first dedicated Family Adventures brochure was launched. By this time the company had been sold to the big package holiday operator First Choice, and is now part of TUI.

Package holiday operators were swallowing up not only smaller competitors in the late 1990s, but also specialised companies such as Exodus. Nigel Jenkins, a founder of the Unijet company which was sold to First Choice, took control of First Choice's specialist division in 2004. 'Buying adventure operators made sense, as net margins are typically 5-6 per cent whereas on mainstream packages, they are only 2 per cent,' he explains. 'The idea was to buy up as many adventure companies around the world as we could, not necessarily to integrate them but to keep them autonomous. We bought operators such as The Adventure Company, Peregrine and Quark Expeditions, plus ski and school travel companies. Many of these brands survive, but not mass market brands such as Unijet. There is much more loyalty towards specialist brands, whereas the package holiday customer is mostly interested in price.'

Today's adventure travel industry is increasingly corporate in outlook and increasingly international, meaning a typical tour group could have half a dozen nationalities represented. Big companies such as Australia-based Intrepid Travel (which had a short-lived joint venture with TUI called Peak Adventure Travel Group) operate from many countries. Intrepid is one of the world's leading adventure operators, taking over 100,000 travellers a year to over one hundred countries and operating in twenty countries worldwide including the UK.

Adventure operators remain true to their principles of operating small group tours which interact with the local community, and in recent years a strong focus on sustainable travel has emerged. But as he looks at today's scene, Derek Moore – who is chairman of the Association of Independent Tour Operators – feels the spirit of the pioneering days has been diluted.

'I'm an un-reconstructed tour leader, but by the time we put Explore up for sale in 2000, I was spending too much time doing risk assessments, budgets and forecasts,' he says. 'Explore needed investment to take it to the next level, and it now hires people from other parts of the travel industry. Explore is a different animal nowadays, and as it has to function in the world of today it is a lot more like Kuoni. But if you look at the annual Adventure Travel Show in London, there are many small companies offering all kinds of activities. In some ways the industry has gone back to where it started, but without the hard edges.

'Many customers today are in their Fifties or Sixties. Young people want an adventure, but they wouldn't go in a Transit van to Morocco, and they aren't looking for cheap holidays any more. It was a master-stroke for Exodus, and then Explore, to start offering family adventures. Adventure travel is now far more diffuse, no longer a fringe business but part of the mainstream.'

However, a few operators are willing to offer more unusual destinations or activities, and one of these is the appropriately named Wild Frontiers. It was set up by travel writer Jonny Bealby in 1999 after epic journeys through some of the same places that inspired the Hippy Trail – Afghanistan and the Northwest Frontier province of Pakistan. He was struck by the total lack of tourism in this troubled region, seeking advice from a Pagan tribe called the Kalash who said they would welcome visitors.

To quote Wild Frontiers' website: 'On 11 September 2001, Jonny was actually with a group high in the Hindu Kush and, as isolated as they were, they didn't hear about the cataclysmic events in New York until 14 September. When they walked into a hotel in Chitral, and saw a newspaper with the headline "Doomsday for the USA", Jonny slumped in a chair and pondered darkly, "Doomsday for Wild Frontiers, more like!" As things transpired Jonny could not have been more wrong. Ironically, far from being the end of Wild Frontiers, this was really the beginning.'

Wild Frontiers has built its reputation in places many would consider off the tourist map. Although it now offers an unusual twist on destinations ranging from Europe to the Polar regions, Pakistan – shunned by most operators and more dangerous than when Wild Frontiers started – is still a major focus.

'After three epic journeys and writing three books, I decided that what I would most enjoy doing is taking tour groups,' explains Bealby. '9/11 put the kibosh on Pakistan for a while, but we are still taking groups there. We operated 120 tours to fifty-five countries in 2015, looking beneath the surface and not just taking photos of pretty scenery.

'Pakistan is a big country, with some areas more risky than others, but northern Pakistan is a true adventure travel playground with diverse people, wonderful scenery and good infrastructure. It reached its lowest point in 2014 with the school massacre in Peshawar, but that was a turning point with everyone galvanised to make it a safer and better place. We know the country very well and have good contacts there. We are not gung-ho, but we partner with the Control Risks Group and aid workers, and we make an assessment. We take advice from the Foreign Office, and we have a bespoke travel insurance policy that doesn't become null and void if the Foreign Office says don't go there.'

Bealby regards Iran as a major opportunity for adventure operators, as the country whose closure killed off the Hippy Trail opens up to tourism again after its nuclear accord with the West. With Syria and Libya dropping away even for the most hardened adventure operators, Iran has grown quickly to become Wild Frontiers' second biggest seller. Central Asia, Mongolia, the Caucasus and South America are other regions in growing demand.

Are there any other places considered just too dangerous to include? 'We have run trips to Iraqi Kurdistan, but even though we had bookings for 2016, we considered it was just not worth the risk,' says Bealby. 'It really is too close to where the action is.'

17

Life Coaching

Unsuspecting visitors to an English seaside hotel in November might stumble across something bizarre – a function room hosting a full-blown Christmas Day or New Year's Eve celebration. The revellers are all over sixty and they have come by coach, on what are marketed as Turkey and Tinsel breaks. Why people would want to have a Christmas or New Year experience in November is open to question, but rock-bottom prices are reason enough. November is a very quiet month for both coach tour operators and hotels – it's a question of using your assets.

Turkey and Tinsel breaks do reinforce a rather negative image of coach holidays, however, which means that people who might well enjoy them would never consider this option. But coach tours have been established for a century and are still important today, ranging from the budget break in the UK to a four- or five-star touring 'experience' in Europe or North America. Coaching is the only type of holiday organised by tour operators where the main destination is the UK rather than abroad, but as early as the 1920s, people were venturing across the Channel by coach.

Pioneers included the much loved Wallace Arnold, whose coaches were known affectionately as 'Wally's Trolleys'. A Leeds man called Robert Barr started organising day trips into the countryside in 1912 using a vehicle called a charabanc – essentially a wagon equipped with seats rather than a load of goods, open to the elements but providing an excellent view. Barr's vehicles acted as freight carriers from Monday morning to Friday evening, when seats were fitted for the weekend's jollities. The suspension was certainly not what a modern customer might expect as they were real bone shakers. By 1926, when he bought out the Wallace Arnold Tours business of Wallace Cunningham and Arnold Crowe, Barr already had twenty-five vehicles with the first covered coach not introduced until 1927. Destinations in the 1920s included Devon (a three-day journey from Leeds), Scotland and Wales, and in 1933 the first European tour was organised, to Germany.

By the outbreak of war Wallace Arnold was already a major tour operator, so resuming operations after the end of hostilities was relatively straightforward. The Barr family would remain in charge until the 1990s as Wallace Arnold maintained its position as one of the market leaders, picking up passengers from all over the country. Vehicles were steadily improved, with sun roofs introduced in the 1950s and taller coaches by the 1970s meaning much more luggage could be stowed underneath. By the 1990s, luxurious Grand Tourer coaches with generous leg-room made their debut. Wallace Arnold was much loved by not only customers but drivers, who also acted as couriers, many of whom worked for the company for much of their lives. At its sixtieth anniversary in 1986, Wallace Arnold celebrated with eighty-four-year-old Elsie Pullan who took her first tour as a twenty-five-year-old in 1926. She had been on holiday with the company almost every year ever since.

A man with one of the longest management careers in coaching is John King, who joined Wallace Arnold in 1964 for a ten-year stint, returning in 1985 after working for competitors including National Holidays. 'When I started you couldn't reach Torquay in a day from Leeds, and a lot of our holidays were touring rather than staying in one place for a week,' he says. 'In those days only one or two people in a typical street would have been abroad, but some customers who had travelled with us around the UK were prepared to risk going abroad with us too. We were also operating overnight coach holidays from Ostend to Spain, Italy, France, Yugoslavia and Austria. Hotels were three-star, with no private bathrooms. Even in the 1980s I felt we didn't need to offer private bathrooms, but by the 1990s they became essential.

'Until people started taking package holidays abroad, no one would ever have considered wanting a private bath in a hotel. In the 1960s there weren't many large hotels, and in some places – Rothesay in Scotland, for example – we put a coachload into three or four guest-houses. But if one guest-house served one rasher of bacon at breakfast and others served two, people would complain! All the changes were customer-driven, because of what they had experienced on package holidays – and those changes continued into the twenty-first century. But even today, many UK hotels are tired in comparison with those abroad. There may be more modern chain hotels, but they are soul-less.'

Wallace Arnold was one of a few large companies, but most coach tour operators were small and served a strictly local market. 'Coaching was a cottage industry, as you travelled with operators having a strong local identity,' says King. 'So when I started work at National Holidays in 1977, we set up a vast network of local pick-up points that gave us the appearance of being a local operator. And because you could also join our tours using the National Express network, we could claim tens of thousands of picking-up points all over the country.'

The biggest companies set up 'hub and spoke' operations, with local pick-up points feeding passengers into interchanges. Coaches would congregate here, and passengers and luggage (some of which would inevitably go astray) were exchanged between vehicles to continue their journeys. This meant that a choice of around fifty holidays might be available from a pick-up point in a village, a major selling point. For Wallace Arnold, these interchanges were at Leeds, South Mimms (by the M1/M25 north of London), Gordano (Bristol) and Dover.

National Holidays – not the same company that owns this name today – was formed in 1973 by the state-run National Bus Company (NBC), made up of many regional operators that also ran bus services. Fourteen NBC companies operated their own tours, so there was some resentment when National Holidays was imposed on them. A 'great deal of suspicion' was directed at King and others who had previously worked for arch-rival Wallace Arnold.

'National Holidays had only 75,000 passengers a year when I joined but became market leader with 325,000, but as it was state-owned we never knew if it made a profit,' says King. 'Wallace Arnold suffered badly as a result, going down from 180,000 passengers to only 60,000 when I went back in 1985. The Barr family was ready to pack it in, but I was head-hunted and brought in my own team so we could start with a clean sheet.'

Although Elsie Pullan had started taking coach tours aged twenty-five in 1926, the typical age range of the customer became progressively older as the century wore on. Younger people were more attracted to package holidays and coaching became saddled with the image of being for the over-Sixties, which it has never shaken off. 'I was told it was a dying market when I started in 1964, and if so then it is still dying more than fifty years later,' says King. 'Wallace Arnold's market was from fifty-five to dead, and that hasn't changed. But people's expectations have increased enormously. Eight- to ten-day holidays used to be the norm, and although eight-day holidays still exist, the vast majority are now for only five days.

'There have always been single people on tours because they are a good way of making friends, and a lot of them are widows. But single room supplements have always been a problem and that has got worse, as so few hotels are built with single rooms. Quite a few marriages have taken place between people who met on coach tours, some as old as ninety. Some coach drivers followed their fathers into the job, and they became passengers' guide, philosopher and friend, as Robert Barr used to say. Some passengers would book a tour when they knew a particular driver was on it, and some single ladies did become very friendly with the drivers.'

One of King's colleagues at Wallace Arnold and National Holidays was Stephen Barber, who in 2015 was director of coaching at trade association the Confederation of Passenger Transport (CPT). He feels the industry is in decline with a smaller number of local companies involved. A key event was the 'big bang' of Tory-inspired deregulation, when the whole of the UK's coach and bus industry was opened to competition in 1980. Until then a strict licensing system policed by traffic commissioners' courts had the effect of protecting established operators and denying would-be competitors entry, but deregulation was not the boon that many small companies might have expected.

'The glory days were in the 1950s and 1960s when there was low car ownership, and many people didn't see the benefit of flying,' says Barber. 'The licensing regime was very strict, but it did protect the many local and regional operators. Companies such as Bee-Line, Norfolk Motor Services, East Kent, Southdown, Hants & Dorset, Excelsior, Devon General, Salopia, Western Welsh, Midland Red and Eastern National banded together against newcomers. Cosmos was a big operator of European tours and was desperate to get into UK tours too, but never succeeded. Some operators got around the licensing restrictions by advertising tours starting in Calais.'

Under the old licensing system, applicants had to prove they could offer something different before getting approval, and established operators could easily undermine their plans. After 1980 local operators gained the freedom to operate whatever tours they wished, but the big companies also had much more freedom. A nationwide battle between Wallace Arnold and National raged, with many local firms going into decline. But some new operations also hit the road, an example being budget operator David Urquhart Travel which started in 1983.

'Deregulation sorted out the sheep from the goats, and gave everyone the ability to run a tour programme however good or bad,' says Barber. 'The CPT's Bonded Coach Holidays section still has over sixty members, but my advice to many small companies today is to stop running tours as they aren't making any money. Their major problem is that some big companies have gone into hotel ownership. If you own hotels you have to fill the beds and if tours are sold at a loss, so be it. The rest of the industry can't compete on price, but one option is to go up-market to include better hotels and more excursions.

'The market has changed, and a lot of people who would have previously gone on a coach holiday wouldn't go on one today as there are so many alternatives. What hasn't changed is the average age of the coach tour customer, which is still seventy-plus with three ladies to every man. Another problem is that British seaside resorts which were once the bedrock of the business have gone into decline – places like Margate. Many resorts haven't kept up-to-date – what do you do when it rains? If you look at Torquay, most of the hotels are like rabbit warrens because they have expanded into neighbouring properties. Their prices have been pushed down so there is no investment, and they look and feel tired.

'Many destinations have changed. Since the independence movement, English people don't see Scotland as such a friendly place. There has been a resurgence to Ireland since the end of "The Troubles", but prices have shot up. There are few Irish people working in hotels, and the magic of Ireland has suffered as it becomes much like anywhere else. Ryanair hasn't helped, as it is now so cheap to fly there and hire a car.

'Coach operators have started to specialise to get more people on board, with holidays focusing on line dancing, gardening and other activities. The traditional eight-day holiday is disappearing with older people travelling on short breaks midweek, and some younger people travelling at weekends to special events. But the top end of the market – people who used to travel in a jacket and tie on Wallace Arnold holidays to Torquay – has disappeared.

'When they reach about fifty-five, some people pass through a sort of golden archway when they will start to enjoy a coach holiday,' adds Barber. 'There are no more holiday decisions to make and you are content to follow the herd. There are some wonderful vehicles on coach tours and a higher standard in some hotels, although congestion on the roads is getting worse. There is a drip-feed of people who may still go on package holidays, but will do five days on a coach as a second holiday.

'But what has really hammered the coaching business is the popularity of cruising, especially now that cruise lines offer coach connections [Cruise Connect has fifty pick-up points for customers of P&O Cruises, Cunard and Princess Cruises.] People used to have to travel to airports or ports to join a cruise, but now they come to you. On a cruise, people have a nice bedroom that they don't need to change during the holiday – the world comes to them. The disadvantages of a coach holiday are that you have to move around, and the standard of hotels. With cruising, as with coaching, you are in a secure environment with like-minded people.'

The battle between Wallace Arnold and National Holidays was to rage for many years, but National changed ownership in 1986 as part of the privatisation of the National Bus Company and later adopted the name Shearings.

'At regular intervals in the mid-1990s, Wallace Arnold tried to buy Shearings and Shearings tried to buy Wallace Arnold,' says Barber. 'In 1997 the family trust owning Wallace Arnold decided to sell to the venture capitalists, which decided to buy Shearings as well and put the two together in 2005. Sadly, they killed the goose that laid the golden egg as the Wallace Arnold name disappeared in a couple of years. They put two and two together, but only made three. It was sad, because according to market research Wallace Arnold was known as the roast beef and Yorkshire pudding of coaching, while Shearings was the burger and chips. At the merger, the combined coach fleet of the two companies was well over 400 – today, it is about 250. No one else has grown to take that lost business, although Leger Holidays took a lot of Wallace Arnold's Continental passengers.'

Many loyal customers regarded dropping the brand as a betrayal, although there are still eight travel agencies owned by Shearings trading as Wallace Arnold. Its disappearance certainly contributed to Leger's growth, with Leger also taking families to Disneyland Paris and operating a major programme of battlefield tours.

The origins of today's biggest company, Shearings, are highly convoluted, as it has grown out of mergers between several smaller companies all based in the North West of England, often regarded as the heartland of coach tours. Herbert Shearing set up his company in Oldham in 1919, and as it grew through various changes of ownership over the next sixty years, one of its main competitors was Wigan-based Smiths. This was founded even earlier in 1914, and by the 1970s it was operating as Smiths Happiway Spencers following mergers with other firms (Happiway was run by package holiday pioneer Ted Langton in the 1930s). Mergers were common because of the strict licensing regime, as small local companies joined together to offer a wider range of tours.

Paul Sawbridge started with Smiths in 1969 when it also operated package holidays by air, mainly to campsites in Spain. 'Licences were valuable commodities, much like landing slots at Heathrow today, but they could not just be sold on and as a result there were numerous mergers and acquisitions,' he explains. 'Profit margins were high as a result of the restricted capacity, and this golden period of profitability lasted from the late 1960s until the 1980 Transport Act put an end to the licensing regime. The need to merge to gain additional licences resulted in some inordinately long names including Smiths Happiway

Spencers and Shearings Pleasureways Ribblesdale. By late 1981 there were four large players, all based in the North of England – National Holidays and Wallace Arnold in Yorkshire, and Shearings Ribblesdale and Smiths Happiways in the North West.'

In 1982 Smiths Happiway Spencers became part of Associated Leisure, a public company, gaining major financial muscle. '1984 was a tumultuous year when Shearings almost collapsed,' recalls Sawbridge. 'But Associated Leisure stepped in and took over Shearings to merge it with Smiths Happiways, and shortly afterwards, Associated Leisure was itself taken over by Pleasurama plc. In 1985, the new Smiths Shearings brand was in operation. It became clear that the National Bus Company was to be broken up, so in 1986 we purchased National Holidays.'

More changes in ownership followed as Pleasurama was taken over by Mecca Leisure and Mecca was taken over by the Rank Organisation, with the Shearings name being adopted for all operations. A management buyout from Rank happened in 1996, and the Shearings Group now includes value brand National Holidays, Caledonian Holidays and around fifty Bay Hotels and Coast & Country Hotels. Sawbridge left Shearings to start a new company, Alfa Travel, in 1990. It now has forty-six coaches and twenty-one Leisureplex hotels, and has grown to take around 100,000 people on coach holidays every year – proof that there's still room for a medium-sized company.

A colleague from Smiths days, and still at Alfa today, is Neil McMurdy. He comments that coach tours were well established by the 1930s, but had to suspend operations during the war when vehicles were used to carry troops and workers. 'The 1950s saw the blossoming of coach holidays as operators started investing money in their fleets and the restrictions on fuel and rationing eased,' says McMurdy. 'The 1960s saw the speed limit for coaches raised, and with the development of motorways it was possible for coaches to go from Lancashire to Cornwall in one day and not require an overnight stop. Since the 1990s there has been contraction in the UK coach building industry, and an increase in higher specification coaches built in Europe. Itineraries have become more inventive, but the principle has remained unchanged since the 1930s.'

Another company that made its debut after deregulation was Grand UK Holidays, set up in 1984 by Paul Bennett who previously worked for Saga, itself a major coach tour operator in its earlier days. Grand UK operates exclusively for the over-55s with most of its customers being considerably older. Sales director Harold Burke is confident about the future of coach holidays although Grand UK has had to adapt with rail journeys, air holidays, European river cruises and self-drive breaks at its own hotels.

'In the 1970s, lots of people took coach tours during Wakes Weeks in industrial areas when whole towns went on holiday, and the age profile was younger,' he says. 'The over-55s now have time to go on holidays all year round, but are more used to taking holidays individually. You have to build a tour around a special event or special interest to persuade them to leave the car at home. Probably only about 20 per cent of people turning fifty-five would now consider a coaching holiday, but while the market has shrunk in some respects, it has grown in others. People take more short breaks now. About 20 per cent of our programme is to Europe but it's not all by coach, and river cruising is now very popular. The standard of hotels has improved and entertainment is more varied. The traditional coach tour customer was happy with a singer, a comedian or a quiz, but we now have more entertainment themed tours such as Gilbert and Sullivan.'

John King now runs dancing breaks as KingsHill Holidays, but while coach tours were the norm when this started in 2000, people now drive themselves to hotels. 'Coaching is in decline, and if you put aside National Holidays who are the Aldi or Lidl of the business and the market leaders, it is difficult to identify other operators of substantial size,' he says. 'Coaching has always been the poor relation of the travel industry, and getting media coverage has always been a struggle. But it never bothered me that it wasn't regarded as glamorous.'

The global connection

Most coach tour companies had their roots in regional operations, concentrating on UK holidays with European tours added almost as an afterthought. Even in 1991, research commissioned by Wallace Arnold showed that while nearly two million people were taking coach tours at home, the number taking a tour abroad was only around 800,000.

But soon after the Second World War, a different type of coach tour operator started with Europe as the main destination, some having no UK tours at all – a situation sometimes dictated by licensing restrictions. These companies were based mainly in the London area, drawing their customers not just from the UK, but from English-speaking countries all over the world including the US, Canada, South Africa, Australia and New Zealand.

One was called, appropriately, Global. It was a travel agency selling lots of holidays for Blue Cars, a coach tour operator owned by Ted Langton who also became one of the pioneers of package holidays by air. Langton had started selling UK coach tours in the 1930s using the name Happiway, but when he started European tours, in 1934, he joined forces with a Belgian company called Les Cars Bleu. Blue Cars brought people into Britain as well as taking them to Europe, and by 1948 it was attracting passengers from the US. Langton sold Blue Cars in 1953, when he launched Universal Sky Tours.

Global soon started its own tours. Sidney Perez, who joined in 1950, says: 'After the war, there was a great public hunger for travel, particularly by coach and train. However, the Government imposed exchange control restrictions on foreign travel and when booking through a travel company, a V Form was required that stated the value of services paid in a foreign currency. At various times the travel allowance was reduced and in 1952 the value was just £25. To cater for this new travel restriction, Global revamped its coach tour programme within twenty-four hours based on the lower travel allowance – and bookings boomed.'

Global opened offices in Australia, South Africa and the US to bring tourists to Europe via London, but plenty of passengers were British too with a holiday in the early 1950s typically costing 29 guineas (£30.45) for a twelve-night tour to Switzerland. This country was not only a desirable holiday destination but the starting place of two large travel companies that are still market leaders today, Kuoni (see chapter eight) and Globus.

Eyewitness: James Saunders
A professional tour manager based in Canada, London-born Saunders works for Globus, the parent company of Cosmos Tours and Cruises.

I've been in this business for nearly thirty years and I've seen a lot of change in the customers, as when I started we had a lot of World War 2 veterans who wanted to visit the places in Europe where they had fought. They were easy customers to deal with because they were happy just to have a hotel room, never mind a hotel room with free wifi. Years ago they would be happy to save money by booking a tour not including breakfasts, but now they would complain.

By the early 1990s, people were becoming more sophisticated. I used to get a lot of questions, but now people do more research before they go. But in some ways, people today pay less attention. I've been doing city sightseeing tours while customers are playing games like Candy Crush on their iPads.

The tours we offer have improved in quality, especially the standard of coaches and hotels. Gone are the days when we used "Mama and Papa" hotels as people prefer chain hotels such as Best Western these days, and a sole proprietor hotel can't make it any more. Food is better too, as a sausage in a bun is no longer considered a good lunch. People want more leisurely tours nowadays, but they don't realise what huge distances have to be covered in a country like Canada. For tours to be made cheaper, they have to be made shorter.

Attractions are much better run than they used to be, but people's expectations are much higher. The quality of museum displays has to be good now that you can see everything online. Things are more politically correct, and visiting the indigenous people of America is now a cultural experience.

This profession is a way of life, and I am still in touch with people I guided in the 1980s and 1990s. Very few people do this job as a first career, but it appeals to some who have retired or are ex-airline cabin crew.

Globus has been owned by the Mantegazza family since starting in 1918 with boat trips around Lake Lugano, buying a fleet of coaches in 1928. The UK office was opened in 1961 and the company was called Cosmos, at a time when space exploration was under way. Right from the start Cosmos operated package holidays by air as well as coach tours, and was to become the fourth biggest package holiday operator. Coach tours, drawing customers from across the world, were always more profitable, but the Mantegazza family set up a UK airline, Monarch, and stuck by package holidays through thick and thin for over fifty years. Only in 2014 did they finally sell off the package holiday side, to venture capitalists, and the Cosmos name disappeared from package holidays. But Cosmos Tours and Cruises continues under the Mantegazza family's control, including major coach tour programmes to Europe and North America.

Global decided to broaden its appeal with a keenly priced programme aimed at the British customer, which was launched in 1957 as Global Overland. Tony John joined that year as an office boy, but was soon acting as a courier before moving into management. Overland proved a great success and John was to stay in the coach tour business all his working life.

'I was creative – I could look at a map and come up with ideas,' he says. 'Coaches would only do about 200–300 km a day in the pre-motorway era, and it would take half a day to negotiate the

Arlberg pass – scenic, but a slog. People took the train to Dover and then a coach from Ostend, and it was very successful. But Cosmos was the demon entity that haunted us. It had started up suddenly and grown very quickly, finding hotels in places we had never heard of, and their coaches were good. We used to bribe the baggage porters at Ostend to tell us their passenger numbers, in return for a jar of Nescafe and a packet of sausages!'

John moved on to Southbound in 1967 but returned to Global in 1976, during a period of great change. Chain hotels such as Holiday Inn were introduced, and air suspension and air conditioning made coaches more comfortable. Longer, three-axle coaches joined the fleet, but John says: 'I was against larger coaches, which turned a convivial experience with forty-eight passengers into a crowd, with up to sixty-five. Operating costs and the purchase price were higher, and the benefits these coaches introduced were marginal. You couldn't use them in some cities where they wouldn't fit down narrow streets. Maybe I'm old-fashioned, but the on-board experience has to be good if you're travelling up to 600 km a day.'

Inbound business was still important but Overland's business went down, as more people started flying. Coach tours were always more profitable than package holidays, but when Global was sold to Harry Goodman's International Leisure Group in 1985, the aim was to build package holiday volume not develop coach tours. The Global brand was sold on to Wallace Arnold, which soon closed it down. John moved on to Insight International, and worked for brands owned by the Travel Corporation until his retirement in 2007.

He is keenly aware that coaches, like aircraft, cruise ships and large hotels, may undermine some of the places tourists set out to see. 'I would go somewhere, think it was fantastic, and then start to think about how we could accommodate a coach party of forty-eight,' he says. 'The next year we would put two coaches on the same tour, and the grumbles would start. Places like Lucerne, where you can get one hundred coaches with over 4,000 people arriving at once, have been ruined. But I don't see these places ever trying to limit numbers.

'I don't see a great future for coach tours, as they are getting more expensive and cruising has drawn a lot of people away. Drivers' hours regulations have been around since the 1970s, but in the 2000s they were tightened up massively with new regulations for time on duty, not just time at the wheel. Companies catering for the inbound market have a good future, but the British market is limited. There are some successful niches, however – like battlefield tours.'

The three main brands of John's former employers, Travel Corporation, serve mainly the inbound market – Trafalgar Tours, Insight and Contiki. Trafalgar debuted in 1947 as Industrial Recreational Services, starting European coach tours in 1958 with a 21-day 'Young Commonwealth Special' and changing its name to the more lyrical Trafalgar in 1959. Its first overseas offices were in South Africa, with other English-speaking markets following in the 1970s. Tours were usually for two or three weeks as people from far away tried to pack in as much as possible, spending up to five weeks touring Europe. By the 1990s Trafalgar had added North America and South Africa as destinations, and today Travel Corporation operates to many countries around the world.

Gavin Tollman, Trafalgar's chief executive, says: 'Our business model is really no different to the 1950s – getting like-minded people from English speaking countries together for a journey of discovery. But what we do while travelling has changed. Our guests want not just the must-see sights but to get below the surface of a country. Authenticity is the word, and this trend started in the mid-2000s. The median age of people on our tours is fifty-two, and the fastest percentage growth is of people in their mid-Forties. They don't want one night in each place but a more in-depth experience.'

Trafalgar's 'At Leisure' tours include a minimum of two nights in each place, while an example of the in-depth experiences on offer is a meeting with a member of country singer Johnny Cash's family on the Tastes and Sounds of the South tour in the USA. 'Hidden Journeys' is another new Trafalgar range, to offbeat destinations, while 'Be My Guest' is a series of dining experiences with local families or suppliers. 'We don't see our travellers as a group, but as forty individuals,' says Tollman. 'These are not tours but guided experiences.'

Contiki started as a coach-camping operator for the 18–35 age group in the 1960s. It continues to serve that age bracket today although most of its very international groups stay in budget accommodation or Contiki-owned properties, including chateaux and villas. Travel Corporation director David Hosking, who joined Contiki in 1975, says: 'Our customers have always been young people having fun, but the more simplistic way of touring doesn't sell any more. We now get Mexicans and Brazilians as well as Americans, Australians and British, and it's all about how we connect with our audience now that over half use mobile phones for online booking. Blogging and social media are critical – young people will believe their peers, so having them talk about us is more important than us talking about ourselves.'

The biggest growth area for tour operators is still the over-Fifties, however – often newly retired people who have what Insight International boss John Boulding describes as 'fifteen golden years' before old age and possible ill health catch up with them. Insight is the premium operator in the Travel Corporation stable, with a maximum group size of forty (meaning much more leg-room in the same size coach as a 49- or 53-seater). It also offers a la carte dining, four- and five-star hotels and similar 'immersive' experiences to Trafalgar, such as meeting an olive grower in Umbria or an art expert at the Rijksmuseum in Amsterdam. 'The Baby Boomers born in the 1950s and 1960s don't want to be herded around, and are the largest consumer sector that has ever existed,' says Boulding. 'The proportion of retired people is increasing every year, and those that have sold their shares and seen their kids leave home are all potential customers. This is absolutely the prime time to tick off your bucket list.'

Coaching's Days in the Sun

For a brief period in the 1980s, package holidays by coach to beach and skiing destinations became all the rage. This type of holiday was particularly popular from the UK provinces which didn't then have the wide choice of flights available in the South, and prices by coach were very keen. The downside was an overnight journey of at least twenty-four hours to reach the Costa Brava in Spain, but rather less to reach the South of France or the ski slopes.

Although this type of holiday started in the 1950s before the era of cheap air travel, at least one and possibly two nights had to be spent en route before the motorway network was developed. Coaches were not designed to travel long distances in a day, but by the 1980s more luxurious vehicles were available with on-board toilets, drinks machines and video entertainment.

The biggest company was NAT Holidays, which had started life as adventure operator North African Tours and was known by its sometimes jealous detractors as 'Never Again Tours'. It diversified into camping and later skiing, but then saw a major opportunity to introduce sunshine holidays to campsites, mobile home sites and hotels.

Warren Sandral, NAT's charismatic Australian boss, says: 'These holidays were very cheap, and I remember doing a £10 holiday offer with Lunn Poly that had hundreds of people queuing outside their shops. We were the first company to bring double-deck Neoplan Skyliner coaches to the UK, which could do one million km in a year. When people heard there was a toilet on the coach, they thought we were joking.'

NAT was already big in skiing, and when it acquired ski operator Neilson it became even bigger. But in 1989 Sandral sold up to Granada, with NAT passing almost immediately to Harry Goodman's International Leisure Group (ILG). One of NAT's rivals, Sunscene Holidays, also became part of ILG and was caught up in ILG's spectacular collapse (see chapter seven). Sunscene started in the early 1980s, when it was selling coach-camping holidays from Scotland to the South of France costing only £69 for ten days or £82 for two weeks, based on four sharing a tent. Its owner Paul Cresswell, who also ran a coaching operation in Leicester, says it attracted many people going abroad for the first time.

'The campsites were very basic, just rows of tents, a cafeteria and an amenities block,' he says. 'Coaches would leave early in the morning and get to their destination by midday the following day if it was the South of France, or about 2pm if it was Lloret de Mar. We also operated to Rimini in Italy and Peniscola south of Barcelona, and these journeys really stretched passengers. They were all as happy as Larry going down, and when the sun came up and they got their first glimpse of the sea, it really lifted their spirits. But on the way back home, they were not happy people.

'We started Sunscene for families who could just scratch together enough money to afford a foreign holiday which was cheap, cheerful and always next to the sea. People who were more used to taking holidays on the Ayrshire coast really were innocents abroad, and sunburn was a big problem especially if they fell asleep after drinking. We used to employ three girls from St John Ambulance to look after them.'

There was, says Cresswell, an 'aggravation factor' about this type of holiday. People gradually moved away from camping into hotels, but prices had to go up. The price war between package holiday operators in the mid-1980s started to kill off the overnight coach market, and there wasn't much left of it by the time low-cost airlines came on the scene. But you can still take this type of holiday, as prices from provincial towns can still be attractive compared to flying, especially in high season for a family with lot of luggage. Siesta International, which dates from 1980, is the market leader.

NAT Holidays and Sunscene both disappeared after ILG went bust in 1991, but not before ILG's visionary boss Harry Goodman had tried to set up a network of scheduled coach services across the Continent called Coach Europe, to mirror his Air Europe operation. Services to Poland did start operating, but Coach Europe never got beyond the embryo stage.

18

The Rail Way

Railways created mass tourism in the nineteenth century, and are seeing a revival in the twenty-first. But despite the opening of the Channel Tunnel in 1994 and the growing number of high-speed routes in Europe and parts of Asia, railways are not involved in organised tourism from a British point of view. While some people use Eurostar and other high-speed networks to get to their destinations quickly, the vast majority go on gently paced tours to enjoy the scenery and culture, and to have an experience akin to the grand era of leisurely rail holidays.

Many British seaside resorts owe their existence to the frenzy of railway construction in the 1840s. Suddenly it was possible for people who lived sometimes only a short distance from the coast to glimpse the sea for the first time, at first mainly for day trips but then for longer holidays too. Resorts such as Blackpool used to welcome dozens of special trains every summer day, bringing workers from grimy industrial areas. 'Wakes Weeks' were born as whole towns laid down their tools for a few days, and before car ownership became widespread in the 1960s, most went on holiday by train. The heyday came in the post-war period when everyone had a legal right to holidays with pay. On rail routes through Devon it was estimated that twenty times the number of trains ran on summer Saturdays, compared to a normal weekday.

Trains were also widely used for holidays to the continent, despite the then very formidable barrier of the English Channel. Bradshaw's tourist guides and railway timetables, recently made famous again by the *Great Railway Journeys* TV series presented by Michael Portillo, were first produced in the 1850s with editions covering Europe following in the 1880s. The reprint of the 1913 *Continental Railway*

Guide is a delight, including advertisements for ferry routes, resorts, hotels and tour operators such as Henry Lunn Ltd, better known as a skiing pioneer but now advertising rail tours as far afield as Russia (25 guineas, via Denmark and Finland).

Then, as now, most people going on holiday by train travelled independently rather than on a package, often with tickets and hotel reservations provided by Thomas Cook. But tour operators soon got in on the act, and by the 1950s they were booking rail-based resort holidays as far away as the South of France, Italy and Spain. Today, you can reach France by Eurostar in just over one hour from London – but picture how much of an obstacle the channel used to be. Dover Marine station was the main transit point, where you had to haul your luggage off the train and up a ramp to board the ferry, doing the same thing in reverse a couple of hours later in France or Belgium. But before flying and the private car became commonplace, the only alternative was the coach and many people preferred the extra comfort of the train.

The 1962 brochure of Swans Tours sets out typical holiday journeys, via Newhaven rather than Dover. Departure from Victoria station in London was at 09.30, with the ferry reaching Dieppe at 14.50. Paris was reached at 18.08 in time for dinner, with a departure at 19.45 reaching Barcelona at 13.00 the next day. An onward journey by coach would get you to Benidorm by 17.30, but if you wanted to go to Mallorca you had to wait in Barcelona for the 22.00 ferry, reaching Palma at 08.00 on the third day, nearly forty-eight hours after leaving London! With the journey time by air to any of these Spanish destinations coming down to two hours within a few years, holidays by rail were shunted into the sidings.

Panorama Holidays, which grew into a package holiday operator, started by selling holidays to British Railways employees who had concessionary tickets. Ten-day rail holidays to the Costa Brava cost from eleven guineas in 1963, and you could add a night in Paris with lunch, dinner and sightseeing tour for £4. But despite the hardships rail holidays were cheaper in the early days of air travel, and as late as 1972 Global Overland was organising 20,000 rail holidays a year claiming that they had a bright future. One reason, said Global, was that 'you can't dance all the way on air journeys as you can on our train to Italy!'

The railways themselves organised holidays, with British Railways setting up Golden Rail, the Italian state rail company owning British tour operator Citalia, and French rail operator SNCF setting up French Travel Service, while also operating motorail car-carrying trains from Calais. Bill Smallwood, who now owns French Travel Service, joined

SNCF in the late 1960s when it operated a string of holiday villages and hotels mainly along the Côte d'Azur.

'SNCF used the villages to fill up the trains, and used to run specials to Nice from Calais, Amsterdam, Brussels and Germany,' he recalls. 'We chartered special trains from Victoria to Folkestone for six hundred people and took their luggage for them, with dinner and breakfast on the train before you got to Nice by 10.30 a.m., and a choice of sleeper or couchette. We were charging only £50 for ten days' full-board including connecting trains from any British Railways station. People came year after year although you could fly to Spain in a couple of hours, but there weren't many air packages to France. By the 1980s it started to drop off, as air packages were becoming cheaper and more widely available.'

French Travel Service was sold off and later closed down, but revived in 1992 a couple of years before opening of the Channel Tunnel. This led to a revival of interest in rail holidays, with many city break companies using Eurostar for Paris, Brussels and other Belgian cities. When the internet made it easy to book simple breaks yourself, French Travel Service switched to more complex itineraries. Now it is expanding again, adding holidays to Germany, Holland, Italy and Spain for 2016.

In a reversal of the situation fifty or sixty years ago, rail holidays are now more expensive than air packages. A four-night break in Barcelona costs from £429 in 2016 – and despite high-speed travel all the way with a change of stations in Paris, it still takes nearly all day to get there. Nor could high-speed rail journeys be considered scenic – you don't see much of the countryside at nearly 200 mph. 'Our clients tend to be retired, and have flexibility,' says Smallwood. 'Eurostar is very expensive if you can't choose when you travel, but we avoid peak time departures.'

High-speed rail (generally considered at least 150 mph), started in Europe in 1981, France leading the way with TGVs (Trains a Grand Vitesse). Spain also has a big network, and with high-speed routes also available in Italy, Germany, Holland and some other countries, Britain lags far behind. Our first purpose-built, high-speed line from London to Folkestone didn't open until 2007, thirteen years after Eurostar started by using existing lines on this side of the Channel. The HS2 high-speed route from London to Birmingham won't open before 2026.

Eurostar quickly became established as the preferred means of transport from London to Paris and Brussels, winning even more traffic from airlines after 2007 when journey times were cut to around two hours. Direct trains also operate to Lyon, Avignon and Marseille, and to Alpine resorts in winter. Eurostar is introducing new trains which can operate to other countries, with Amsterdam services due to start in 2017 followed possibly by Germany and Switzerland. German Railways (DB) has yet to realise its ambition to operate from London, and a challenge faced by both operators is that on routes such as Germany, it is still faster – and cheaper – to fly.

Eurostar is upbeat about the appeal of high-speed rail, which many people prefer because of its lower carbon footprint compared to flying. But despite a small increase to 10.4 million passengers in 2014, this figure is less than half what Eurostar expected to be carrying when services started in 1994. While the drive-on Shuttle has proved a success, rail freight operating through the tunnel has also been a failure.

Eurostar's hope of reaching over twenty million passengers a year by 2015 included the very costly mistake of building trains to operate overnight sleeper trains from Scotland, Wales and the West Country through to Paris, and also from London to Frankfurt and Amsterdam, which never went into service. It also built extra trains to operate daytime trains from Scotland, northern England and Birmingham to Paris and Brussels, which likewise never started. Journey times from anywhere north of London to Paris or Brussels are not competitive with flying, a major factor for the all-important business travel market that planners failed to recognise. Eurostar has not overcome its image of being a London-centred operation, which won't change even when new high-speed lines are built in Britain.

The return of luxury

The year after the first high-speed train ran in Europe, a very different train service started which would revive the concept of luxury tours by rail. This was a restored Pullman train, the Venice Simplon-Orient-Express, the start of a dynasty which now covers several countries and has inspired similar, if less expensive trains all over the world.

There's something essentially 'naughty' about quaffing a glass of champagne and tucking into eggs benedict for breakfast as your Pullman train heads through the suburbs of London, while thousands of grey-faced commuters pack onto standing-room-only trains travelling in the opposite direction. This is central to the appeal of luxury trains, which are now incorporated into tour itineraries throughout the world. You are joining an exclusive club harking back to the golden era of rail travel, before airlines opened up travel to the masses, when you are on the inside looking smugly out.

The *Orient Express* occupies a romantic platform in our imagination, largely due to Agatha Christie's novel *Murder on the Orient Express* and films derived from it. When the original train first ran in 1883 it operated from Paris to Romania, where passengers joined another service to reach Varna in Bulgaria then sailed across the Black Sea to Constantinople, now Istanbul. The *Orient Express* was much celebrated with the king of Romania and Ottoman sultan waving it off, and was known as 'The Train of Kings, the King of Trains'.

In 1921 it began running right through to Istanbul, with a journey time of fifty-six hours from Paris, crossing six frontiers. Its reputation for mystery, spying and intrigue started before Christie's novel appeared in 1934, when it was operating to Venice via the Simplon tunnel under the Alps, for onward travel via Eastern Europe. Sleeping cars ran from Calais for the convenience of British high society. But after the Second World War, with much of Europe in ruins and air travel becoming more popular, the *Orient Express* went into decline. Migrant workers and backpackers were the main passengers when it ceased in 1977.

It took a lot of money and imagination to relaunch it, but when the *Venice Simplon-Orient-Express* (VSOE) started running in 1982 it was a triumph for James Sherwood, who had made his fortune with a company called Sea Containers. He bought and restored some of the 1920s Pullman carriages to start a regular service from Calais and Paris to Venice, with occasional departures to many other cities. The original *Orient Express* didn't have a connecting service in Britain, and the *Night Ferry*, which ran between 1936 and 1980, was the only train with through carriages to the Continent before Eurostar, carriages being shunted onto a ferry. But Sherwood also acquired some British Pullman carriages to run from London to Folkestone, passengers continuing by sea.

The *VSOE* has proved to be a major success story, proving that there are plenty of people prepared to pay the high prices (from £2,735 for four days in 2016 including one night on board, two nights in Venice and return flight). The company, then known as Orient-Express Hotels and now known as Belmond, later launched luxury trains, hotels and river cruises around the world.

The *British Pullman* (as it became known) continues to take passengers down to Folkestone, while also operating luxury day trips to many other places. Two more trains were added in Britain, the *Northern Belle* and ultra-luxurious *Royal Scotsman*, while it also launched the *Eastern & Oriental Express* between Bangkok and Singapore, and the *Hiram Bingham* (named after the explorer) between Cusco and Machu Picchu in Peru. A luxury train in Australia was not a success, but in 2016 the first new train for several years joins the company's roster when the *Grand Hibernian* starts in Ireland.

The *VSOE* was the catalyst that inspired many new – or revived – tourist trains around the world, although some have more modest standards and are therefore more affordable. South Africa's *Blue Train* started in 1946, but was upgraded in 1997. The *Palace on Wheels* started in 1982, the same year as the *VSOE*, and was the first of several luxury tourist trains in India. Sometimes, as here, the train offered a comfortable way of travelling between major sights in a country with poor roads and (then) a poor standard of air services. In other countries, especially Canada and Australia, the prime attraction is scenery.

Canada's *Rocky Mountaineer* started in 1990, while Australian rail operators revived historic trains such as *The Ghan* (named after Afghan camel drivers who opened up the outback), which now runs all the way from Adelaide to Darwin via Alice Springs. Many countries now have at least one tourist train of high standard, others including Rovos Rail's *Pride of Africa*, and the *Golden Eagle* running through Russia and Central Asia. But there remain comparatively few in Europe, and none of note in the US.

Tour operators were fairly slow to start incorporating rail journeys into their itineraries, but in recent years these have become common and often offer passengers a relaxing break as part of a hectic tour mainly by air and coach. One of the first to see the potential, even before Sherwood, was Philip Morrell, whose early career was spent organising package holidays for Thomson but who left in 1978 to form his own company, Voyages Jules Verne.

He not only used rail travel as part of his tours but, in a publicity coup, organised a train trip all the way from London to Hong Kong as one of his first ventures in 1979 – the *Central Kingdom Express*. In his autobiography *Return Ticket Home*, he describes a lively scene at London's Victoria station where a Coldstream Guards band gave passengers a send-off, with lots of journalists and TV crews watching. There might have been only eighteen passengers travelling on a drab, ordinary British Rail train, but the station announcer called out stops on their journey including Paris, Berlin, Moscow, Ulan Bator and Beijing.

Voyages Jules Verne became a major escorted tour operator with rail travel among its unusual ideas, which Morrell eventually sold to Kuoni (see chapter fifteen). 'When I left Thomson, I saw trains as a different means of romantic travel and also came up with a Cape to Cairo itinerary and the Centenary Orient Express tour in 1983,' he says. 'Voyages Jules Verne was all about journeys, not package tours.

I did things that appeared to be too difficult to organise and which didn't make money, and we appealed primarily to travellers.'

Today a growing number of companies specialise in rail tours all over the world, using not only dedicated tourist trains but often ordinary rail services, which are much better value and offer a different experience. Some have romantic names (Amtrak's long-distance American trains such as the *Southwest Chief* or *Coast Starlight*, for example) while others are for the more adventurous, especially in developing countries. An experienced courier accompanies you throughout, although a few tour operators also put together tailor-made rail holidays for independent travellers, mainly in Europe.

Ffestiniog Travel is one of the oldest established, being founded in 1974 and owned by a charitable trust which supports the Ffestiniog and Welsh Highland narrow gauge steam railways in North Wales. Although it operates a few rail tours in faraway countries such as India and Burma (Myanmar), most of its itineraries are in Europe including little visited countries such as Moldova and rural Romania. The company with the most extensive programme is Great Rail Journeys, with tours all over the world from England to Germany and from America to Vietnam. Nearly all holidays to Europe start with Eurostar from London, and it also offers 'No Fly' holidays by rail and either river boats or ocean-going ships.

The number of people taking rail tours has increased enormously in the twenty-first century, helped by favourable media coverage and negative publicity about security and other delays at airports. Ex-politician Michael Portillo has played a major role, fronting the BBC2 series starting with *Great British Rail Journeys* in 2010, *Great Continental Rail Journeys* in 2012 and *Great American Rail Journeys* in 2016. Portillo, a former Conservative minister of transport, summed up the appeal of rail travel at a presentation for European rail ticket agency Voyages-SNCF in 2015: 'Travel should be a sociable experience. I don't expect to meet people on a plane, but on a train I do. My tip is to carry a picnic – uncork your wine, and offer it to the people around you.'

Thomas Cook, whose first trip was a train excursion for teetotallers in 1841, might have agreed – but not with the wine!

Where Do We Go From Here?

Tour operators face four big challenges as we head towards 2020, and they should all be of major concern to anyone who enjoys foreign holidays. In some ways we have never had it so good; in other ways, some very harsh times might be already here. The world is our oyster yet parts of it are, literally, bad. But whatever the outlook, we are highly unlikely to stop travelling. What could change is where we go, and how we set about booking it. In a worst case scenario, we could be putting our safety and security at risk if we make the wrong choices.

Crystal ball gazing is futile in such a fast-changing world, but as future historians look back at the start of 2015 they will identify four major interlinked issues facing the travel business – safety and security; making sure our money is secure; sustainability, or the green agenda; and the online future. If we can negotiate these challenges, then another golden age of foreign holidays could be dawning. If we can't, there's a very real possibility that in the short- or medium-term, holidays abroad could go into decline. Thomas Cook warned at the end of 2015 that the travel industry faced the worst turmoil for thirty years.

Safety and Security

The travel industry has become wearily familiar with the threat of terrorism ever since the 1970s, when the hijacking of aircraft became a regular occurrence. Then, as now, the threat emanated from the Middle East – but unlike then, the Middle East is now a major mass-market holiday destination. On-board security might have been ramped up to the point where hijackings almost never happen, but, as may be conclusively proven, it is still possible to plant a bomb on board. That was the likely cause of the destruction of a Russian Metrojet flight that had departed from the holiday resort of Sharm El Sheikh in Egypt in October 2015, killing all 224 on board.

Terrorists strike not only in the air but on the ground, and not only in the Middle East. Often those attacks are aimed at tourists, especially Western tourists. In June 2015 an attack occurred in the purpose-built Tunisian resort of Port El Kantaoui, near Sousse, which hit British tourists in particular, slaughtering thirty-seven people on the beach and around the swimming pool at the Riu Imperial Marhaba Hotel.

British tourists have proved remarkably resilient to terrorist attacks in the past, with bombs planted by Basque separatist group ETA at Spanish beaches and airports having no impact at all, despite a couple of fatalities. British tourists in particular – but often not Americans – have soon returned to the scene of atrocities, whether in New York or Paris. They will return to Tunisia too, in 2017 if not 2016, but will the 2015 attacks be a game changer? However much you might like Tunisia or Egypt, or want to support local people who have lost their jobs in tourism because of attacks, do you really want to lie on a beach with armed guards as well as waiters hovering among the palm trees?

The benefits of travelling on a traditional package holiday rather than a holiday you put together yourself were again proved by the massacre in Tunisia, and the prolonged ban on flights to Sharm El Sheikh in Egypt following the Metrojet disaster. People who had booked package holidays with tour operators were looked after, at no cost to them but at huge cost to the travel companies (an estimated £38 million cost to TUI, just because of Tunisia). Those who had booked flights and hotels separately often had to make their own arrangements, at their own cost, to fly home early or stay on until they could fly anywhere at all.

Thirty-three of the thirty-seven people who died in the Tunisia massacre were customers of TUI, which owns the Thomson and First Choice brands. The TUI group's then joint chief executive, Peter Long, deservedly won many plaudits for how it handled the crisis, as TUI (and other big tour operators whose customers weren't at this hotel) evacuated all customers from Tunisia.

'The Tunisia attacks were horrendous beyond belief,' he says. 'The world is a much more uncertain place today, but our customers know that when there is a problem, we have an absolute warranty to look after them. The biggest challenges we face today are geo-political, whether it's terrorism or political upheaval. When the British government banned flights to Sharm El Sheikh, you could see from interviews with people stranded at the airport that they weren't happy trying to contact the airlines they had booked with. Even if these airlines had someone at the end of a phone line, they were overwhelmed.

'Our reputation is built on how we look after people, but it is a negative message to say, "book with us in case there's a problem". In a world of social media and instant news coverage, inferior organisations are found out and rumbled very quickly. With Tunisia, our customers will tell us very clearly if we should go back in, whatever the Foreign Office might say. We might have a programme to Tunisia that is 20 per cent the size of what we had before, and I don't see that changing any time soon. I feel very sad for Tunisia, but we lost thirty-three of our customers there. That hits us more than anything and was our worst crisis ever.'

As with Thomas Cook and other major tour operators, TUI has started moving flights back to more familiar destinations, especially Spain, as a result of what happened in Tunisia and Egypt. 'Demand for Portugal, the Balearic Islands, the Canaries and also mainland Spain is strong,' said Long, as he looked ahead to 2016. 'People don't want to go to North Africa at present. Demand for Turkey is still good, and I hope that will continue to be the case.'

Terrorists were also targeting tourists in Turkey as 2016 began, with an attack that killed ten Germans in Istanbul. Worryingly for major tour operators Turkey is now one of their top sellers, and the remoteness of its Mediterranean beach resorts from the conflict zone around the Syrian border may not save them from attack. Many other Middle Eastern and North African countries, ranging from the United Arab Emirates (including Dubai) to Morocco, could be targeted. Big tour operators were looking to sell more holidays to Spain in 2016, but the British were not alone and hotel beds in Spain and Greece were in short supply with prices rocketing. At the time of writing, Russia had banned all holiday flights to Turkey as well as to Sharm El Sheikh.

Terrorism is one reason why some people are going back to package holidays, and a whole raft of other health and safety issues could indicate you are better off booking a package than putting together a holiday yourself. The carbon monoxide poisoning case that hit a family holidaying with Thomas Cook in 2006 was tragic, but it does highlight that you should be safer on a package holiday than if you booked a flight and hotel separately. Thomas Cook failed its customers on that occasion, and although it has now acted to improve monitoring of hotels and to raise awareness of carbon monoxide generally (see chapter fourteen), that won't bring back the two dead children.

Ever since 1990, when ABTA tightened up its rules ahead of European-led legislation making tour operators liable for the health and safety of holidaymakers, it has been possible for aggrieved customers to bring a case before British courts. When a hotel anywhere in the world appears in a tour operator's brochure you should be able to assume that it has passed rigorous safety checks. Even the smallest tour operator is liable, and they can insure themselves against a claim and employ specialist companies to do safety checking for them. But if you booked that hotel through any number of websites, you may have no redress if things go wrong and no choice but try to seek justice through a foreign court. The law, as handed down by the European Commission and enacted by all EU countries with varying degrees of stringency, is specific. If you've booked a package, you should be protected. If you haven't, you're probably on your own.

Andy Cooper, a lawyer who has worked for Airtours and Thomas Cook and now runs a consultancy, says: 'If there was ever a ruling that there had to be carbon monoxide alarms in every room, even where there are no boilers and no risk, hotel groups would refuse and tour operators would be exposed. Thomas Cook came out of this case worse than it should have done, but there have been only four deaths in over thirty years from carbon monoxide poisoning in holiday hotels. People might criticise tour operators, but they then book accommodation with organisations such as Airbnb with no safety monitoring at all whether it's fire risk, carbon monoxide, swimming pools, balconies or road traffic hazards.

'There will have to be regulation of organisations like Airbnb, and the average cost of complying with health and safety regulations is small. I like to think that people will trust tour operators more because of terrorist atrocities like Tunisia, and TUI got a lot of plaudits. But is it enough to bring people back? Many people booking holidays have short-term memories.'

Another travel industry lawyer, Alan Bowen of AGB Associates, says tour operators must be rigorous to distinguish themselves from new online competitors: 'The only way tour operators can survive is to give customers something they can't get themselves, and I very much doubt whether a bedbank has inspected all 10,000 hotels they might represent,' he says. 'With many online bookings, there is a whole chain of organisations saying the booking is not their responsibility, so people making these bookings are taking a lot of risks. People tend to assume that hotels have effective fire alarms, sprinklers, water supply and other safety features, but total safety isn't possible on some kinds of adventure holidays. In that case tour operators should ask accommodation providers to put up a sign saying the accommodation doesn't meet those standards, so be aware.

'Unfortunately, the message is not getting through about how much tour operators protect you, and a lot of people will book a cheaper non-protected holiday just to save £50. Tour operators are bad at marketing so everyone buys on price, and the same is now happening with cruising. When you are booking a package you won't necessarily get a bargain, but someone will have checked out the accommodation and there'll be someone at the end of a phone line if you have a problem.'

Bowen adds that most court claims against tour operators are because of food poisoning, a problem that increased with the proliferation of all-inclusive hotels where some food might be recycled. But he warns that terrorist attacks could result in court cases against travel companies in the UK, and that they must be vigilant. 'Islamic State is different to anything we have seen before, and there is a risk people will lose confidence in travelling,' he concedes. 'One of the benefits of buying a package is that tour operators will offer you an alternative holiday if required, and while EasyJet offered refunds when it had to stop flying to Sharm El Sheikh, many people who couldn't get there found the hotels they booked separately had 100 per cent cancellation charges. There is no legal case against tour operators unless they take big risks. But even if the Foreign Office says somewhere is safe, then tour operators need to take action if their resort staff become aware of a risk.'

John de Vial, ABTA's head of financial protection, has also done much work on health and safety – but now feels tour operators are often at a disadvantage. 'The European Package Travel Regulations introduced in the 1990s meant many hotels had to do a lot of work to continue dealing with tour operators, especially on fire safety, swimming pools, balconies, and food and water hygiene,' he explains. 'Major events such as the ash cloud crisis and terrorist attacks have reminded people of the value of taking a package, but you're not protected if you don't book a package. The ABTA brand that most travel companies subscribe to is all about confidence, expertise and trust. People don't want to know how it all works behind the scenes, but they do know they are less likely to be let down if they book with an ABTA member.'

Many of the new Online Travel Agents (OTAs) are not part of ABTA, and are coy about explaining how they protect customers. Steve Endacott, the former Airtours executive who is now chairman of Teletext Holidays, admits that most of these companies don't offer the same level of customer care as package tour firms. 'OTAs handled the Tunisia and Sharm El Sheikh crises badly, because unlike big tour operators they rely on third party airlines to bring people home,' he explains. 'At Teletext we worked with hotels to look after customers, but we depend on airlines to communicate with them.

'You get a cheaper holiday through an OTA, but we can't control delivery of that holiday so it's horses for courses. But we are working together closely on mobile apps, so we can follow our customers into resorts. We are evolving and filling some gaps, but events like the attacks in Tunisia and Egypt strengthen the role of tour operators because they have back-up people in resorts. People tend to go back to traditional tour operators when terrorism happens, but OTAs could also set up 24-hour duty offices.'

Financial Protection

Holidays can be an emotional subject, and if we lose them because a company goes bust or if that happens while we're away, it's bad news. But ever since the 1960s, and particularly after the Court Line collapse of 1974, tour operators have been working to protect the money we pay out. Their record in protecting the public is second to none, although that doesn't apply to airlines or other travel arrangements that aren't part of a package. Other forms of protection might be in place, including when you pay by card, and various types of insurance. But now, while tour operators still have that protection in place, the internet is making mugs of them. Lots of online companies offer inadequate financial protection or none at all, whether they are selling packages or simply flights or hotels.

The Civil Aviation Authority (CAA) has been in charge of licensing package holidays by air since 1972, and the phrase 'ATOL-protected' is now widely used in TV, print and online advertising although most people have no idea what it means. ATOL stands for Air Travel Organiser's Licence, and companies have to meet strict financial criteria to get one. If the financial guarantees they provide aren't enough, the government-backed Air Travel Trust is a safety net funded by a levy on holidays. ATOLs also cover some types of airline tickets sold through travel companies, but not when a booking is made direct with an airline. The ATOL regime doesn't cover holidays by surface transport, which may be covered by ABTA; the Confederation of Passenger Transport (CPT), for coach tours; the Cruise Lines International Association; or trust funds.

So far, so boring, you might think, but here's the rub. According to the CAA, well over 90 per cent of package holidays by air were covered by ATOL in the 1990s, falling to 75 per cent by 2006. Now it stands at about 67 per cent, having gone up from 58 per cent in 2012 as the ATOL rules were tightened. That means one in three people taking a package holiday isn't covered, and their money could be lost. Even if you do get your money back when a non-ATOL company goes bust, that won't get you a replacement holiday. You might have to settle for Margate rather than Mallorca.

New regulations coming in by 2018 could resolve the situation, and will mean more airlines will have to protect passengers on package holidays including when you 'click through' to third party websites and details of your airline booking are passed on. But as with all regulations affecting the travel industry over the last fifty years, there are holes ready to be exploited. A particular concern is that a company offering package holidays or tours to UK customers can decide to base itself in any of the twenty-eight EU countries, although it might have a sales office and phone number in the UK, and a co.uk domain name. Some companies have already 'gone offshore' to countries where the financial protection rules are far less stringent than in the UK, and that could well increase in 2018.

The CAA went on record in 2014 to express concern about the protection offered by one major online player, which had moved its operations to Mallorca, Spain the previous year and backed out of ATOL protection. While stressing that it wasn't advising against booking with the company, the CAA queried whether the financial protection offered in Spain was adequate.

David Moesli, deputy director of the CAA's consumer protection group, says: 'People are confused about whether their holidays are protected because there are so many badges in the travel business, such as ATOL, ABTA, AITO, IATA and so on, with IATA (International Air Transport Association) offering no protection at all. But as a result of court cases and changes to ATOL by the Government, more people are protected and most major online players are covered. It could become more common in future for travel companies selling in the UK to base themselves in other EU countries. We have advice on our website saying people need to ask questions about these companies, and find out how their protection works.

'The changes happening in 2018 are the biggest in financial protection since ATOL started over forty years ago. People will be able to buy a wider range of holidays from companies based in other EU countries, but it important that you know where you stand if things go wrong. There have been a lot of failures in the travel business, and they are often very public, affecting something that people dream about. If you buy a sofa and it doesn't arrive, you're fed up. But if your tour operator goes bust while you're in Turkey, you could be out on the street.'

Whether the ATOL system continues after 2018 is a matter of debate, with travel industry bodies including ABTA pressing for a single government-approved body to protect all kinds of holidays. This was considered in the 1990s but ruled out because of cost and government unwillingness to get involved, while proposals to widen the safety net and include airline tickets also foundered. As more bookings are made online a clear distinction is emerging between companies that come under ATOL and those that don't, but the situation could get more confused if online giants such as Google and Amazon become more directly involved in travel.

Many more operators may 'go offshore' because of the cost of providing financial protection under UK rules, while more companies based in Europe might start selling in the UK. They not only avoid strict financial criteria imposed by the CAA and other bodies, but avoid having to pay VAT on their profit margins as demanded by HM Customs & Excise. This alone could add up to £20 to the cost of a holiday, a significant amount. Cut-throat price competition has always existed, but is so much more intense in the online world with most people going for the cheapest deal.

Travel industry lawyer Alan Bowen, of AGB Associates, says: 'The good thing about the new regulations coming in 2018 is that much more will be classed as a package, including a hotel or car hire added to a flight booking within twenty-four hours. The regulations create what's called a linked travel arrangement, but although that will be financially protected, it won't help if the airline itself goes bust, but only the company putting it together, and there will be no liability for health and safety. It's ridiculous that in some ways, the new rules go backwards on what we have now.

'It would be good if there was a single organisation to license all packages, as happens in countries including the Irish Republic, but I doubt whether the Government would be interested in extending the CAA's role. It is a real worry that a company can set up in business anywhere in the EU, as there are only eight out of twenty-eight countries where you have any chance of getting your money back. Even in Germany, protection is inadequate.

'It is very difficult to take legal action against companies based abroad, and the whole point of regulations introduced in the 1990s was to allow you to take action against tour operators in British courts,' adds Bowen. 'Your money may be protected if you book with a card, but if a company goes bust within a couple of weeks of your holiday starting then you won't get another one, and you'll spend the next few weeks filling in forms. The travel industry protects people better than most other sectors, and in future you will get much more information about what you're booking, in black and white. But it will be a shame if some things go backwards.'

It's no wonder that the public are confused, and whether 2018 will bring clarity remains to be seen. Many put their trust in ABTA, with research in 2015 indicating that 73 per cent of people booking a holiday felt more confident when they see the ABTA symbol. The association's 1,200 members have a combined turnover of £32 billion and include nearly all the big names in tour operating, but not some of the online brands. While ABTA insists that members provide financial protection on package holidays (as does the Association of Independent Tour Operators – AITO), ABTA itself only provides protection for holidays not involving flights, such as by coach or rail. Nor does ABTA protect air tickets or simple hotel bookings done by members, but most people believe it offers blanket protection when it doesn't.

John de Vial, ABTA head of financial protection, says: 'With the growth of online brands and low-cost airlines, it's been clear for some time that the rules aren't working. The Government realises that reform is needed and that the scale of risk is not covered by the back-up funds available, so during 2016 it is consulting about the way forward. ABTA feels that there needs to be a single set of regulations and a single authority to deal with, so it would be easier to understand for the consumer and the trade. Airlines have become more active in selling holidays, and I believe we will see more of them following British Airways, Virgin and Jet2 by setting up holiday divisions that protect people properly.

'Customers believe there is more protection than there really is, especially with airlines. They become angry when they lose their money, but so far, not enough to apply political pressure for change.'

Steve Endacott, chairman of online operator Teletext Holidays, estimates that nearly eight million of a possible twenty million package holidays sold each year are arranged by online firms, and if all these holidays were to drop out of the ATOL system then there could be a huge hole in financial protection. 'The cost of VAT alone is up to £20 on the price of a holiday, and although that has no real impact on a tour operator's price, it has a big impact on online companies when a family of four could save £80 by booking with them,' he explains. 'It is perfectly legal to be based in another European country.'

Endacott feels some low-cost airlines will become major players in package holidays, while others will continue to think that this isn't their business. 'It makes sense to have a package holiday division as you can cut holiday prices when you need to, whereas if an airline cuts ticket prices, other airlines react and you have a price war,' he says. 'Many low-cost flights are already incorporated into other companies' packages, but people don't realise that.'

Tour operators are happy with competition – after all, they have been at each other's throats since package holidays started. But the thing they say over and over again is that they want a level playing field, and not to be burdened with extra costs and rules that low-cost airlines and new online players are not.

Derek Moore, chairman of the Association of Independent Tour Operators, says: 'The bottom line is having a level playing field – either we all have to offer the same protection to the public, or no one does. Things are still not clear. Personally I feel a £1 levy on everything, including air tickets, would be the answer as it would build up a huge compensation fund. But the airlines are powerful lobbyists and have said no.'

Noel Josephides, ABTA's chairman, adds: 'We have done a lot of lobbying, both at Westminster and in Brussels, and we need to ensure that any new rules are enforced. Airlines might try to side-step the new rules, but in that case they will have to tell people their holidays aren't protected and that's not a good stance to take.'

If you care about your holiday money, the confusion might continue. Let the buyer beware.

Sustainability, and the Green Agenda

As we have become more aware of protecting the environment, climate change and other ways in which taking a holiday could have a damaging effect on people and the country they live in, we have been demanding more sustainable holidays. You could argue that it's too late to protect heavily developed coastlines such as mainland Spain or the Balearics, but it is never too late to do something positive even here. Demand for more sustainable holidays has intensified as tourists have spread to the most fragile places on earth, and due to greater awareness of a whole range of environmental issues.

The whole of the global tourism industry, including governments, developers, hotels, airlines, tour operators and cruise lines, has come under withering and often justified attack from environmentalists, including demands that tourist numbers should be restricted in places at greatest risk. But people keep on travelling, and only a small minority consciously choose more sustainable options such as travel by rail rather than air, or smaller scale accommodation which recycles waste. Sustainability is often thought to be a twenty-first century issue, with online portal Responsibletravel.com being set up in 2001 and charity the Travel Foundation in 2003. But another campaigning group and charity, Tourism Concern, was operational by 1991, and tour operators started to consider the impact of what they were doing even earlier.

Roger Heape, a former Thomson, Intasun and British Airways Holidays executive, started working on the green issue with Tour Operators Study Group (later the Federation of Tour Operators) as package holidays faced an increasingly bad press. Out of this, in 1990, came the Tourism for Tomorrow awards, developed with the *Wish You Were Here* TV programme. 'At BA Holidays in 1991 I worked very closely with Hugh Somerville, the airline's head of environment, including a study of tourism impact in the Seychelles, all-inclusive hotels in St Lucia and consumer donation schemes,' he says. 'BA then took over the Tourism for Tomorrow awards, which became more global.'

By the end of the 1990s came the first signs of a wider industry approach with Heape later becoming chairman of the Travel Foundation. The focus was on projects and training in the 'three pillars of sustainability'– environmental, economic and social. Funding was raised by an 'opt-out' levy on holidaymakers as BA had found that 'opt-in' donation schemes didn't work. The foundation has carried out thirty-five projects in twenty-four countries and trained large numbers of travel industry staff.

'Tourism has the potential to help solve the problem of widening inequality between nations,' says Heape, now retired. 'It is an efficient way of transferring wealth from rich to poor nations. Tourism is relatively corruption-free, although there is still a need for getting a higher proportion of money through to the staff on the ground rather than business owners. But with the emergence of huge numbers of middle classes in both India and China, a huge boom is likely with tourism becoming the largest industry in the world. Airlines' contribution to CO2 emissions and global warming will continue to rise in spite of more fuel-efficient aircraft. The development of hotels risks widespread resort degradation, unless tighter environmental assessment is enforced.'

ABTA plays a leading role in making the travel industry more aware. Nikki White, its head of destinations and sustainability, is keen to stress that the emphasis is not only on protecting the environment but on a range of other issues including workers' rights, child protection and animal welfare. Training is offered to all ABTA members on these issues, and about 1,500 hotels in over forty countries observe responsible tourism standards through ABTA's Travelife auditing scheme. Most big tour operators also subscribe to Travelife, and people can choose a sustainable hotel by consulting the Travelife website.

'Sustainability started with people becoming more environmentally conscious, but it has now developed further and is no longer a niche but a whole way of doing business,' explains White. 'We help our members have a policy on preventing child exploitation, working with ECPAT (End Child Prostitution and Trafficking), and on animal welfare. We estimate that 60 per cent of resort excursions include animals whether to zoos, marine parks, on safari or boat trips. If we say something is an unacceptable practice, we suggest alternatives.

'Human rights are also a growing issue, including workers' rights in tourist destinations such as Sri Lanka or the Maldives. There are always issues to deal with, and we urge countries to develop ways of dealing with them. Unfortunately, sustainable tourism is sometimes pushed aside by political issues, as in Egypt.'

Often, says White, hotels can do little things to help guests feel more in tune with their surroundings, such as supporting the local community by helping train staff in local restaurants, or inviting local traders in to display their wares. 'Generally, ABTA believes that tourism is beneficial to countries and contributes greatly to their economies,' she says. 'To lose tourism would be very damaging, as we have seen in Tunisia and Egypt. There is a lot of concern about carbon emissions, but people aren't going to stop flying. A flight with every seat sold is a very efficient way of moving people around.'

The rapid growth of all-inclusive hotels, which often occupy previously pristine environments and use a lot of resources, especially water, is of particular concern. Studies have shown that tour operators using all-inclusive resorts can harm local communities by discouraging people from leaving hotels except on excursions organised by the operator, as in a paper on the Dominican Republic presented at Reading University by Michelle Palmer. She visited the country many times staying mainly with local people, and only fell ill when she stayed at an all-inclusive hotel. 'The promotion of particular images of a destination does impact on tourists, who may desire a more authentic holiday experience but lack the confidence to move beyond the environmental bubble of the organised mass market experience,' her paper concludes.

'There are good and bad ways of doing all-inclusive, and if people think there's nothing to see outside the resort, they won't go out,' says White. 'But the Travel Foundation has shown that all-inclusive can benefit communities through the supply chain, and these hotels are a great source of employment.'

Her colleague at ABTA, John de Vial, says a turning point for big tour operators' approach to sustainability was when they became public companies, as happened soon after he joined Thomson in 1997. 'To have roles such as a full-time responsible tourism manager was ground-breaking at that time, but as a public company Thomson had to be best in class,' he says. 'Environmental activists such as David Bellamy came to talk to us, with the view that it was better for the environment to have tourists clustered together in big resorts, or travelling in one coach carrying fifty people, rather than spread about or in twenty-five taxis carrying two people in each.'

Tour operators handle sustainability in various ways, and if acting more responsibly helps save money as well as gaining recognition from those customers who do care, they see this as a winner. TUI claims that Thomson Airways emits less carbon than most airlines in Europe, with its new fleet of Boeing 787 Dreamliners strengthening that claim. Customers are urged to engage in sustainable tourism through kids' club activities, school education initiatives and donation schemes, while many of the hotels used by TUI are accredited to Travelife.

Thomas Cook has adopted the Travel Foundation's Make Holidays Greener campaign and runs an excursions programme called Local Label, which benefits local communities and provides customers with a more authentic experience. It could be argued that sustainability is even more important in fragile Third World countries, and Kuoni, among other initiatives, has a supplier code of conduct including rules on preventing bribery and corruption, making work places safe and protecting animals. It observes ABTA's animal welfare rules and runs a 'Water Champion' programme at hotels in countries including Kenya and Thailand, and supports wildlife charity Born Free. Escorted tour operators also have initiatives, such as Travel Corporation's TreadRight Foundation. This supports more than thirty sustainable projects worldwide, and is fronted by documentary maker Celine Cousteau of the famous explorer family.

But in many ways smaller tour operators have a better record on sustainability, and the Association of Independent Tour Operators (AITO) can trace its involvement back to the mid-1980s, almost year dot in the sustainability calendar. AITO's 120 members follow a sustainable ethos and publicise many projects on its website, while offering guidelines to holidaymakers on how to act in harmony with the environments and people they are visiting.

Sustainability adviser Dick Sisman helped develop AITO's approach thirty years ago, and also worked with the International Green Flag Organisation's approach to the travel industry. 'Small tour operators tend to have a lot more concern about the impact of tourism, as unlike the big companies they can't just move their holidays somewhere else if there's a problem,' he says. 'Small tour operators have done most of what they can do, and my focus now is to get more local communities working with tour operators, as with a company called Gambia Experience in Africa. We want to create long-term sustainability, rather than just build a new well or a new school.

'It is easy for holidaymakers to give money to charities, but that doesn't absolve them of responsibility. Only about 10 per cent of travellers are what I would describe as "true greens". There will always be people telling the travel industry what to do, but we must understand that tour operators need to make a profit, and are often constrained by regulations. But travel is an inspirational industry that can make things better, and if there are problems in a country, tourism is often one of the first industries to recover.'

The Final Call – In Search of the True Cost of Our Holidays is sometimes regarded as an attack on the tourism industry. But the book, written by former *Guardian* journalist Leo Hickman and published in 2007, is a well-reasoned account of the ills of mass tourism from Benidorm to Cancun, and from the backpacker trail in Thailand to Tallinn in Estonia, a city much favoured by stag parties ('Kamikaze Sex and Kalashnikovs'). Hickman describes tourism as one of the most unregulated industries in the world, adding: 'It is still making extraordinary claims – that, for example, tourism nurtures world peace, love and understanding. There seems to be little evidence to me that tourists and those that serve them engage with each other on a balanced, harmonious footing ... it is in grave danger of trashing the very assets on which it depends to survive ... it could become the slapstick cliché of the man up a tree, sawing through the branch he is sitting on'.

Hickman feels the travel industry has made some progress since he wrote the book, but since then all-inclusive hotels have mushroomed. 'There is now a deeper understanding of the social and economic impact of tourism, but whether that is greenwash or sincere, I don't know,' he says. 'All-inclusive hotels and large cruise ships are the two areas that give me most concern, because of the socio-economic impact. If an international hotel chain operates lots of all-inclusive hotels in a country such as Mexico, there is no economic benefit to the local community except for jobs. There is no real opportunity for hotel guests to go out and spend in local shops and restaurants, as they may never get their wallet or purse out on the whole trip. There's reduced opportunity for cultural exchange too, as the only local people you will meet are those paid a very low wage to serve you.

'In the longer term, homogenised, international resorts where you feel you could be anywhere in the world could cause major resentment. But the whole of the tourism industry is very short-term in its thinking. Countries should diversify and not go for one type of tourism. Look at Tunisia and Egypt, where terrorism is undermining their business model.'

The big question no one can answer is how many tourists really care and perhaps, as Sisman says, it is only 10 per cent. Andy Cooper, the former Airtours lawyer who headed the Federation of Tour Operators, says: 'Sustainability is a much bigger issue for holidaymakers in Scandinavia than it is in the UK. Here the big tour operators, except TUI, are relatively indifferent. Trade associations have dragged their members kicking and screaming through the sustainability agenda, not because they don't see it as important but because of the perception that customers aren't that bothered.'

The Online Future

People have been predicting the demise of tour operators since the first online holiday bookings were made in the late 1990s, and the demise of travel agents since way before then. The number of high street travel agents has certainly dropped, with more operating online or as part of homeworking organisations, but the number of tour operators has increased with many very small companies operating online at low cost. Anyone predicting that tour operators could be wiped out is foolhardy, but no one knows how the internet will develop and whether price-is-everything online operators could be undermined if Google and Amazon, to name just two, start taking travel bookings.

As if all the online competition wasn't challenging enough for more traditional tour operators, along comes another threat – the so-called 'sharing economy' or peer-to-peer marketing. Major online players such as Airbnb and HomeAway offer accommodation ranging from a spare room in a flat to fully fledged commercial lettings. Not only the travel industry, but also mainstream hotels, could be hit as the sharing economy develops.

Horror stories abound, including fraudsters hacking into websites and posing as accommodation owners to take people's money; and people who rent an apartment to throw a wild party for hundreds who trash the place. Barcelona is one of several cities trying to impose restrictions, as rowdy youngsters run amok in quiet residential areas. Once again, tour operators are disadvantaged by all the regulations heaped on them – while much of the accommodation offered through the sharing economy hasn't had even the most basic safety checks. While no one might begrudge a private individual marketing accommodation online, many of the rooms are in fact owned by commercial letting organisations.

Noel Josephides, chairman of ABTA and specialist tour operator Sunvil, says: 'Huge organisations such as Airbnb, and major hotel reservations websites such as Booking.com, don't have to follow the same rules as us. Some of these organisations don't pay tax in the UK and don't take any responsibility for bookings made, yet consumers have embraced them. We need to see some regulation as tour operators and hotel groups are getting very worried.'

Hugh Morgan, who celebrates fifty years in tour operating in 2016, adds: 'Peer-to-peer is a huge threat, but Booking.com is an even bigger worry. Wherever you want to go, you can find a hotel or apartment online within seconds. The reach of Airbnb is phenomenal, and an owner can get £200 a night for a good apartment and pay only 13 per cent in commission. I use low-cost airlines, Booking.com and Airbnb, but these organisations are totally unregulated.'

Travel industry thinkers are predicting that Google and Amazon may start taking travel bookings themselves sooner rather than later, including Teletext Holidays chairman Steve Endacott who probably has more experience than anyone selling holidays online. He also says that the concentration of power in the hands of a few, as happened with tour operators in the late 1990s, is now being replicated on a global basis in the online world.

'Google may not actually complete a booking, but that doesn't mean it isn't an Online Travel Agent (OTA),' he explains. 'We are now seeing a big switch in holiday bookings to mobile devices, meaning people spend even less time choosing a holiday, but links to Google on mobile devices don't work so well. You can already access Google Maps, Google Flights and Google Hotels and now Google Destinations is coming. You can compare prices now, but not actually complete the booking with Google. But the move to mobile bookings will push Google to becoming an OTA itself.'

Endacott says that in the US, 65 per cent of online travel bookings are controlled by just two major players – Expedia, which owns Travelocity, Hotels.com, Orbitz and HomeAway; and Priceline, which owns Booking.com, Kayak and Rentalcars.com. Expedia's move into the sharing economy by acquiring HomeAway is seen as very significant, meaning customers can search for hotels or private accommodation through the same organisation. TripAdvisor's acquisition of sightseeing website Viator follows a similar logic, while Priceline is thought to be looking for further purchases.

'All the major US players seem to be following the same consolidation programme, aimed at maximising existing customer databases or Google spend,' says Endacott. 'As they run out of opportunities in the US, it is logical that they will expand in Europe, including the UK. OTAs ushered in a new age of tour operating early in the century, and the last ten years have been rather like the Wild West as with traditional tour operating back in the 1960s. Now the online sector is maturing and consolidating. The merger of Airbnb or Uber with one of the OTA giants has a lot of logic, but is highly unlikely to occur in the short term.'

Endacott expects UK-based OTAs to make acquisitions in Europe first, and adds: 'The first of these pan-European deals is likely to be the sale of the trade-only Hotelbeds group by TUI, which was valued at £1 billion. The strategic benefit of its massive hotel buying power, particularly in the traditional beach hotel sector, is a prize few of the major US players will want to miss out on.'

It's a scenario that many people find hard to comprehend, and enough to make some old tour operators – who often started, like Harry Goodman, sweeping the floor in a small business – look on in disbelief. As ever, theories are rampant about acquisitions and mergers, or alliances between major companies, including possible cooperation between one of the travel giants and one of the big low-cost airlines. Where will all these scenarios leave tour operators? No one knows, because the world is changing at a dizzying speed.

But at the end of the day, we are still talking about the same type of holiday – combining flights and hotels, and a way of getting between the two – as back in the 1950s. Where *do* we go from here?

Touch-Down

I promised you an exhilarating trip, and I hope you'll say some nice things when you fill in your holiday questionnaire. Our story has become rather serious, but these are the times we live in. We'll be coming in to land in a few minutes, and how things have changed. When we embarked on this trip we were innocents going abroad for the first time, but just look at us now.

We set off in a bumpy old DC-3, and it took four hours just to get to Mallorca where we stayed in a funny little hotel or at a campsite. Now we're on a Boeing 787 Dreamliner, flying home non-stop from the Pacific coast of Mexico in only eleven hours. We've been staying at an all-inclusive hotel, but we've been out and about too. We've already got two more holidays booked this year, to top up our suntans.

Shortly before writing this book I took two trips which, at first glance, couldn't have been more different. The first was to Butlin's at Skegness, the English east coast resort famously described as 'so bracing' in a railway publicity poster of 1908. It certainly was bracing in December, but that was for a music festival and I didn't go out much! The second trip was to Puerto Vallarta in Mexico, where I lounged about in truly tropical temperatures sipping margaritas.

While at Skegness I peered into the original 1936 chalet that Butlin's has preserved, which is very basic. In Puerto Vallarta I reflected that this chalet would fit three times into my palatial room at ClubHotel Riu Jalisco, but I also felt there were similarities in what Butlin's set out to do then and the swish hotels of today. You can now have a quality holiday at Butlin's, but aren't all-inclusive hotels a type of Butlin's too, with everything happening in one place?

So, where do we go from here? Holidays in space, which Thomas Cook first starting taking bookings for half a century ago, will probably never happen even for the super-rich. Whatever new holiday destinations might come up in future, we will keep going back to tried and trusted favourites particularly in these troubled times. A new golden age could be dawning for the Mediterranean, although climate change might make it too hot one day, and package holidays are now being blamed for an increase in skin cancer. Wherever we go, will there still be tour operators to take us there? I sincerely hope so, but that's it for now – but look at my website www.historyofpackagetours.co.uk for updates.

Fasten your seat-belts please! I wish you a smooth landing, and see you back at the airport soon.

The Family Holiday Association

Many of the people who have built up the travel business have, like me, enjoyed a great time travelling all over the world at little or no expense. But even today, when many people regard a holiday abroad as their right, we should think of those for whom any kind of holiday must seem like an impossible dream. That's why I, like so many people in the travel business, support the long-established Family Holiday Association. It raises funds to help around four thousand families a year to take a holiday, short break or day trip in the UK, and over half these families have never had any kind of holiday before. Please support the FHA to help even more.

The Family Holiday Association is the only national charity dedicated to providing seaside breaks and day trips for families coping with some of the toughest challenges life can bring.

We help UK families struggling with problems such as severe and long-term illness, bereavement, mental health issues, disability and domestic violence. Each family is referred to us by someone already working with them in a supporting role, such as a teacher or social worker.

Evidence shows that our work results in stronger, healthier and happier families and communities.

FAMILY HOLIDAY ASSOCIATION
The charity that gives families a break

Learn more at FamilyHolidayAssociation.org.uk

Registered charity number 800262

Index

Also available from
Amberley Publishing

ISBN 9781844564770B
eISBN 9781445647715